Reading Early Hammett

ALSO BY LEROY LAD PANEK

The American Police Novel:
A History (McFarland, 2003)

Reading
Early Hammett

A Critical Study of the Fiction
Prior to The Maltese Falcon

LeRoy Lad Panek

McFarland & Company, Inc., Publishers
Jefferson, North Carolina, and London

Library of Congress Cataloguing-in-Publication Data

Panek, LeRoy.
    Reading early Hammett : a critical study of the fiction prior to
The Maltese Falcon / LeRoy Lad Panek.
        p.   cm.
    Includes bibliographical references and index.

    ISBN 0-7864-1962-8 (softcover : 50# alkaline paper)

    1. Hammett, Dashiell, 1894–1961— Criticism and interpretation.
2. Detective and mystery stories, American — History and criticism.
I. Title.
PS3515.A4347Z84 2004
813'.52 — dc22

                                                        2004018232

British Library cataloguing data are available

Cover photograph ©2004 Digital Vision

Manufactured in the United States of America

*McFarland & Company, Inc., Publishers
    Box 611, Jefferson, North Carolina 28640
        www.mcfarlandpub.com*

For Roger

Contents

Preface

Victim, martyr, hero of the 1950s red scare and Senator Joseph McCarthy's House Un-American Activities subcommittee. Advocate for civil rights in the days of legal segregation, lynching, and institutionalized racial prejudice. Marxist during the heyday of American corporate wealth and power. Soldier who reenlisted to defend his country at the age of forty-nine. Bibulous, witty, charming, rich, smart, suave, romantic man about town, and tough, cynical, quixotic private eye in his shared fantasies. Writer of seminal importance in the history of crime fiction. And the embodiment of every writer's fear — success and acclaim followed by permanent writer's block, destitution, dependence. Dashiell Hammett represents a lot of things to a lot of people.

Since the publication of Hammett's last novel, *The Thin Man*, in 1934, every decade has seen a Hammett revival. In the 1940s and early 1950s Spivak published a series of collections of Hammett's short fiction written in the 1920s. In the 1960s Knopf reprinted all of his novels in one volume and also published *The Big Knockover: Selected Short Stories and Short Novels* with an introduction by Hammett's longtime companion Lillian Hellman, and William Nolan began contemporary assessment of Hammett's life and works with his *Dashiell Hammett: A Casebook*. In the 1970s, as a precursor to his neo-hard-boiled Spenser novels, Robert B. Parker wrote his Boston University dissertation on Hammett and Chandler; mystery writer Joe Gores published his novel *Hammett*; and Steven Marcus began what would be a long association with Hammett criticism with his introduction to Random House's reprinting of seven Hammett stories in *The*

1

Continental Op. In the '70s, too, Don Herron began taking aficionados on four-hour walking tours of Hammett-related sites in San Francisco. The early 1980s saw the real beginning of Hammett study with biographies from Richard Layman, William Nolan, and Diane Johnson and with analyses and commentaries from Peter Wolfe, Dennis Dooley, William Marling, and Sinda Gregory. At the turn of the century Knopf reprinted twenty of Hammett's short stories in *Nightmare Town* (1999), and the Library of America issued *Dashiell Hammett: Crime Stories and Other Writings* (2001). Constant throughout the decades, too, have been television reruns of the classic films made in the 1940s from Hammett's *The Maltese Falcon* and those based on his characters Nick and Nora Charles from *The Thin Man*.

Today Hammett is more accessible to readers than he has ever been. But not entirely. Even with recent reprints, a number of his early works from *The Smart Set* and other magazines of the 1920s have never been reprinted — in fact, no one can find his two pieces published in *Experience* in the 1920s. And when biographers and critics discuss Hammett's early works they give little insight into their nature or worth. Layman, in *Shadow Man*, for example, devotes only one sentence to "Esther Entertains," one of Hammett's early experiments with point of view. And Robert B. Parker in his critical-biographical entry in John Reilly's *Twentieth-Century Crime and Mystery Writers*, dismisses all of Hammett's short fiction as unworthy of consideration. While the critics of the 1980s have shed some light on his works, their focus has been largely on Hammett's novels — especially the later novels — and interpretations of Hammett have sometimes been colored by preconceived, retrospective views of the entire hard-boiled detective and film noir genres. A lot of discussions of Hammett also begin the wrong way round, either starting with his political views (made public mostly after he stopped writing) or basing interpretations of his works on motifs from Chandler-colored hard-boiled fiction or focusing only on what happens in *The Maltese Falcon* or *The Glass Key*. The Flitcraft anecdote in *The Maltese Falcon*, for example, looms large in a number of commentators' views of Hammett. It is surely an important and arresting metaphor, but for some it has ballooned to become the key to all of what Hammett was about. Hammett, however, didn't begin with the vision of the construction accident that jolted Flitcraft out of his unexamined middle-class life or with the creation of Ned Beaumont or Sam Spade. In fact, Hammett didn't begin with his nameless detective hero, the Continental Op. He didn't even start off his career as a writer of crime or detective stories. He began as a satirist; he began as a "sex story" writer; he began as a writer with literary aspirations but also as a writer who saw writing as a way to pay the grocer.

Looking at Hammett backwards has led to some pretty grandiose views about his works: that they convey a coherent and particular view of society; that they reflect the core values of American literature; that they inaugurate a new prose style; that his heroes are knights fighting corruption. Some of these arguments have merit and some don't. All readers, however, would benefit from reading Hammett starting from the beginning rather than from the end and from a clearer, more accurate vision of what he actually wrote before he created Sam Spade and before hard-boiled writers became a school.

What follows, then, is a reading of what Hammett wrote before he was famous, before *The Maltese Falcon, The Glass Key*, and *The Thin Man*. While much of this study concerns Hammett's first detective hero, the Continental Op, it also examines his writing before, during, and after he created his first important detective hero. A lot his work was not about detectives. But all of it had something to do with the detective he created, the detective stories he was writing at the time, and those stories he would go on to write.

Like all books, this one has depended on the help, indulgence, and forbearance of many. Especially helpful were the librarians at McDaniel College's Hoover Library. My thanks go to them, to Christine for her inevitable and invaluable help, to Alex and Claire, and to Dr. D., prince of Lorain, Ohio.

1

Hammett's Magazine Writings

Dashiell Hammett did not start out as a hard-boiled detective story writer. He made himself into one. Before he wrote the Continental Op stories and while he wrote them, Hammett tried his hand at a number of different kinds of writing in a number of different venues, literary and otherwise — mostly otherwise. Before "The Cleansing of Personville" in 1927 and the publication of *The Red Harvest*, the Continental Op stories in *The Black Mask* amounted to less than half of Hammett's total output. Thus, before mid–1927, excluding letters to the editor of *The Black Mask*, Hammett had written 34 pieces that did not feature the Continental Op (versus his 24 Op stories) and his work had appeared in 17 magazines besides *The Black Mask*: they appeared, alphabetically, in *Action Stories, Argosy All-Story, Bookman, Brief Stories, The Editor, Experience, The Forum, The Judge, New Pearsons, Saucy Stories, The Smart Set, Stratford Magazine, Sunset Magazine, True Detective, Western Advertising, Writer's Digest,* and *10 Story Book*. In addition to these, he also wrote eight stories for *The Black Mask* that did not feature the Continental Op as hero. Seven of the places where Hammett's pre–1927 work appeared (*Action Stories, Argosy All-Story, The Black Mask, Brief Stories, Saucy Stories, True Detective,* and *10 Story Book*) were ephemeral pulp magazines; indeed, the magazine that accepted "A Man Named Thin" went out of business before the story was published (Layman 72). In terms of quantity, after *The Black Mask*, the largest number of Hammett pieces appeared in *The Smart Set* (seven items, from "The

Parthian Shot" in October 1922 to "The Green Elephant" in October 1923), followed by five in *Brief Stories* (from "The Sardonic Star of Tom Doody" in 1923 to "Esther Entertains" in the following year).

Perhaps significantly, a number of the periodicals in which Hammett appeared in the early 1920s had connections with H. L. Mencken. Mencken and George Nathan edited *The Smart Set*—"A Magazine of Cleverness" that included "Burlesques, Epigrams, Poems, Short Stories, etc." and the first magazine to accept Hammett's writing. Between October 1922 and October 1923 Hammett appeared seven times in *The Smart Set* and then left the magazine at the same time that Mencken left it. In addition to *The Smart Set* Mencken and Nathan founded the pulp magazines *Saucy Stories* and *The Black Mask* to finance their more high-brow publishing ventures. They started the former, a "naughty magazine," in 1916 as competition to *Snappy Stories* (Mott vol. V, 261), and began the latter, an "Illustrated Magazine of Detective, Mystery, Adventure, Romance, and Spiritualism," in 1920. Mencken called it "boob bait" and he and Nathan sold *The Black Mask* off for a hefty profit after several issues. In his first full year as a writer, Hammett had stories appear in both *The Black Mask* and *Saucy Stories*. While he would continue to try other outlets, *The Black Mask* was to become Hammett's principal publisher until he made himself into a novelist. In addition to these three connections, Mencken's partner, George Nathan, was on the staff of *Judge*, a satiric journal, in which Hammett's "The Advertising Man Writes a Love Letter" appeared in 1927. It is notable that during his first year as a writer Hammett used his own name only in *The Smart Set* (with the exception of the anti–Ku Klux Klan story "The Crusader" for which he used the name of his infant daughter, Mary Jane Hammett) and adopted pseudonyms for his early appearances in the pulps: he began with the pseudonym Daghull Hammett for his first pulp publication "Immortality" in *10 Story Book*, and adopted Peter Collinson for "The Barber and His Wife" in *Brief Stories* (December 1922) and used it for his first three *Black Mask* stories (including the first Continental Op tale, "Arson Plus").

Hammett's most prolific years in magazine publishing were 1923 and 1924. Hammett broke into print in 1922 with five appearances—two pieces in *Smart Set* and one each in *10 Story Book*, *Brief Stories*, and *The Black Mask*, with "The Road Home," his first appearance in that magazine. In 1923 there were four somewhat longer *Smart Set* stories (his earlier two *Smart Set* pieces took up a page or less; "From the Memoirs of a Private Detective" lasts four pages and "The Green Elephant," six); a return to *Brief Stories* with two stories; seven pieces in *The Black Mask* (five of which were Continental Op stories); and one appearance each in *New Pearsons*, *Saucy*

Stories, and *Action Stories* for a total of 16. Hammett reached his magazine peak in 1924 with 17 publications: eleven were in *The Black Mask* (eight of them Op stories); two were in *Brief Stories*; and he appeared once each in *Argosy All-Story, Forum, True Detective,* and *Writer's Digest.* In 1923 and 1924 Hammett also busied himself writing letters to the editor of *The Black Mask* and ten appeared during those years. He both wrote fewer pieces and narrowed his publishing focus in 1925, concentrating on *The Black Mask,* which published six stories all about the Op, and focusing on regional publications with two pieces in *Sunset Magazine—* along with his final appearance in *The Forum* and one in *The Editor.* Along with these eleven pieces, he wrote only one letter to the editor of *The Black Mask* in 1925. 1926 saw very little of Hammett in print. There were three stories in *The Black Mask—* one about the Op — and his first publication in *Western Advertising.* But the next year, the year "The Cleansing of Personville" appeared, Hammett wrote more: there were three Op stories in what was now *Black Mask,* two articles in *The Stratford Magazine,* one in *The Judge,* one in *The Forum,* and one in *Bookman,* along with five reviews in *Saturday Review of Literature.*

Separating out the Continental Op stories, Hammett's literary production before *The Red Harvest* falls into several relatively distinct categories. His first efforts were submissions to *The Smart Set* and fall under the rubric of that magazine's contents—clever "Burlesques, Epigrams, Poems, Short Stories, etc." During Hammett's first year as a writer, he also began to write what he termed "sex" stories with "The Barber and his Wife" in 1922. These would continue with "The Joke on Eloise Morey" (June 1923), "Holiday" (July 1923), "The Dimple" (October 1923), "Esther Entertains" (February 1924) and "The Ruffian's Wife" (October 1925). In 1922 he also began what was to be a short flirtation with the adventure story with his first *Black Mask* piece "The Road Home." This he followed with "Laughing Masks" in 1923, "Nightmare Town" in 1924, and "Ber-Bulu" in 1925. Before "From the Memoirs of a Private Detective" came out in March 1923, Hammett entered the world of crime fiction by writing criminal stories with "The Sardonic Star of Tom Doody" (February 1923). He followed this with four more criminal stories: "The Man Who Stood in the Way" (June 1923), "Second Story Angel" (November 1923), "Itchy the Debonair" (January 1924) and "The New Racket" (February 1924). In the mid–1920s Hammett wrote three detective stories featuring detectives other than the Continental Op. They were "The Nails in Mr. Cayterer" (January 1926) about Robin Thin (he wrote a second Robin Thin story entitled "A Man Named Thin" at about the same time but it was not published until the 1960s) and "The Assistant Murderer" featuring Alec Rush. Throughout the pre–*Red Harvest* period, Hammett also wrote reflections and several poems.

While the pulps remained Hammett's meal ticket until the publication of *The Red Harvest*, throughout his early years he occasionally but consistently kept an eye on other more "respectable" and more literary magazines. After leaving *The Smart Set* in 1924 Hammett submitted a brief review letter of Joseph Hergesheimer's novel *Balisand* to *The Forum*, a journal of events, and *Writer's Digest* published his "In Defence [sic] of the Sex Story." The next year another short review letter, this time of Mary Austin's *Everyman's Genius*, appeared in *The Forum* under the header "Genius Made Easy." In 1925, too, under the heading "Contemporary Writers and Their Work" in *The Editor*, Hammett discussed the composition of his own story "Ber-Bulu," which had appeared that same year in *Sunset Magazine* (a publication founded by the Union Pacific Railroad to encourage western travel). In 1926, while working for Samuels Jewelry, Hammett saw himself as an "advertising man" and wrote "The Advertisement Is Literature," the first of several pieces that he would write for the journal *Western Advertising*. The next year the satirical magazine *The Judge* published "The Advertising Man Writes a Love Letter." By 1927, he analyzed crime fiction in a place other than *The Black Mask* by becoming a semiregular reviewer for one of the voices of the eastern literary establishment, *The Saturday Review of Literature*.

The Smart Set Pieces

"THE PARTHIAN SHOT"

In October 1922 Hammett appeared in print for the first time. "The Parthian Shot" is an 18-line block of prose printed in two columns at the top of page 82 of *The Smart Set*. The same issue includes "Portrait of an American Citizen" by Mencken, "A Ballet of Opinion" by Nathan, "Repetition Generale" by both of the editors, a novelette by Harold Armstrong, and sundry other "Burlesques, Epigrams, Poems, Short Stories, Etc." Hammett's piece is among the shortest of the magazine's selections.

"The Parthian Shot" recounts a wife's decision to leave her husband and infant son. Paulette Key finds her husband and son to be objectionable both in their appearance and their behavior. Harold Key's behavior is the sticking point: his wife bridles under his "stupid obstinacy." Their child takes after his dad with his "obstinate demands." Fed up with Harold's domination, Paulette "...took the little boy to church, had him christened Don, sent him home by his nurse, and boarded a train for the West (82). Get it? Don Key: donkey. That's Hammett's first published work.

One wonders why Mencken and Nathan published it in the first place in their "magazine of cleverness." Different times, perhaps? One also wonders about the source of the title. Did Hammett find out about the Parthian practice of shooting arrows at their enemies while retreating during his hours spent trying to make up for his lack of formal education or did Mencken and Nathan supply it? What the editors of *The Smart Set* probably saw in this throwaway piece of prose was not the pun but the piece's narrative double twist and its satiric bent. In the 18 lines of "The Parthian Shot," Hammett superficially develops support for Paulette Key as a clever and independent woman who leaves an obstinate and domineering husband and obnoxious child, and that this abandonment serves both of them right. Within the narrative, however, he weaves in suspicion that the whole episode springs not from Paulette's long suffering but from her arrogance and selfishness when one learns that her objections to her infant son rest on the baby's "inarticulate demands for its food, its toys." The fact in the final sentence that she "sent him home by his nurse" underlines the suggestion that the wife and mother is a coddled middle-class woman. Thus, in "The Parthian Shot" everybody gets the business—both the wife and the husband. In sum, this story was a precursor to Hammett's run of sex stories (narratives that center on relationships) in the early 1920s; it introduced his inclination in his early work to depend on the surprise ending in his storytelling, and it debuted the fondness for irony that dominates almost all of his works.

"THE GREAT LOVERS"

In the November 1922 number of *The Smart Set,* Hammett made his second appearance in print. Moving up, "The Great Lovers" is the second piece in the magazine — on page 4 — and this time there is a whole page of text, even if there is generous white space at the top and a type ornament at the bottom. In the issue there are Mencken and Nathan's usual pieces, Nathan's review of "various new plays" and assorted other ditties, serious and otherwise — Douglas Ford's "Six Cold Bottles of Pilsner" would seem to fall into the latter category.

"The Great Lovers" consists of a long, one-sentence introduction followed by twelve brief anecdotes gleaned from history that illustrate not love but monstrously exaggerated self-love. Here's the last, and longest, of them:

> And Thomas Hart Benton, who, when his publishers consulted
> him concerning the number of copies of his book *Thirty Years' View*,
> to be printed, replied, "Sir, you can ascertain from the last census
> how many persons in the United States can read, sir"; and who
> refused to speak against Calhoun when he was ill, saying, "When
> God Almighty lays His hands on a man, Benton takes his off! ...
> [sic]" [4].

Hammett cites similar expressions of arrogance from the Earl of Chatham,
Louis XIV of France, William Rufus, Prince Metternich, Joseph II of Aus-
tria, Charles IV of Spain, the Prince of Kaunitz-Rietberg, Virginia Oldoini
(the Countess of Castiglione), Lord Brougham, and Paul of Russia. It's all
very bookish — reminiscent of an hour or two of idle amusement spent
rummaging through *Bartlett's Familiar Quotations*. Indeed, in the whole
piece Hammett contributed only 48 of his own words (the introductory
sentence) to "The Great Lovers":

> Now that the meek and humble have inherited the earth and it
> were arrogance to look down on any man — the apologetic being the
> mode in lives— I should like to go monthly to some hidden gallery
> and, behind drawn curtains, burn perfumed candles before the
> images of: ... [4].

In "The Great Lovers," then, Hammett tries out for the second time
(in a pretty ham-handed manner) the double perspective of irony. Thus,
the piece argues both for but also overwhelmingly against the inflated self-
love expressed by the collection of historical big shots. All things considered, "The Great Lovers" is pretty much like fishing with dynamite.
Arrogance, however, was something very much on Hammett's mind at the
time. It's the subject of this piece and his next *Smart Set* story, "The Master Mind," as well as the paragraph-length fiction entitled "Immortality"
that appeared in *10 Story Book* in the same month that "The Great Lovers"
appeared in *The Smart Set*. The 171 words of "Immortality" set forth the
last testament of grocer Oscar Blichy who maintains that, in spite of his
apparent anonymity, he will be immortal because he has saved $17,000
that, at the time of his death, "is to go to the writer of the best biography
of me!" (www.miskatonic.org/rara-avis/biblio/lazy-gink)

"THE MASTER MIND"

Hammett's third *Smart Set* piece appeared in January 1923. It's another
one pager, appearing on page 56 with generous white space at the top and
a type ornament squeezed in at the bottom. It's Hammett's first foray into

crime and detection, but, instead of one based on his experiences, it's a tongue-in-cheek obituary of the fictitious Waldron Honeywell, the "Master Mind" detective.

It begins with "Whenever crime or criminals were discussed by enlightened folk, the name of Waldron Honeywell could be heard" (56). Honeywell's international reputation encompasses both the theoretical and the practical: "He had punctured Lombroso's theories at a time when the scientific world regarded the Italian as a Messiah" (56), and demonstrated that Arthur Conan Doyle would not have made a successful detective. On the practical side, Honeywell

> unearthed and frustrated the Versailles bomb plot before it was well on its feet; ... he recovered the aircraft program memoranda; ... [he succeeded in] finding the assassin of the emperor of Abyssinia ... [and] he coped with the epidemic of postal robberies [56].

Hammett loads most of the two-column piece with examples of Honeywell's prowess, almost in the manner of the self-promoting puffery characteristic of Alan Pinkerton's efforts on his own and his agency's behalf. Many of the examples are also reminiscent of the kind of gigantic criminal exploit that Hammett found so absurd in the thrillers he read and reviewed. In the manner of all of his early work, Hammett's last paragraph turns the thing around. In spite of having amassed a considerable fortune ("his monetary rewards were enormous"), Honeywell's estate consisted of $186.65 and a bundle of worthless securities issued by failed and fly-by-night companies. In other words, he may have been the scourge of evildoers around the globe, but he was also a sucker for big-stakes swindlers who peddled worthless stock. This, to be sure, undercuts all of the detective's vaunted achievements and perspicacity; equally, it implies a definition of crime that includes not simply felons, terrorists, and spies, but also unscrupulous speculators and scheming get-rich-quick entrepreneurs.

"FROM THE MEMOIRS OF A PRIVATE DETECTIVE"

In March 1923 *The Smart Set* ran a series of 29 short observations and brief anecdotes that Hammett wrote drawing upon his experiences as a Pinkerton operative. Few of them deal with being a detective or how to be a detective. Most of them involve observations about crime and criminals. All of them depend on satire or irony. Since a number of Hammett's observations shed light on specific pieces of fiction, discussion of "From the Memoirs" will occur later in this chapter.

"THE CRUSADER"

With this piece Hammett moved to the front of *The Smart Set*; in the August 1923 issue "The Crusader" is the opening piece of the magazine. In length the vignette actually boils down to about one double-column page, but it is spread over pages 9 and 10 with the magazine's title at the top of page 9 and type ornaments and supposedly witty anti-feminine epigrams ("Brunettes believe in suffocating their victims. Blondes accomplish the same effect by attrition") set at the bottom of page 10. "The Crusader" appears under the name Mary Jane Hammett, the name of Hammett's daughter born on October 15, 1921.

"The Crusader" is an anti–Ku Klux Klan story. It begins when Bert Pirtle's wife finishes sewing his first white robe and hood. Trying on the costume, Bert stares in the dresser mirror and conjures up visions of the crusades and a crusader: there is color and pageantry and he imagines that "It was not a man who stood in the mirror now, but a spirit: the spirit of a nation, even a race" (9). From seeing himself with the mantle of the crusader Bert shifts to imagining the sight of Sir Galahad — "out of the saffron cloud came a single rider all in white upon a white charger — another who rode in the Cause" (10). These visions supersede the more realistic — but not yet satiric — picture of Bert's initiation into the Klan:

> Never had he known such exultation, not even at the initiation the night before, when he had stood on Nigger Hill among a white shrouded throng, grotesque in the light of a gigantic bonfire, listening to and repeating a long, strange, inspiring, and not easily comprehensible oath [10].

The satiric punch line, however, comes, as usual, at the end. Bert's toddler son comes into the bedroom:

> The child's eyes widened at the sight of the figure before the bureau, two pink palms beat the air, a shriek of pure ecstasy came from its mouth. It tottered toward the man, gurgling joyously: "Peekaboo! Papa play peekaboo!" [10].

"THE GREEN ELEPHANT"

This was the last and longest piece (it runs from page 103 to page 108) Hammett wrote for *The Smart Set*; it appeared in the October 1923 issue. The story is not about elephants, green or otherwise. It's about crooks and money — $250,000 in cash is the item that becomes as much of a burden as carrying around an elephant. "The Green Elephant" was a logical successor to "From the Memoirs of a Private Detective," for in it Hammett began to explore in fiction one of the tenets about crime and detection he had established seven months earlier: criminals are stupid. The story concerns Joe Shupe, a dim-witted ex-counterman at a diner, who becomes "an unskilled laborer in the world of crime" (164). Indeed, crime, Shupe is told, is an unprofitable occupation:

> Making a living on the mace ain't duck soup! Take half these guys you hear telling the world what wonders they are at puffing boxes, knocking over joints, and the rest of the lays— not half of 'em makes three meals a day at it! [165]

Lounging in a doorway after an unsuccessful visit to the employment office, Shupe witnesses a robbery and in the ensuing shoot-out and hubbub, a valise lands at his feet. Snatching up the bag, he makes a hasty exit from the scene, ducking through buildings and changing streetcars. Upon opening the valise Shupe discovers that it contains $250,000, unimagined riches. But he has no idea of what to do with it and immediately becomes paranoid about both having the money and losing the money. He moves from hotel to hotel and finally goes from Spokane to Seattle, hoping he will be able to enjoy his new riches there. But he cannot. Afraid of asking for advice, afraid of spending the money, afraid of going to banks, Shupe becomes a derelict, wandering the streets hugging the bag of money to his chest. Because of his suspicious behavior, two Seattle detectives— who had recently been called on the carpet for not "getting results"—follow, question, and arrest Shupe and charge him as one of the robbers of the Fourth National Bank. Once convicted, Shupe becomes "his normal self again, both physically and mentally" (175).

In writing "The Green Elephant," Hammett looked back to his Tacoma days with the Pinkertons— the action of the story takes place in nearby Spokane and Seattle and the small bit about the Seattle police department's rebuke to the two detectives for not being energetic enough rings true. As a precursor to Hammett's series of criminal stories, it establishes that criminals are stupid, that crime quite literally doesn't pay, and that most crooks are easily caught, and introduces readers to snatches of thieves' argot: thus in the passage quoted above "puffing boxes" is blowing-up safes. He would come back to these things a number of times in succeeding stories.

Hammett achieved some success in writing for *The Smart Set*. From the minimal "The Parthian Shot" his pieces became longer until his last *Smart Set* entry was an actual short story rather than a vignette. While his pieces were longer, their attitude remained the same — satiric and, as satire inevitably is, condescending. In technique, all of the *Smart Set* articles, except "From the Memoirs of a Private Detective," depend on the snappy, witty conclusion. Perhaps Hammett's most significant development over the course of his submissions to the magazine lay in his choice of subject matter. Toward the end of his short career with *The Smart Set,* Hammett shifted his attention from general satire to a world he knew intimately: the world of crime and detection. To be sure, his attitude in "The Master Mind," " From the Memoirs of a Private Detective," and "The Green Elephant" remains as supercilious as in the other *Smart Set* appearances, but it did provide a focus for Hammett as a writer as well as an identity — the detective who was a detective story writer — that made him famous and that he probably lived to regret. One of the most intriguing questions about Hammett is why he moved on from *The Smart Set.* Was it because he needed more money than he could make from writing frothy bits for *The Smart Set*? Did someone coach him and point him toward writing other kinds of fiction than those featured in "the magazine of cleverness?" Or was it because in October 1923 — in the same issue that carried Hammett's last *Smart Set* story — Mencken announced that he was quitting his job as editor of the magazine?

Sex Stories

Numerically, sex stories come in second (albeit a distant second) to detective stories in Hammett's repertoire during the period leading up to the publication of *The Red Harvest.* Looking at his earliest output, moreover, it appears as if Hammett's first impulse as a writer was to concentrate on stories about marital relationships, to write, in the terminology of the time, "sex stories." Relations between wives and husbands is the subject of his first, miniscule *Smart Set* piece, "The Parthian Shot." Hammett's second story to be published outside of the pages of *The Smart Set,* however, is his first real "sex story."

"The Barber and His Wife"

This story appeared in the December 1922 issue of *Brief Stories.* It takes place in an unnamed East Coast city and recounts the final break up of the marriage of Louis and Pearl Stemler. Their relationship is particularly poisonous. "The Barber and His Wife" begins with the Stemlers' morning rituals, whereby each partner tries mightily to irritate and dominate the other. Louis ostentatiously exercises by the open window, splashes in the bath, and sings while dressing, all designed to be "sufficiently irritating to Pearl" (54). She rushes to the kitchen to have breakfast on the table before Louis finishes dressing: "It was a point of honor to her never to rise until her husband had his trousers in his hand, and then to have his breakfast on the table in the kitchen ... by the time he was dressed" (55). Hammett describes the Stemlers' relationship as "warfare" in which each partner has his or her particular offensive and defensive weapons.

After the morning interlude, Louis Stemler's character becomes the principal focus of the story. The proprietor of an exclusive barbershop, Stemler, robust of health, prides himself on being a he-man. Thus, his self-conscious exercises in the morning and his pride in his practice of walking to his shop: "He always walked downtown in the morning, covering the twenty blocks in twenty minutes—a feat to which he would allude whenever the opportunity arose" (57).

When he meets his brother, Louis advises him to "get out and walk; let me take you down to the gym; take cold baths" (58). Hammett makes Louis's interests "manly" ones: prizefights, racing, and burlesque. When the crisis of the story arrives, Louis believes that the answer to his problem resides in manliness: "For these situations men had fists and muscles and courage. For these emergencies men ate beef, breathed at open windows, held memberships in athletic clubs, and kept tobacco smoke out of their lungs" (59). But it does not.

Pearl Stemler has been having an affair. Louis learns this from his brother and confronts his wife with it. Far from denying the affair, Pearl justifies her actions as a response to Stemler's "manliness": "He reads things besides the sporting page. He doesn't go to prizefights. He likes the movies. He doesn't like burlesque shows. He inhales cigarette smoke. He doesn't think muscle's everything a man ought to have" (60).

Dismissing Pearl's outburst, Louis seeks out his wife's lover and, in good manly fashion, thrashes him. Afterward Louis believes that this has provided "a sensible, manly solution of the problem" (62). Except that when he returns home after a night out with the boys, he finds that his wife has left him. The brief conclusion to "The Barber and His Wife" shows Louis losing his confidence in his view of manliness—"his calm certitude ran out of him" (63). But to the last sentence he continues to define the world in terms of physical strength: "Why, a man might just as well be a weakling!" (63).

"The Barber and His Wife" recapitulates the situation from Hammett's first publication, "The Parthian Shot." In it he portrays a boorish man whose insensitivity essentially forces his wife to leave him. Only here it's a short story and not an epigram. Hammett pays particular attention to drawing Louis Stemler as objectionable. Stemler, of course, is an evangelist for old-school manliness, an attitude that encourages pomposity, vanity, arrogance, exploitation, rudeness, and downright bad taste. With regard to the latter, Hammett makes a point of noting Stemler's pride in his new shirt — "a white silk one with broad cerise stripes." With regard to the former, Hammett centers Stemler's vices on his pride in his physical vigor and well-being — attributes he believes can be gained and possessed through personal effort and willpower. That assumption, of course, would seem particularly delusional to someone who was chronically ill, as Hammett was. The undercutting of "manliness," then, is the principal focus of the story, but it also contains a minor note about drudgery and routine. Indeed, aside from being a pompous ass, Stemler is a nascent Flitcraft from *The Maltese Falcon*— the man habituated and self-defined by rituals.

"The Joke on Eloise Morey"

Six months after "The Barber and His Wife," *Brief Stories* came out with another one of Hammett's sex stories, "The Joke on Eloise Morey." One of the differences in this piece from Hammett's earlier sex stories is that, between "The Barber and His Wife" and "The Joke on Eloise Morey" he had begun to think about his experiences as a detective and about the crime story, witnessed by the intervening publication of "The Sardonic Star of Tom Doody" in *Brief Stories*, "The Vicious Circle" in *The Black Mask*, and "From the Memoirs of a Private Detective" in *The Smart Set*.

Hammett drew the relationship in "Eloise Morey" as more poisonous and vitriolic than that in "The Barber and His Wife." The story begins with

> "But, good God, Eloise, I love you!"
> "But, good God, Dudley, I hate you" [71].

Warfare here is out in the open as opposed to the devious sniping in the earlier piece. Hammett directs readers' sympathy toward the husband, an artist whose ambitions and abilities are ridiculed and crushed by his wife:

> "You were a genius; you were going to be famous and wealthy and God knows what all! And I fell for it and married you: a milk-and-water nincompoop who'll never be anything. An artist! An artist who paints pictures that nobody will look at, much less buy. Pictures that are supposed to be delicate. Delicate! Weak and wishy-washy daubs of color that are like the fool that paints them" [72].

Eloise has the verbal edge in the one-sided combat in the story. Dudley doesn't fight back. First of all, Eloise is both more forceful and bigger than her husband. She is two inches taller and Dudley is short and slight. He is in love with his wife and possessed of a nature too refined to engage in marital combat: "His was too sensitive a nature to permit any of the answers he might have made. Where a cruder man would have met the woman on her own ground and hammered his way to victory ... he was helpless" (71). After being verbally bludgeoned by his wife, Dudley goes to his studio and commits suicide, leaving a pathetic note expressing undying love for Eloise. Shocked by the implications of the note — not her husband's death — Eloise destroys it. Shortly thereafter she is questioned by the police and circumstantial evidence (including overheard outbursts in which she wished for her husband's death) leads to her arrest for his murder.

With "Eloise Morey" Hammett fused the sex story and the crime story in which the machinery of the criminal justice system provides the denouement. From this the story contains the destruction of evidence, testimony from the Morey's maid, the introduction of police officers, and even official warning about self-incrimination ("You're arrested for the murder of your husband, and anything you say may be used against you" [77]). Eloise's callousness, domineering nature, and psychological abuse of her husband are punished by the law. All of this, of course, drips with irony in that Eloise's concern about her image as a wife has caused her to destroy the piece of evidence that would have literally but not figuratively exonerated her. Just as misunderstood manliness is Stemler's undoing in "The Barber and His Wife," in "Eloise Morey" the main character is superficially done in by her perverse notion of social propriety. In both cases, however, the real reason for the main character's fall resides in part upon sadism. Thus, with Eloise, "these not unfamiliar, and in this case anticipated, indications of pain infuriated her even as they pleased her" (71). Part of it, too, comes from lack of humanity and Hammett shows this in "Eloise Morey" by describing her eyes as "twin points of steel" and her mien as that of a panther. In all of Hammett's pieces written to this point, irony is the principal method and object of his fiction. Indeed, his use of "joke" in the title of this piece, as well as using the term "sardonic" in the story he published four months earlier ("The Sardonic Star of Tom Doody"), highlights the irony that was a constant in Hammett's published pieces.

"Holiday"

This story, published in *New Pearsons* in July 1923, is the most atypical — and autobiographical — of all of Hammett's sex stories. Partly this comes from the tone of the story, which is dispassionate and gray. Unlike the other sex stories, it does not concern relationship problems. Rather it is about not forming relationships.

"Holiday" recounts a 12-hour period in the life of Paul Hetherwick. Hetherwick is a veteran patient at "United States Public Health Hospital No. 64" outside of San Diego, the same hospital where Hammett was treated for tuberculosis in 1921. He asks for and receives a one-day pass to San Diego. There, he hurriedly cashes his monthly compensation check ($80) and catches the bus for Tijuana, Mexico. Once in Tijuana, Hetherwick hightails it for the racetrack. He wins some but mostly loses at the track; neither winning nor losing nor even drinking liquor unavailable to him in the United States makes much of an impression on him. From the track Hetherwick goes to a saloon where he spends most of his remaining money buying drinks for a bar girl ("A sub-harlot ... holding out false promises of her monstrous body to bring about that stimulation of traffic in liquor for which she was employed" [116]) in whom he has only a passing, albeit weird, interest. "If he ever turned to a woman of this particularly sordid world it would be to some monster as the one down the street. Given a certain turn of temper, there would be a savage, ghoulish joy in her" (118).

Careful not to spend all of his remaining money on this woman, he leaves intending "to buy a drink or two for the girl with the amazing red hair at the Palace" (116). With her, as well, Hetherwick has ambivalent feelings. They experience "a certain definite delight" smiling into one another's faces. Yet Hetherwick, while by no means sure that she is a prostitute, nonetheless feels that "the desires of too many men had rendered her no longer quite desirable" (117). On his way out of Tijuana, he buys postcards and sends them to friends with the following message: "They tell me the States have gone dry." He gives 40 of his last 85 cents to a panhandler. Back in San Diego, in passing he sees "the most beautiful face he had ever seen." And then he returns to the hospital. Hetherwick blows his entire month's compensation during the twelve hours in Tijuana, but he doesn't care. He gets mildly intoxicated in a place where buying alcohol is legal, but that, too, is only a mild entertainment. He passes the evening with two women, but he is content to make do without either of them. For a holiday it's a pretty gray affair.

In some ways Hetherwick is a precursor to Phil Truax in "Laughing Masks" and Steve Threefall in "Nightmare Town," both veterans whose lives were rendered purposeless after their service in the Army. Unlike those two characters, however, Hetherwick finds no new definition in adventure. The irony of "Holiday" comes forth most forcefully in the story's title, and the fact that his day out of the hospital for Hetherwick differs little from the dreariness of his days in the hospital. He does things in Tijuana that should brighten his spirits—or at least get his adrenaline and hormones flowing. But Hammett does not permit Hetherwick or the readers these excitements because of his stripped-down, objective narration. The only place in the story that Hammett allows readers glimpses of anything beyond the bare statement of facts comes in his presentation of Hetherwick's attitudes toward women. On his holiday he encounters three women: the "sub-harlot" in the first Tijuana bar, the red-haired girl at the Palace, and the woman with "the most beautiful face he had ever seen" on the street in San Diego. Much of Hetherwick's attitude toward these women revolves around his unresolved thoughts about the public and private ramifications of women's beauty. Thus, he stifles his inclination to become attached to the red-haired girl, even though "she had a freshness that withstood" her job as a drink hustler. And with the beautiful woman he glimpses in San Diego his fascination is not so much with her but with the arrogant and threatening attitude of her escort:

> He did not know he was staring until the beautiful face's escort in the uniform of a petty officer whispered to him, with peculiar, threatening emphasis: "Like her looks?"
> Paul went on down the street slowly ... wondering just what would be the mental processes of a man who under those conditions would ask that question in just that tone [119].

But his curiosity about how that man or about how he himself resolves the conundrum of how beauty can be both a public possession and the basis of intimacy goes unanswered other than in his earlier thoughts about sex with the first bar girl he met and that "given a certain turn of temper, there would be a savage, ghoulish joy in her." But in "Holiday," Hetherwick finds no such joy, only a trip back to the hospital during which "the fog-laden air rushing into the automobile chilled him and kept him coughing almost continuously" (119).

While Hammett never specifies the cause of Hetherwick's hospitalization — to make him a tuberculosis patient would have been too self-indulgent — the story makes clear that his is a chronic illness. It is also a chronic illness for which hospitalization is at best ineffectual. What this means, then, is that the grayness Hetherwick encounters during his holiday simply recapitulates the world he leaves and returns to at the hospital.

"The Dimple"

Hammett's only appearance in *Saucy Stories* (October 15, 1923) is more morally shocking than saucy. "The Dimple," not even a thousand words long, is a double-layered vignette involving death and adultery. It begins when writer, Walter Dowe, breaks off from his work at 3:15 A.M. and discovers that his wife, Althea, has not yet returned from the theater. He telephones friends and learns that there had been a fire at the theater and that victims of the fire had been taken to local hospitals. At City Hospital he can learn nothing about Althea's fate. Dowe turns for help to his friend, Murray Bornis, who is the police commissioner. He does so even though he believes that Bornis has never been one of his wife's favorite people:

> She never liked Bornis. His frank sensuality, and his unsavory reputation for numerous affairs with numerous women, had offended her strict conception of morality. To be sure, she had always given him the courtesy due her husband's friend; but it was generally a frigid giving. And Bornis, understanding her attitude, and perhaps a little contemptuous of her narrow views, had been as coolly polite as she [90].

Dowe and Bornis search the city's hospitals to no avail and as a last resort they go to the morgue. There Bornis, not her husband, recognizes Althea's corpse, even though it was "a face that stampeding leather heels had robbed of features; a torso that was battered and blackened and cut, and from which the clothing had been torn. All that was human of it were the legs; they had somehow escaped disfigurement" (90–91). Bornis identifies Althea's corpse from a dimple on her knee. This, obviously, also identifies Bornis as her lover and places a new and different interpretation on their behavior in front of her husband.

Beyond the desire to provide shock and sensationalism, not a whole lot can be said about "The Dimple." As in "The Joke on Eloise Morey," Hammett used an artist husband as the victim. Were the story not so short, a case could be made for arguing that the writer's absorption in his work caused him to neglect his wife: "She never interrupted him when he was at work, and he was usually too engrossed by his labors to hear her footsteps when she passed his study door" (88). Nonetheless, he is passionately devoted to his wife: "He was on the verge of hysterics. He must take hold of himself. He must not collapse before he found Althea" (90). Unlike the ineffectual Dowe, Althea's lover possesses power (he's the police commissioner after all), sensuality, and a socially unsavory, dangerous reputation. Added to these, moreover, he has passion and Hammett makes it clear that he loved Althea when he identifies her corpse with "a vibrant, anguished voice" that at once identifies the body, exposes adultery, and reveals his love for his friend's wife. What this means, then, is that, short as it is, "The

Dimple" displays a degree of implied moral complexity not found in most of Hammett's earlier sex stories.

"ESTHER ENTERTAINS"

This piece occupies two-and-a-half double-column pages in the February 1924 issue of *Brief Stories*. It consists of an interior monologue with five short interruptions of one-sided dialogue. The substance of the monologue revolves around the principal's shifting attitudes toward Esther, his mistress. For most of the piece his attitude toward Esther suggests that her chief use is for convenient, semiregular dirty weekends. He finds her to be growing physically unappealing: "Even in this light, diluted and tinted to friendliness, she failed to appear quite young. Her figure, too, was less youthfully slim now than merely thin" (524). Her actions irritate him. She fidgets, she slobbers up the ends of the cigarettes she insists on lighting for him, she plays the radio or phonograph ("that damned talking machine"), and she is intrusive: "...Why did women always want to know what you were thinking about?" (525). Added to this, she seems to be a drama queen, theatrically investing their relationship with exhibitionistic "solemnity," "seriousness," and "reverence."

As was Hammett's trademark, toward the end of the monologue the man's attitude changes. First he becomes aware that she does possess sexual allure and that in their relationship they are both playing roles: "And she did kiss well; she was undeniably delectable in spite of her gestures, her dramatics.... After all, the difference between her acting and his was only a matter of degree" (526). In his new attitude toward her he glimpses in Esther the fundamental power and magnetism inherent in all women ("It was as if something — some same thing behind all of them — was looking out through their faces; some aboriginal — but that was fantastic" [526]). Only he sees this as not merely the creation of fantasy and, in the end, Esther overwhelms him:

> Sincere or affected, she was devilishly fascinating, nevertheless.
> ... If only she —
> ... By Jove, she was glorious! [526, Hammett's ellipses].

"Esther Entertains" is about as risqué as Hammett gets—and that's pretty risqué for 1924. Four months later he would defend the story from charges of immorality on the grounds that it examined the universal theme of the relationship between the sexes. And that it does. It exhibits the transforming power of women's sexuality: she changes from a scrawny, aging, trivial odalisque into something delectable and glorious, and he abandons his aloof rationality for passion. While none of this is especially profound, "Esther Entertains" is the deepest exploration of the theme than Hammett had undertaken to date. It also demonstrates two other things. The first is that Hammett was experimenting with narrative style. "Esther Entertains" is the first time he tried the first-person narrative in his sex stories and, insofar as it is effective, the point of view makes it so. The second interesting aspect of the piece is that it shows that Hammett very much viewed himself as an avant-garde writer — a sophisticate who dared to handle themes shocking to middle-class sensibilities.

"In Defence [*sic*] of the Sex Story"

The June 1924 number of *The Writer's Digest: A Monthly Magazine for Writers of Short Stories, Photoplays, Poems, Popular Songs, Etc.* carried a piece by Hammett entitled "In Defence [sic] of the Sex Story." In this short outburst, Hammett presents, as the editors tell us,

> a discussion of an article by H. Bedford-Jones which appeared in the October Writer's Digest, entitled "Sex Deftly Handled." Mr. Jones held that the writer could not afford to write them, as it affected both his reputation and his mental fibre [7].

Hammett seems to have viewed Jones's piece as a personal affront, one probably connected with his last sex story, "Esther Entertains." He identifies himself as having written about the subject: "I've written altogether three stories that are what are sometimes called 'sex stories,' and two — or possibly three — that might be so called if you stretched the term" (7).

Hammett asserts that writing about "the relations between the sexes" is one of the prominent themes in great literature past and present, citing Shakespeare's *Measure for Measure* and, his contemporary favorite, Anatole France. In the piece following Hammett's, Bedford-Jones rejoins that "my argument is not against the story worth telling, but against the story deliberately written with a smutty pen to get the dinero. Your record shows that you're not that sort of writer" (8).

In all, this piece is a naïve attempt at self-justification — and self-promotion on Hammett's part. What it shows, however, is that, at this point in his career at least, Hammett had not yet identified himself exclusively as a detective story writer, or, indeed, a writer fastened to any particular genre. He identifies himself as a literary person trying to engage with universal literary themes. Writing this also, perhaps, made Hammett think a bit more deeply about the serious purposes that he had achieved and could achieve in writing about relationships.

"THE RUFFIAN'S WIFE"

Hammett published the last and, in many ways, the most complex of his sex stories in *Sunset Magazine* (October 1925). Written in a more figurative style than the earlier stories, "The Ruffian's Wife" combines elements of his stories of adventure, his stories about criminals, and his stories about relationships between men and women, or, in this case, women and men. It recounts the return home of Guy Tharp from a life of danger, adventure, and mayhem, and his wife's changing views of her husband, of herself, and of their relationship.

Guy Tharp, the "ruffian" of the title, is made of the typical stuff of adventure heroes. He's big, he's handsome, and he's charming. He is a soldier of fortune whose life has been spent in the world's most exotic and dangerous places: Tharp regales his wife, Margaret, with tales of roughhousing, gambling, mayhem, and slaughter; of storms and moonless nights; of India and Indochina; of berzerk natives and fellow adventurers. As the story begins he has just returned from a caper that was supposed to have netted him and his backers "half a million rupees" but which apparently went sour: "We turned the island upside down from Dambulla all the way to Kala-wewa, and got nothing" (63). But he has picked up $15,000 on his way home to San Francisco in payment for an unspecified (but dangerous and illicit) job: "I did a thing a man needed done" (64). At the end of the narrative he's off to grab up a pearl concession in Bolivia. Throughout the story the metaphors of "bull," "raging beast," and, most often, "red wolf" become attached to Guy. And at the beginning of the story, through Margaret's eyes, Hammett contrasts the lives of danger and domesticity with the honors going to danger.

> What ... would it be like to have for a husband a tame, housebroken male who came regularly to meals and bed, whose wildest flying could attain no giddier height than an occasional game of cards, a suburbanite's holiday in San Francisco...? [58].

At the beginning of the story Hammett emphasizes Margaret's absolute devotion to her husband, to his manliness, and to his dedication to adventure. Thus, she eagerly anticipates the disorder he will bring into her scrubbed and tidy house — his outrageous laughter and curses; his cigars, cigar butts, and ashes; the litter of empty liquor bottles rolling under foot and piled on the front porch; and the jumble of clothing, equipment, and weapons strewn around the house. In every respect Margaret idolizes her husband and believes that he "alone was firmly planted in a whirling universe" (59).

But then the appearance of Leonidas Doucas, a first sketch for Caspar Gutman of *The Maltese Falcon*, turns Margaret's world upside down. Doucas, the financier of Guy's last, apparently failed, exploit, enters and demands the fortune with which he claims Guy absconded. They argue over this in the Tharp living room, there is a fight, and, assisted by Margaret's turning off the lights, Guy kills Doucas. During all of this, Margaret's feelings about her husband change. As she listens to the two men argue in her living room, questions torment her:

> They had to do with the existence or nonexistence of this gilding
> courage, without which a rover might be no more than a shoplifter
> on a geographically larger scale, a sneak thief who crept into
> strangers' lands instead of their houses, a furtive, skulking figure
> with an aptitude for glamorous autobiography [63].

Indeed, in stories like the Op's "The Tenth Clew" there is in Hammett's early work a fairly strong motif of people being corrupted by lives of adventure in foreign lands. Margaret's new assessment of the image of the "soldier of fortune" diminishes her husband in her eyes—"Guy seemed to become abruptly smaller" (65) and turns, for a time, to loathing of both Guy and herself. Her attitude, then, changes to a most sane and realistic appraisal of herself and her husband: "The plain truth was she had never seen Guy as a man, but always as a half-fabulous being" (65). As a result of this new view, Margaret turns off the living room lights, which allows Guy to wrestle Doucas's gun away from him and to strangle him in the ensuing melee. It is then that Hammett turns to Margaret's feelings for the third time. Seeing the effects of the struggle, "she stared at him in horror, her back pressed against the wall, sick with her own part in this death, sick with Guy's callous brutality of voice and mien" (67). With the final twist, Guy neither sees nor understands his wife's feelings. He wipes the blood off of his hands and face and prepares to rush off to Bolivia in search of Doucas's pearl concession.

"The Ruffian's Wife," then, reevaluates the adventure story hero, heroes of imperial romances like those of John Buchan. The soldier of fortune, rather than being a swashbuckling hero whose engagement with danger proves his worth and whose actions achieve high ends of civilization, becomes in Hammett's story the "sneak thief." Possessed of this view, it is small wonder that Hammett didn't write more than a few adventure stories. "The Ruffian's Wife" also follows up on Hammett's short stories about criminals, the burden of which is that criminals as a class are neither admirable, perceptive, smart, nor especially efficient. Guy Tharp, dispassionately considered, is a blowhard who can't even get the drop on an asthmatic fat man and needs his wife's help to get him out of a jam. In addition to the recapitulation of these motifs from his other kinds of stories, Hammett in "The Ruffian's Wife" presents a fuller picture of the disintegration of a relationship than he had in his other sex stories. Margaret Tharp experiences not one defining moment in her relationship with her husband, but several, going from blind adulation of Guy at the start, to shock and loathing, to mature recognition of human frailty, to shock and loathing again. This emotional and intellectual roller coaster presents a fuller and more realistic view of a dying relationship than one finds in the other sex stories. Finally, Hammett seems to have devoted more attention to figurative language in the composition of "The Ruffian's Wife." In the opening paragraphs of the story, for instance, he uses compound word descriptors: "the sunpainted west wall," "the next-door chickens." There's the clock simile — "the clock's hands pointed like one long hand to a few minutes past seven." There's the comparison the narrator uses to describe Doucas's speech: "sighing puffs of breath spaced his words, cushioned them, gave them the semblance of gems nestled separately in raw cotton." And there is the personification of "the fragrance of magnolia in the breeze tickling her cheek with loose hair-ends." His attention to character and theme and style make this a fitting farewell to the sex story, one of Hammett's principal vehicles during his early years as a writer.

No doubt it was very avant-garde and daring to write about sex in the 1920s. And Hammett fit right in: two of his stories deal pretty openly with adultery and in one of them, "The Dimple," his main objective patently is to shock his readers. Then, too, treating relationships between men and women as examples of human folly was something that, for Hammett, corresponded with the emphasis on irony and satire of his first publisher — *The Smart Set*. The sex stories, however, give few clues about what he would later become as the writer of detective stories except, perhaps, in the negative sense: they demonstrate the messiness as well as the literal and figurative psychological violence of relationships that his detectives consciously avoid in order to do their jobs. Rather than the misogyny that can be seen in some of the detective stories, however, several of the sex stories demonstrate sympathy and even compassion for women and their roles in sterile and destructive relationships. Thus, in the two stories with "wife" in their titles ("The Barber and His Wife" and "The Ruffian's Wife") the female characters attract far more sympathy than the men do. Indeed, in the first story Hammett included a strong anti-machismo theme and throughout punishes traditional views of "manliness" and encourages sympathy for the artistic, if not the domestic, male character. While the subject of adultery comes up, the themes of obstinacy and arrogance carried over from his *Smart Set* pieces weigh more heavily in Hammett's delineation of relationships in the sex stories.

The sex stories got Hammett into print; they allowed him to examine, albeit mostly superficially, the ways in which people behave, and they provided a place for him to work out motifs important for his other kinds of fiction. "The Joke on Eloise Morey" served as a practice run for the criminal stories he would write, and "The Ruffian's Wife" gave Hammett the opportunity to make a final comment on the popular action/adventure story.

Adventure Stories

In discussions of Hammett, the name of the character Philo Vance often turns up. It shouldn't. Hammett began writing fiction when the Golden Age of the detective story was just beginning in Britain: Christie's first novel, *The Mysterious Affair at Styles,* appeared in 1920 but was not published in the United States until 1927 — the same year as Hammett's move from short stories into novels. American Golden Age writers, moreover, did not begin to publish until after Hammett had become an established feature in pulp fiction: S. S. Van Dine's first Philo Vance story, *The Benson Murder Case,* came out in 1926 and Ellery Queen's first effort, *The Roman Hat Mystery* (1929), did not appear until after the publication of *The Red Harvest.* If it's a question of influence, one should look not to middle-brow detective fiction — which did not exist in America when Hammett began to write — but to thrillers and imperial romances. Books by British thriller writers dominated popular fiction in the first quarter of the twentieth century. Books like Sax Rohmer's *The Mystery of Dr. Fu Manchu* (1913); John Buchan's *Thirty-Nine Steps* (1915) and *Mr. Standfast* (1919); and Sapper's *Bulldog Drummond* (1920) and *The Black Gang* (1922) came into print in the United States shortly after they came out in Britain. As a reviewer Hammett would later have little but scorn for thriller writers, and in "The Gutting of Couffignal" he showed this when the Continental Op settles down with a copy of M. P. Shiel's *The Lord of the Sea* (1901) and finds it to be "as real as a dime." Nonetheless, when Hammett turned to writing fiction in 1922, one of the main kinds of fast-selling fiction was the thriller, which was generally a story, set in an exotic locale, about an above-average average man pitted against the deep plots of a mastermind intent on executing heinous schemes. Forget about Philo Vance then.

"THE ROAD HOME"

After beginning with sex stories, Hammett tried his hand at action/ adventure stories with "The Road Home," which appeared in *The Black Mask* in December 1922. To label it a short story is hyperbole — "The Road Home" is only 1,300 words. Set in Asia, the story focuses on a dialogue between Hagedorn, the hero, and Barnes, the villain. From start to finish Hammett freights the piece with the exotic, principally by bringing in foreign words and phrases. Thus, the story takes place on a boat in the middle of a river somewhere in Asia, and at the beginning the hero looks "over the teak sides of the *jahaz* to where the wrinkled snout of a *muggar* broke the surface of the river" (31). And almost at the end the hero has an exchange with the owner of said *jahaz* (or boat) in "his broken Burmese": "'I go after him. You wait three hours,' pointing over-head, 'until noon — *ne apomha*. If I am not back then do not wait — *malotu thaing, thwa. Thi?*" [34].

In the wilds of Asia (probably Burma), then, Hagedorn has found and captured Barnes, and the story centers on Barnes's efforts to talk Hagedorn out of taking him back to New York to answer for his crimes. The crime in question, as Barnes would have it, consists of a holdup that went wrong and during which a messenger was killed: "Why, I thought of that hold-up as a lark when we planned it! And that messenger yelled and I guess I was excited, and my gun went off the first thing I knew" (33).

After the manner of the Pinkertons' much-publicized chase of Butch Cassidy and the Sundance Kid into the wilds of Mexico, Hagedorn is an agency detective who has taken on the job of tracking Barnes down in the wilds of Yunan and Burma. Hammett repeatedly calls Hagedorn a "detective" and Hagedorn says that he has "promised my people" to find Barnes. Insofar as he can in such a short piece, Hammett emphasizes that, for the hero, being a detective is more than a job. As the Continental Op would later define himself using some of the same language, Hagedorn tells Barnes that "maybe manhunting isn't the nicest trade in the world but it's all the trade I got" (32). Being a detective, "The Road Home" emphasizes, means persistence — Hagedorn, readers learn, has been searching the jungles for Barnes for two years. Being a detective, too, means understanding criminals. Hagedorn knows that Barnes is both brutal and a liar. Thus, when Barnes tries to justify his crime as the result of youth and circumstance, Hagedorn reminds him of his savage treatment of the Burmese woman he was living with.

Hammett, who at this point in his career saw criminals as a sorry lot (see "From the Memoirs of a Private Detective"), portrays a social difference between Hagedorn and Barnes. Barnes's clothes are shabby and he uses nonstandard diction — slang and incorrect grammar, a characteristic of criminals in most of Hammett's stories. Barnes is rootless versus Hagedorn who thinks of home and a daughter. Added to this, Hagedorn has principles. Indeed, those principles govern most of the story. It begins with emphasis on Hagedorn's commitment to his job and at the crucial point in the story, when Barnes escapes into a crocodile-infested river, he shoots the crocs rather than the escaping felon because

> ...the sudden but logical instinct to side with the member of his own species against enemies from another wiped out all other considerations, and sent the rifle to his shoulder to throw a shower of bullets into the *muggars* [33].

Hammett's whole focus on Hagedorn bends toward sentiment. Hagedorn is dutiful in spite of its great physical cost. He takes the hard choices versus the easy ones. His thoughts center on home and family — thus, the title. He is chivalric and protects human life and deplores Barnes's treatment of women. This is the focus for almost the entire story. In his last thoughts to himself, however, Hagedorn thinks about the rigors of finding Barnes again: "Two years ... it took to find him when he didn't know I was hunting for him. Now — Oh, hell! It may take five years" (34). But then Hammett throws a *Smart Set* curve when the hero adds, "I wonder about them jewels of his" (34), alluding to the bribe that Barnes offered him at the beginning of the narrative. And so having built up a conventional sentimental hero, Hammett leaves the readers with a problematic ending, begging the question of whether Hagedorn has been tempted and tainted by the promise of wealth as opposed to being solely motivated by the stern demands of duty.

"LAUGHING MASKS"

By October 1923 Hammett had published three Continental Op stories in *The Black Mask*, and with the second, "Crooked Souls," had stopped using the pseudonyms he had used in all of his pervious fiction. The next month, November 1923, his "Laughing Masks" appeared in *Action Stories,* and with it Hammett reverted to his old pseudonym Peter Collinson. "Laughing Masks" is considerably longer than anything Hammett had written to that date — at 20 pages in the original it's twice the length of the earlier Op stories in *The Black Mask*. It is also Hammett's attempt to write a substantial adventure story.

"Laughing Masks," retitled "When Luck's Running Good," has a hero with a real hero's name: Phil Truax. Hammett portrayed him as a typical member of part of the post–World War I generation.

> Since his discharge from the army he had been drifting, finding himself at odds with the world, gambling, doing chores for political clubs— never doing anything very vicious, perhaps, but steadily being more and more enmeshed in the underworld [105].

Mostly, however, this comes into the story as a past that the hero can surmount through moral commitment: "Well, that was all past! After this tangle came to an end he would get a job and go back to the ways he had known before the war interrupted his aspirations" (105). But vices can also be virtues. At the start of the story readers find Truax on his way home from a poker game with $400 of winnings in his pocket. He is a skilled and inveterate gambler and throughout the rest of the story Hammett uses poker as a defining metaphor for his hero. Again and again the narration comes back to the hero's poker face — when he negotiates with the villain and even when he is threatened with torture. Like the poker player, Truax possesses the ability to judge his opponents acutely and, more than that, he has the gambler's faith in luck.

> Times come, as every gambler knows, when a man gets into a streak of luck, when everything he touches proves fruitful; and his play is to push his luck to a fare-you-well — make a killing while the fickle goddess is smiling [94].

In typical thriller fashion, at the start of the story Truax is the "average" man leaning an aimless and unexamined life. By accident and inclination, he attempts to intervene to save a woman in distress. This results not in saving the woman but in a bump on the head and discovery of a black silk handbag containing a few baubles and an indecipherable letter written, it turns out, in Russian. When a Russian aristocrat turns up to claim the bag, Truax, more on impulse than reason, insists on returning it to its owner, not her uncle. When Uncle Kapaloff brings his niece to Truax's apartment it's love at first sight: "To Phil she seemed the loveliest creature he had ever seen" (103). And there is mute communication that there is something seriously wrong — the beautiful Romaine Kapaloff's eyes, for a split second, display abject fear and helplessness to the observant (and smitten) hero. So Phil withholds the purse and several nights later goes to the Kapaloffs' house to get to the bottom of things. In an inept attempt at housebreaking, Phil falls into the hands of the villain — who knew what he was up to all along. He is threatened with torture, is rescued by Romaine, and is involved in a shoot-out in the darkened mansion. At the end, in addition to the machinery to set the world aright, Phil, somewhat inarticulately, promises to reform: "Then I'm going to convince him [Romaine's guardian] that I'm — that I'm not too tough an egg. And then we'll see" (126).

In "Laughing Masks" it's the villain who runs the story. If not from phrenology or some allied method, Phil intuits that Boris Kapaloff is out of his league: rather than the low forehead and jutting jaw of the criminal, Kapaloff has a broad forehead, aquiline nose, and a well-defined chin and jaw, and he exudes worldliness and power of a sort that Phil has never experienced. Indeed, Kapaloff comes both from the tradition of the master criminal — characters like Sapper's Carl Peterson or better yet, Collins's Count Fosco — and from that of the gentleman crook, à la Raffles. Truax admits that Kapaloff is smarter than he is. In the suspense part of the story — when the hero invades the villain's lair — Kapaloff knows beforehand what Phil is planning and outwits him. Not only that, Kapaloff possesses the autocrat's contempt for human life. After shooting one of his own lifelong servants, Kapaloff flips the corpse over with his foot and fires four bullets to obliterate the man's face. Kapaloff's house, where the concluding action takes place, possesses the same Gothic accoutrements found in most villains' lairs. There are wolfhounds roaming the grounds ("not the sedate, finely bred borozois of my lady's promenade, but great, shaggy wolfkillers of the steppes, over half a man's height ... and more than a hundred pounds of fighting machinery" [107] and hulking, brutish servants. Vicious and evil he may be, but Boris Kapaloff is also a gentleman and a sportsman. He speaks to Phil, even when threatening to apply a hot knife to the soles of his feet, with suave courtesy. Near the surface of the entire story, in fact, is the motif of the game, the poker game, in which deportment may be just as important as winning. Hammett makes this clear when Kapaloff addresses Phil as a fellow sportsman and describes their whole encounter as a sporting contest with its own set of Queensbury rules.

This is the note upon which Hammett ended the story. "Laughing Masks" finishes with a farewell written by the defeated and mortally wounded Kapaloff. It congratulates Romaine and wishes her happiness in the future with Truax and ends with "And I who have never shown a sign of weakness in my life am vain enough to desire that I leave this gentle world with that record intact" [121].

A good bit of what goes on in "Laughing Masks" connects back through the turn-of-the-century thriller to the nineteenth-century sensation novel. Although crudely rendered, the principal emotional impact of the story is Truax's emotional struggle to maintain an aloof demeanor when confronted with danger. As mentioned above, the story has the requisite Gothic embroidery. The first sentence in "Laughing Masks" is "A shriek, unmistakably feminine, and throbbing with terror, pierced the fog" (91). The dark and spooky Kapaloff house, the wolfhounds, the servants, and more fit into the Gothic tradition of the sensation novel. As in the sensation novel, a secret coated with intrigue and passion becomes the motivation for the story. Like many sensation stories from *The Woman in White* to "The Speckled Band" that grew out of the Victorian debate surrounding what was to become the Married Women's Property Act, in "Laughing Masks" the secret is an unscrupulous attempt to steal an innocent woman's inheritance. It's a motive that Hammett would use again in "The Assistant Murderer." But he would do it better the second time.

In the editors' note appended to "Laughing Masks" (or "When Luck's Running Good") in the anthology *A Man Named Thin*, Ellery Queen surmises that

> If Mr. Hammett were writing now, he could not possibly have
> concocted a plot like the one you have just read — no more than a
> present-day motion picture studio could produce "The Perils of
> Pauline" or "The Exploits of Elaine." Action alone is not enough.
> Damsels in distress and heroes in the tarnished (or untarnished)
> armor of toughness are not enough [127].

Whether or not Hammett realized this, his third adventure story written a year later did some things the same way and some things differently.

"NIGHTMARE TOWN"

The December 1924 issue of *Argosy All-Story* featured Hammett's novelette "Nightmare Town." In it Steve Threefall arrives in Izzard, Arizona, where he finds a girl, Nova Vallance, who catches his fancy living in an unusual, and then sinister, and then mysterious, and then dangerous, and then, as he discovers, wholly corrupt environment. He saves the girl and they flee together. Threefall looks like a hero: "He was a large man in bleached khaki, tall, broad, and thick-armed" (3). In a place where just about everyone packs a gun, he carries only a thick, ebony stick, which he wields expertly when the need arises; this was a weapon and skill Hammett expressly linked to Robin Hood. Like Phil Truax from "Laughing Masks," Threefall is a gambler. He has wound up in Izzard as the result of a bet made at a poker game: that he could not drive across the desert with only alcohol to drink. Threefall's past comes from both Truax, the hero of "Laughing Masks," and Hagedorn, the hero of "The Road Home." Like

Truax he lacks roots and purpose. Like Hagedorn, he is overmatched by the villains. Just as Hagedorn has wandered around Asia for two years, Threefall has traveled in exotic lands: the bet at the poker game that set the whole adventure going comes as a result of Threefall talking about his experiences in the Gobi Desert. Indeed, readers discover that his background consists of "thirty-three years of life and eighteen years of rubbing shoulders with the world — its rough corners as well as its polished" (10). Nonetheless, Threefall is a somewhat more fully developed character than Hammett's earlier adventure heroes. He displays a bit more self-consciousness than Truax — something that isn't very hard to do as Truax's consciousness focuses chiefly on immediate circumstances. Thus, in one of his early attempts to impress Nova, he wonders why maturity and seriousness slip away and instead he jabbers and fools around like a moonstruck adolescent. There is not only that, but Hammett also made Threefall somewhat less gullible than the hero in "Laughing Masks." While Nova attracts him, he does question her behavior when she seemingly interferes with his capture of a mysterious intruder. And, beginning in the middle of the narrative, albeit without results, he "puzzles" and "meditates" and "reasons" over the strange and violent things happening around him. In the main, however, Threefall is not much different than the heroes of Hammett's two earlier adventure tales.

The same thing could be said of the villains in "Nightmare Town" and it would be partly true. There is a good bit of the "master criminal" formula in the story's background. There is the blind man living in a shack at the edge of town, for instance, who turns out to be playing a role to cover his real identity and function as a master criminal. More important in the story is Larry Ormsby. Ormsby is suave, handsome with (once again) aquiline features, a finely muscled frame, and impeccable clothes that are all gray. He is also sinister. But Ormsby is a sportsman who sees the rivalry with Threefall for the attention and affection of Nova Vallance as an exciting game. When the contest for Nova comes into the open, he says, "I'd like to shake hands with you — a sort of ante-bellum gesture. I like you, Threefall; you're going to add materially to the pleasures of Izzard" (25). During the course of the story Threefall witnesses Ormsby intimidating others and committing murder. In spite of this and his involvement in the wholesale corruption of Izzard, however, Ormsby, like Boris Kapaloff in "Laughing Masks," has style and, in the end, is a gentleman — dying, he again asks to shake hands with Steve. Before that sentimental departure, moreover, Ormsby warns Nova and Steve of the town's imminent explosion and he sacrifices his life so that they can escape.

The difference on the evil side in "Nightmare Town" lies in the fact that there isn't one corrupt and evil character but an entire town of them. From the gigantic town marshal to the banker to the doctor to the undertaker, all of the citizens of Izzard are bad. Indeed, the town was an enterprise founded for the purposes of criminal activity. Overtly organized to collect and process "soda niter" (sodium nitrate — "You scoop it up off the desert, boil and otherwise cook it, and sell it to fertilizer manufacturers, and nitric acid manufacturers, and any other kind of manufacturers" [11]),

> Izzard is a plant! The whole damned town is queer. Booze — that's the answer. The man I knocked off this afternoon ... organized the scheme. You make soda niter by boiling the nitrate in tanks with heated coils. He got the idea that a niter plant would make a good front for a moonshine factory. And he got the idea that if you had a whole town working together it'd be impossible for the game ever to fall down [22].

Law and law enforcement in Izzard is illusory, established only to keep outsiders out. And corruption leads to corruption. Not content with the immense profits of bootlegging, the citizens of Izzard cheat their eastern backers, and are about to put into practice insurance fraud on a grand scale. This gigantic enterprise echoes the grandiose schemes found in the turn-of-the-century thrillers that Hammett would later scorn. But here, the demands of updating an archetypal story outweigh the demands of credulity. In the manner of thrillers all of this comes to naught — but not through the actions of the hero. As the crooks plan the final coup — burning down the entire town for the insurance money — they fall upon one another: "The game was too rich for us. Everybody is trying to slit everybody else's throat" (36).

What Hammett did in "Nightmare Town" was to change not the hero but the environment of the manly and sentimental adventure story. In "Nightmare Town" Steve Threefall is attacked by the wicked and ably defends himself. He is present at the murder of his friend Kamp ("Not a thousand words had passed between them, but they had surely become brothers-in-arms as if they had tracked a continent together" [15]), and he saves the girl. But he has nothing to do with the outcome of the story — he never figures out what's behind all of the bad things that happened — Ormsby reveals all of this just before the story ends. If the hero doesn't expose and defeat evil, then who does? As he makes clear in "Vamping Samson" (May 9, 1925), Hammett based his story "Ber-Bulu" (1925) an updating the biblical story of Samson. In "Nightmare Town" he did the same thing with the biblical account of the character and destruction of the Cities of the Plain, Sodom and Gomorrah. Izzard is the city in the

desert whose iniquity leads to its destruction. The town's spurious econ-
omy is ironically based on sodium nitrate, one of the uses of which is for
the manufacture of explosives. Threefall searches not only for the just men
of the bible but for a just woman, whom he finds in Nova. Threefall and
Nova are threatened throughout the story and finally must fight their way
through a mob of miscellaneous citizens to escape. When the sweethearts
flee the town, they look back "where they had left Izzard, a monstrous
bonfire was burning, painting the sky with jeweled radiance" (41). But, of
course, along with the modernization and given that in the providential
scheme of things evil is self-destructive, they don't turn into salt.

In "Nightmare Town" Hammett happened on something he could
use. It wasn't the characters—Threefall is too youthful, the villains too
sentimental and outmoded, Nova too improbable. It wasn't the plot
either—readers see only glimpses of the machinery whereby the citizens
of Izzard destroy their creation and themselves. It was the idea of cleansing a wholly corrupt environment. He came back to it the next year, 1925,
when he gave it a western twist and created a town to be cleaned up by
the Continental Op in "Corkscrew" (December 1925). And two years after
that he used the same environment to better advantage with "The Cleansing of Personville," the first installment of *The Red Harvest*.

"BER-BULU"

Hammett was pretty proud of "Ber-Bulu" ("The Hairy One"), published in *Sunset Magazine* in March 1925. He chose to write about its conception and execution in "Vamping Samson" in the May 9, 1925, number
of *The Editor*. In the *Sunset* story he returned to the scene of his first adventure story and wrote a yarn that avoided the clichés that burden his other
stories in the same genre.

"Ber-Bulu" takes place on the island of Sulu, a portion of the Philippines that the United States had a most difficult time subduing after the
Spanish-American War and the site of General "Black Jack" Pershing's first
military successes against the indigenous Moro people. In "Ber-Bulu"
Hammett seeds in a few fairly well-known anthropological and ethno-
graphical details such as the prevalence of Islam (and polygamy) among
the Moros, and the use of Mexican dollars as currency (the Sultan of Sulu
was paid in Mexican dollars by the United States), along with a smattering of Moro words (*ikat* = bind, *telanjang* = naked, etc.). In the early part
of the story the narrator refers to the easing up of government restrictions
"since the late nineties," the date when U.S. occupation of the Philippines
began. When he wrote this piece Hammett, of course, had never been to

the Philippines—or anywhere else outside of the United States for that matter. It is interesting, then, to speculate about where he got his background information: from Spanish-American War vets? Filipino workers at the VA hospital?

In "Vamping Samson" Hammett would later maintain that the kernel of the story lay in his comic conversion of the biblical story of Samson — the man whose strength was linked to his hair. In "Ber-Bulu," when Jeffol and associates shave the gigantic but pea-brained Levison, their victim presents an absurd figure: "A gorilla with a mouse's head wouldn't have looked any funnier than Levison without his hair; and the anger that purpled him made him look funnier still. No wonder he had hidden himself behind whiskers!" [189].

Embarrassment drives Levison off the island and two lovers are then reunited. Both in the essay about the story and in "Ber-Bulu" itself, Hammett reveals that he made most of the other characters from stereotypes. Thus, that Jeffol is a Moro explains his character — Moros, Hammett holds, are smart, crafty, and violent. And as for the woman, Dinihari,

> Dinihari's race matters as little. She was a woman, complaisant woman, of the sort whose no always becomes yes between throat and teeth. You can find her in Nome, in Cape Town, and in Durham, and in skin of any shade [176].

The missionary, Langworthy, is also a cliché, an example of muscular Christianity who is concerned with the island's morals and, other than having a solid left hook, is largely ineffectual in changing the natives' habits. Peters, the narrator, however, is the most interesting character in the story. He's a picaro, a likable rogue who drifts about the islands making his living as a gambler—a profession (or avocation) that ties him to the heroes of Hammett's other adventure tales. He is an uninvolved commentator who makes observations about the people and events on the island. And, as he is the one who describes the principal actors—Jeffol, Langworthy, Levison, and Dinihari—for readers, it is his ironic view of the characters and their actions that forms the substance of the story. They are all predictable, trivial, and absurd. And at the end of his yarn about the silliness of people and their relationships, Peters gets the prize of Levison's boat and his goods. In a number of ways, then, "Ber-Bulu" is an anti-adventure story, one that employs an exotic locale but in which the action rather than being titanic is trivial and domestic and in which the hero is not a soldier of fortune whose actions prove his worth but a rogue who observes human silliness and sails off with an unmerited reward.

Adventure stories were hardly Hammett's métier. As Ellery Queen noted, they were old-fashioned. And they were so because Hammett built his heroes and villains on outmoded, sentimental clichés. Hammett realized this and wrote an antidote in "Ber-Bulu." As he wrote his stories about the Continental Op, too, Hammett reevaluated the lure of the exotic that plays a fundamental role in the adventure tales and, in them, coupled the search for riches in exotic places with crime and corruption — see "Slippery Fingers" or "The Creeping Siamese," for example. Adventure yarns may have been saleable in the early 1920s, but they were also the kind of fiction for which Hammett would express contempt in his comments about popular fiction. They were also a world away from his own experience and his more mundane fantasies about how one deals with crime and criminals.

Criminal Stories

Before he wrote about detectives, Hammett wrote about criminals. Of course, having been a Pinkerton during his early adult years, he knew about criminals—but not Napoleons of Crime, or gentleman burglars. Forget about Nicky Arenstein, mostly as a Pinkerton Hammett saw losers, not very smart people who did not very smart things. Thus, in "From the Memoirs of a Private Detective," written at almost the same time as Hammett's first story about criminals, he sometimes gives instances of the stupidity of criminals.

> I have never known a man capable of turning out first-rate work in a trade, a profession or an art, who was a professional criminal [907].

> Pick-pocketing is the easiest to master of all the criminal trades. Anyone who is not crippled can become an adept in a day [908].

And he sometimes gives examples of how criminals are just plain goofy.

> A man whom I was shadowing went out into the country for a walk one Sunday afternoon and lost his bearings completely. I had to direct him back to the city [905].

> I know a forger who left his wife because she had learned to smoke cigarettes while he was serving a term in prison [908].

As he was searching for subject matter during his first full year as a writer, writing about criminals became Hammett's first effort to mine his own experience as a detective for material rather than continuing to write sex stories and adventure stories. His approach to his subject matter in the early stories about criminals, however, remained the same one he used with sex and adventure — in all of his early pieces the reversal of stereo-types and a sense of irony dominate.

"THE SARDONIC STAR OF TOM DOODY"

Two months after "The Barber and His Wife" appeared in *Brief Stories*, that same pulp magazine published Hammett's first criminal story, "The Sardonic Star of Tom Doody" in its February 1923 number. Only several pages long, the story recounts the fall and rise and fall of Tom Doody. Convicted of robbing the National Marine Bank, Doody is sentenced to a long term in the slammer. Interviewed by a reporter from the *Morning Bulletin*, Doody tells of his faith-based reformation and the reporter, though skeptical, writes up his story in an effective manner, "gilding the shabbier of his mouthings and garnishing the man himself with no inconsiderable appeal" (33). The story captures the public's fancy, and, in part because "the football team of the state university — three members of the board were ardent alumni — turned defeat into victory in the last quarter" (34), the parole board grants Doody his freedom. Once he is out, a theatrical impresario puts Doody under con-tract as an inspirational speaker. A speech is written for him, posters are printed, and the hall is hired when Fincher, the impresario, rushes in with a newspaper that announces a deathbed confession of someone who claims to be the real robber of the National Marine Bank. Fincher tears up Doody's contract and demands the return of the $500 advance. When Doody is unable to produce the entire amount, Fincher calls the cops. End of story.

Most of the people in "The Sardonic Star of Tom Doody" are carica-tures. The two cops who arrest Doody at the beginning are ugly: one is "the tall man with the protruding lower lip" (31) and the other is "the fat man under a stiff straw hat" with "folds of his burly neck" (32). Miss Evers, the reporter, has "beady eyes" and is tired and middle aged. Fincher is a raging hypocrite. As for Tom Doody, Hammett starts off by burdening him with the stereotypical sign of low intelligence: a low forehead ("the none too ample area between Tom Doody's eyebrows and the roots of his hair" [32]). Doody's story of reformation springs from little imagination and succeeds because of the writer's skill, the coincidental victory of a football team, and the desire of the police "who for quite perceptible rea-sons, pretend to see in every apprehended criminal an enormously adept and industrious fellow" (35). The inspirational speech that he hopes will allow him to cash in on his accidental celebrity is written by a "young fellow who had been hired to mold and polish the Doody epic" (35). As the final touch, Hammett makes readers guess whether or not Doody actually robbed the National Marine Bank.

But whether he did or didn't rob the bank, the story rests on satire and irony. Hammett skewers a variety of social institutions: the police, prison and parole systems, newspapers, religion, entertainment and the gullible public. Institutions display, by turns, hypocrisy and naïveté. The largest irony in the story, however, is in what happens to its title character. Doody is a loser. Paying for his first crime (or admitting to a crime he did not commit), circumstance and good luck offer him the opportunity for both fortune and the chance to do something useful in preaching about "the criminal's inherent misery and the glory of standing four-square with the world" (35). And then circumstance snatches all of the promise away and Doody loses the heroic aura others had conspired to create and he ends pathetically, about to be charged not with a grand crime but with "obtaining money under false pretenses" (37).

"THE MAN WHO STOOD IN THE WAY"

Hammett's second appearance in *The Black Mask* (June 1923) is a ham-handed story based on the cliché that there is no honor among thieves. "The Man Who Stood in the Way" introduces readers to a character whose background stretches credulity. He is a convicted murderer who has escaped from San Quentin and, using a different name, has been elected, by turns, a state legislator, governor, and U.S. senator. About to be nominated by his party to run for the presidency, he decides to do something about the man who has been blackmailing him for years. He turns for help to Gene Inch, a gnarled, diminutive, repulsive hayseed whose son the senator pardoned for a murder conviction when he was governor. Although ostensibly warned against murder by the senator, Inch lures the blackmailer to a Baltimore hotel room and shoots him as an intruder. He then returns to Dupont Circle and takes over blackmailing the senator from the man he killed.

"The Man Who Stood in the Way" contrasts two despicable characters: the senator, "a massive man, exuding an air of power" (120), and Gene Inch, whose

> unkempt hair, to the extent that it had survived, was a dingy yellow-white which had probably been sandy in its youth; a mustache of the same hue, except where tobacco had stained it a richer shade, straggled over his withered lips. His forehead was low, narrow, and of an almost reptilian flatness [120].

It is difficult to tell who is more deserving of contempt — the man whose power and prestige rests on mendacity and who hires others to do his dirty work or the vicious and calculating social outcast who possesses neither gratitude for his son's release from prison nor the inclination to honor his own commitments. In the manner of his other early pieces, Hammett aimed at irony in "The Man Who Stood in the Way" by defeating expectations at the end of the narrative — having Inch replace rather than remove the blackmailer and become a threat to the senator's career. Here, however, the reversal is not a surprise and is both expected and deserved — nobody wants to see a politician get off and nobody should trust a person who looks "reptilian." The story recapitulates Hammett's Lombrosean leanings: Inch has the same low forehead hinted at in "The Sardonic Star of Tom Doody." Inch's shooting of the blackmailer through bedclothes also puts forth one of Hammett's recurring notions about firearms, repeated in "The Zigzags of Treachery," in that one hits what one is looking at. In the main, however, "The Man Who Stood in the Way" represents backsliding in Hammett's attempts to make himself a writer, and, as Layman says, it is a "pompously written, awkwardly plotted tale" that possesses the "single virtue ... [that] Gene Inch acts like a real criminal" (38).

"THE SECOND STORY ANGEL"

Unlike "The Man Who Stood in the Way," Hammett's next criminal story possesses multiple virtues. "The Second Story Angel" begins when Carter Webright Brigham hears noises in the night. Brigham is a former newspaper reporter who has now turned to writing crime fiction: "'Poison for One' and 'The Settlement' in *Warner's Magazine*, 'Nemesis, Incorporated' in the *National*, and ... stories in *Cody's*" (222). Emboldened by his fiction-writing knowledge of crime, Brigham goes into his darkened living room and tackles the intruder. Turning on the lights he discovers that the burglar is a young woman, Angel Grace Cardigan. Abashed that he struck a woman, even by mistake, Brigham attempts to put her at ease when a burly man enters through the jimmied window, flashes a badge at Brigham and Angel Grace, and prepares to take her away. Brigham, both from chivalry and from self-interest ("The gods do not send a real flesh-and-blood feminine crook into a writer's rooms every evening in the week. The retention of such a gift would be worth contending for. The girl must have within her, he thought, material for thousands, tens of thousands, of words of fiction" [218]), bribes Cassidy to forgo arresting the young woman. He spends the rest of the night listening to Angel Grace recounting her own and her family's criminal history. Fearing that she will be arrested by another copper, Brigham gives her money and train fare to a town where they can get together and he can unwrap those tens of thousands of words based on her tales. But she takes the money and runs. Brigham never sees Angel Grace again. To recoup his expenses, however, he decides to turn his experiences with the female crook into fiction and submit it for publication. He does so, sends the finished piece off, and is called to his publisher's office. There he discovers that four other writers have submitted the same story for publication, all five of them victims both of Angel Grace and their own naïveté.

"The Second Story Angel," then, is not so much about criminals as it is about writers, writers of crime stories to be precise. From his point of view as a former Pinkerton operative, Hammett made his protagonist a young man who is earnest but also one who is terminally naïve about criminals. Indeed, given that Angel Grace and Cassidy not only dupe Brigham but also four others as well suggests a generic naïveté among crime fiction writers. The fact that Hammett gave Brigham three names (Carter Webright Brigham) also suggests an upper-class background and the general innocence of that class about real crime and actual criminals. Brigham, like all of the writers, although he has little experience with it, wants to be able to write about real crime. What attracts these men to Angel Grace, however, is not her reality but her uniqueness (she is, for them, the singular "girl-burglar"). On top of that, her story holds popular appeal ("crook stories were always in popular demand" [224]) and a sentimental angle. The story Angel Grace pitches to Brigham (and the other four writers) depends upon clichés about criminals. One is that criminals have funny nicknames— Angel's father is "Paper-Box John." Another is that crooks talk funny. Thus Angel uses criminal argot in her dialogue: "So besides hiding from the dicks I had to dodge half the guns in the burg for fear they'd put the finger on me — turn me up to the bulls" (221). Even more alluring than this, Angel ostentatiously mixes virtue with her criminal actions— even though Brigham is too much of a gentleman to imagine such a thing, Angel makes it clear that she will not sleep with Brigham to obtain her freedom or to tell her story. Reading backwards, it's clear that Angel's con game depends on her use of stereotypes and the writers' innocence and chivalry.

Maybe even more apparent in the stereotype department is Angel's associate, Cassidy. Especially significant in light of the fact that in the Continental Op stories Hammett consistently presents the police as efficient, honest, and admirable, in "The Second Story Angel" and his other criminal stories he used most of the popular stereotypes about the police. Of course, there is the Irish name, Cassidy. Then there is his hulking appearance:

> A grunt came from the open window by which the girl had
> entered.... Framed in it was a burly, red-faced man who wore a
> shiny blue serge suit and a black derby hat. He threw one thick leg
> over the sill and came into the room with heavy, bearlike agility
> [217].

And finally, there is his motivation by the supposed reward money offered for Angel Grace's arrest and his susceptibility to bribery. Cassidy embodies for Brigham the stereotype of the cop, the same stereotype that Hammett would disprove in his Op stories.

In all, "The Second Story Angel" is the story that Hammett had been trying to write from his first efforts in *The Smart Set*. First of all, it enabled him to use those things he knew about—criminals from his Pinkerton days and magazine writing from his own efforts to find a subject that would get him into print. Next, it gave free reign to his satiric and ironic inclinations in a more sophisticated manner than his previous efforts. The story, therefore, pokes fun at the naïveté of inexperienced writers who see themselves as crime writers. Finally, the wordplay of the title shows Hammett's maturation since the silly pun in "The Parthian Shot." Here readers have to concentrate a bit harder to see the wry humor in the two meanings of "story" in the title. One of them points to floors of a building and the label "second story man" applied to burglars. The other meaning of "story," of course, refers to a fictional narrative and the fact that this is not the first story (the one about Angel Grace's criminal activities) but the second story, the one about how a writer was duped.

"Itchy the Debonair"

This appeared in *Brief Stories* in January 1924. It is a narrative elaboration of Item 23 in "From the Memoirs of a Private Detective." In that entry Hammett wrote about the public's fascination with the idea of the gentleman burglar and contrasted it with what an actual "gentleman crook" might be like:

> Second only to "Dr Jeckyl [sic] and Mr. Hyde" is "Raffles" in the
> affections of the daily press. The phrase "gentleman crook" is used
> on the slightest provocation. A composite portrait of the gentry
> upon whom the newspapers have bestowed this title would show a
> laudanum-drinker, with a large rhinestone horseshoe aglow in the
> soiled bosom of his shirt below a bow tie, leering at his victim, and

saying "Now don't get scared, lady, I ain't gonna crack you on the
bean. I ain't a rough-neck!" [908]

"Itchy" tells of the conversion of a professional criminal into a "gentleman crook." It all happens because during a bank robbery a newspaper
misconstrues Floyd's (or Itchy's) instructions to one of the bank's employees:

> The stenog — one of them goofy kids— has me worried for a minute.
> I'm afraid she's going to try something funny, or let out a squak, or
> something; she's got that kind of look in her eye. So I tell her, sharp,
> "Now you run along with them, sister. I don't want to have to hurt
> you" [64].

Rather than springing from social niceties, Itchy's direction to the stenog-
rapher comes from prudent criminal practice. Hammett, in fact, goes to
some pains to show Itchy as a member of the criminal class that has little
to do with normal society: "There is a stratum of criminal society whose
constituents— either bandits or safe burglars; the latter, once predomi-
nant, now a dwindling minority, are primarily hoboes. They have all the
caste consciousness of those wanderers, all their contempt for the niceties
of gentler modes of life" (67). Floyd's nickname, indeed, comes from having been egregiously flea-bitten at a hobo camp. Nonetheless, the newspapers reinterpret Itchy's comment during the bank robbery and announce
the robbery story with the headline "Debonair Bandit Robs Oakland Bank."
Irritated at first by the ribbing he gets from his partner Pete, Itchy then
uses exaggerated politeness when pulling their next job. Pete, knowing
that Itchy is getting wacky, quits the partnership and Itchy becomes fascinated with the idea of the gentleman burglar. He reads gentleman crook
stories, buys evening clothes, and finally sticks up a theater in his formal
attire. The cops nab him almost at once. At the Hall of Justice Itchy aims
to impress the cops with insouciant repartee, remembering having read
an encounter with the police in which the gentleman crook says, "I'm tired
of you. You bore me. You weary me. You exasperate me. Now get out" (69).
Only he says, in the last line of the story, "I'm tired of you... You weary
me. You bore me. You exasperate me. You are a big slob!" (73).

Patently Hammett here wants to contrast real criminals and those
concocted in the fantasies of popular writers. Itchy (or Floyd) is a workmanlike crook. He and his partner Pete maintain a low profile, living in
anonymous rooms. While Itchy is an efficient and prudent crook, Hammett highlights the fact that he possesses "imperturbable subnormality"
(66). Because one newspaper used the term "debonair" in its headline, the
idea of gentleman crook stories fires his imagination: "He had never

thought of stories having any connection with actuality, any relation with life; but it seemed that they did…. Books had been written about men like him; that was what the newspapers were getting at" (67). When he begins to read these books, however, he finds that "the books weren't, on the whole, satisfactory" (68):

> Still, say what you would about these men in the books—always being surprised at work, neglecting the most simple precautions, showing themselves unnecessarily gullible and only succeeding through the malicious favors of chance—they did have something [69].

Thus, in spite of learning that the facts in the crook stories have little connection with the world of real criminals and that gentlemen crooks are bunglers and incompetents, the style rather than the substance of the fiction seduces Itchy. It leads to his downfall and, in the last line of the story, he reverts to his old self.

"THE NEW RACKET"

This piece, re-titled "The Judge Laughed Last," first appeared in *The Black Mask* in February 1924. In it, a grouchy and cantankerous old con tells a story that illustrates his view of the perverseness of the courts to the younger narrator who is amused by the old con's naïveté. The tale Old Man Covey relates tells of his youthful exploits as a robber. He and his partner moved from town to town in the Midwest, staging armed robberies at diners, garages, drugstores, and other small businesses. While they achieved modest success, Covey convinced his partner that they could avoid the risk of serious jail time if they followed his new scheme. The new scheme was to rob stores without guns and then, if caught, plead guilty to begging, not robbery, since they did not threaten anyone with guns when they asked shopkeepers for money. Inevitably caught and brought to trial, the two robbers, through an inexperienced lawyer, put forth their claim in court and return to jail assured that the judge will convict them only of vagrancy and begging. The judge, however, does them one better. He finds the store clerks whom they had robbed guilty of grand larceny (because they appropriated money without their employer's consent), suspends their sentences and finds the two crooks guilty of receiving stolen goods and sentences them to long terms in prison.

Of course, in "The New Racket," Hammett treated crime and criminals with his characteristic dose of irony. As in the other criminal stories he shows criminals to be both stupid and naïve: throughout the story the old con is unaware both of his own self-delusion and of the fact that the narrator to whom he relates his tale of the law's perfidy sees him as a buffoon. The crooks are markedly undesirable people. Old Man Covey, who tells the story, is both ignorant and bitter, and his partner not only is a criminal but also looks like one: "…he ain't no flower to look at. I seen a cartoon of a burglar once in a newspaper during one of those crime waves, and that's the only time I ever seen a face like Flogger's. A good guy — but we had to be careful how we moved around, because the bulls had a habit of picking us up on account of his face" (162–63). These guys, Hammett tells the readers, act like crooks, look like crooks, and talk like crooks. To demonstrate the latter, he puts in a generous sampling of thieves' slang (judges are "beaks," cops are "bulls," a cash register till is a "damper," etc.) and he even includes a bit of British thieves' slang (Flogger is "what 'Limey' Pine used to call a 'bene cove'" [162]). And on top of this, they end up like crooks, first in the slammer and then, in their old age, subsisting on the charity of relatives. Thus, "The New Racket" reiterates points from Hammett's *Smart Set* treatise on being a private detective and he also glances at society's hypocrisy as he had in "The Sardonic Star of Tom Doody": at the beginning of "The New Racket" the narrator notes that a "street preacher had turned 'Big-dog' Covey from the ways of crime…" (161) whereas both the narrator and readers know that the old man is perhaps even more nasty and bitter than he ever was.

The criminal stories combine Hammett's experience as a Pinkerton operative among real criminals with his inclinations toward satire and irony encouraged by his first success as a writer with his *Smart Set* pieces. While with Gene Inch in "The Man Who Stood in the Way" Hammett suggests that there is such a thing as a biologically determined criminal (a system of belief he undercuts when the Op de-programs Gabrielle in *The Dain Curse*).

At the turn of the twentieth century the authority on criminals was Cesare Lombroso. In his *L'uomo delinquente* (1876), Lombroso held that criminals were evolutionary aberrations, "degenerates," or throwbacks to more primitive stages in human development. One could pick out a criminal, Lombroso held, not solely by his or her actions but by the way that person looked. An awful lot of people bought into this theory and some of them were detective story writers like S.S. Van Dine. In the early stories about the Op it looks like Hammett, too, bought into Lombroso's theories: the lowest class of his early professional criminals look like criminals: they have low brows, jutting jaws, and beady eyes.

In most of his criminal stories Hammett portrays crooks not as degenerates (à la Lombroso) or geniuses or monsters but as naïve, unsophisticated men who are not so much predators or society's victims as much as they are victims of their own ignorance and silly delusions. Their defeats depend not on clever and efficient law enforcement but on their own inability to understand themselves and their world. At the end of all of the criminal stories, Hammett gives the plots his characteristic twist, defeating the main character's expectations and introducing the "lord what fools these mortals be" attitude that he cultivated in his first pieces for Mencken's magazine of satire. While they, too, fit into Hammett's purposes, there is, however, one kind of criminal found in the early stories that doesn't fall into the cretin class of Tom Doody and Itchy, and that is the confidence artist, such as Angel Grace and her partner Cassidy. Thus, in "The Second Story Angel" the boobs are not the crooks but their gullible victims. And this cuts two ways. First of all it is one of the things about criminals that connects Hammett's criminal stories with his detective stories. In both his early detective stories about the Op as well as those about Robin Thin and Alec Rush, the villains turn out to be confidence men — or a confidence boy in the case of one of the Robin Thin stories. Hammett, one suspects, knew from his own experience that most criminals are stupid and that their detection and apprehension is either simple or dependent on circumstance. Unlike the smash-and-grab man, the robber, or the burglar, the confidence artist works at creating an illusion (a fictitious identity, a plausible narrative, a credible set of circumstances) that the detective must penetrate. It's one of the reasons that one does not find gangsters until the midpoint of the early run of Continental Op stories — the confidence artist (whether a bunco shill or a murderer) proves the detective's worth better than any other kind of criminal. The other attractive thing about the confidence man to Hammett at this point in his experience derived from his views on society's perception of criminals. In the criminal stories Hammett returns again and again to the ways in which the public dupes itself about crooks. In "The Sardonic Star of Tom Doody" a newspaper piece cultivates a naïve and sentimental public perception of the criminal that makes victims both of society and of the criminal. In "Itchy" the vogue for reading thrillers and gentleman crook stories serves the same purpose. And in "The Second Story Angel" the same desire for sensational and sentimental reading makes fools not of the criminals but of writers and, by extension, of their publishers and readers.

Hammett's motive, then, in the criminal stories came in part from the ironic outlook he cultivated in most of his early fiction and in part from looking at his own experience for publishable material. The criminal stories are, moreover, as much about the way the public views criminals as they are about describing criminals themselves. They are heavily affected by Hammett's view that criminals are stupid, or silly, or trivial — people who have been misrepresented by romantic inclinations of writers of both fact and fiction. Thus irony and satire were the appropriate ways to convey this, to get the facts as he knew them straight. These tools, however, did not work when Hammett started to write about the other side of his early experiences: his experiences as a detective.

Detective Stories

Between October 1923 and January 1926 Hammett had written 20 stories about his detective hero, the Continental Op. But by 1926 Hammett had given up trying other forms of fiction; while he would use what he had learned in them in his later work, he would write no more sex stories, action stories, or criminal stories. Insofar as he worked as a writer he was either committed to or resigned to being a detective story writer. Two years earlier he wrote as if his efforts as a detective story writer were centered and going to be centered on developing the Continental Op: in his August 1924 letter to *The Black Mask* he wrote that "Whenever from now on, I get a hold of a story that fits my sleuth, I shall put him to work, but I'm through with trying to run him on a schedule" (Layman, 25). He would write only four more Op stories before he began on *The Red Harvest* with "The Cleansing of Personville" in November 1927. Working a full-time job writing advertisements for Samuels Jewelry, in 1926 Hammett published only three pieces of fiction (and wrote one piece that went unpublished until the 1960s). All three were detective stories. One of them, "The Creeping Siamese," was about the Op. The remaining two—and the one that was written but not published—introduced new detective heroes named Robin Thin and Alec Rush.

In external appearance at least, both of Hammett's new detectives differ a great deal from the Continental Op: one is a prissy aesthete and the other is a plug ugly. And the storytelling connected with his two new detectives differed from the kind of narrative style he developed and was developing for the Op, one of the new heroes featured a self-consciously talky first-person narration and the other used third-person narration. With both of the new creations, too, the singularity of the heroes is more prominent, more important, than the story. Thus, as opposed to the matter-of-fact tone of the Op stories, those about Robin Thin and Alexander Rush depend upon the incongruity of the heroes' demeanor or appearance. The creation of his two new detective heroes, to be sure, reflects Hammett's desire to experiment with character, with narrative, with style, and with setting. Indeed, in "The Assistant Murderer" Hammett used Baltimore, his old hometown, rather than the West Coast settings he used in almost all of his other stories. The principal difference between Hammett's stories about new heroes and those he had written about the Continental Op resides in their purpose. The original Op stories aimed to explain and demonstrate to readers how real detectives worked. And even though part of the aim of the "The Assistant Murderer" is depicting a real, non-agency private eye quite different from the agent of the Continental Detective Agency, the principal aim of that story as well as that of the two Robin Thin pieces lay in their novelty. And perhaps, too, it lay in their commercial appeal.

ROBIN THIN

Detective Robin Thin appeared first in "The Nails in Mr. Cayterer" in *The Black Mask* of January 1926. Hammett wrote a second story, "A Man Named Thin," featuring the same detective around the same time, but the pulp for which it was written went out of business before publishing the story, and it did not appear until it was printed in *Ellery Queen's Mystery Magazine* in 1961. In the Robin Thin stories Hammett set out to do something very different. As opposed to the realistic and down-to-earth Op, Hammett made Robin Thin a prissy aesthete who works for his father's detective agency but would rather be writing poetry.

Hammett set the tone for his new detective hero with the first sentence of "The Nails in Mr. Cayterer," which reads "I was experiencing, as one will, difficulty with the eighth line of a rondeau when Papa's firm and not to be mistaken tread sounded outside my door" (40). The second Thin story begins with Robin's poetry and a confrontation between father and son about one of Robin's poems, characterized by the elder Thin as "nonsense" and "Mother Goose Rhymes." Nonsense they may be, but they're hardly Mother Goose rhymes as Robin had submitted the poem in question to an avant-garde sounding journal *The Jongleur*. In terms of poetry, Hammett framed "A Man Named Thin" with a sonnet — the story begins with an editor's request for revisions of Robin's "Fictitious Tears" and ends when the poet perfects the final couplet based on a visual image he encounters in the course of solving the story's crime. In both of the Robin Thin stories Hammett made the point that the hero practices the art of poetry furtively — in "The Nails in Mr. Cayterer" Robin hides his rondeau in progress "under a pile of reward circulars on my desk" (40) and in "A Man Named Thin" he tells readers that he hides his rhyming dictionary behind a copy of Gross's *Kriminal Psycologie*. The real art revealed in the two Robin Thin stories, however, is not poetry but detection, and the contrast between the plodding professionals (especially the police in the second story) and Robin's seemingly effortless solutions to complex problems.

In physicality, Hammett patterned Robin Thin on the ineffectual poet Burke Pangborn from "The Girl with the Silver Eyes." It's not just Pangborn's abstracted and effete nature as poet that the Op calls readers' attention to in the earlier story, it's also his dressing gown — "a mauve dressing-robe spotted with big jade parrots" (146). This is the same kind of foppish fascination with outlandish clothes that made Hammett comment on Robin's fascination with a lavender dressing gown he sees in a haberdasher's window in "A Man Named Thin." Indeed, the brief interplay between the hard-headed Op and flaky Pangborn in "The Girl with the Silver Eyes" probably served as a partial model for the relationship between the Thins, father and son, only this time it's told from the poet's point of view instead of that of the man of the world. The father, "Bob" Thin, is big: in "The Nails in Mr. Cayterer" Robin describes the entrepreneur as "a large man, nearly as large as Papa" (41). In fact, everything about Bob Thin is supersized. "The Nails in Mr. Cayterer" begins when Robin hears his father's tread reverberating outside his office and in "A Man Named Thin" the narrator hears his father's voice calling him from his office "with a force that fairly agitated the three intervening partitions" (335). Not only is he big, but the elder Thin is loud. In the first story he startles a miscellaneous passerby on the street: "Papa's voice was so sharp that a man immediately in front of us jumped, looked back over his shoulder at Papa with startled eyes, and moved over to the curb to get out of his way" (53). And, in his son's eyes at least, Bob Thin is vulgar. In both stories the narrator censures (and censors) his father's curses. On top of this, Papa Thin uses slang and improper diction — he says things like "Hop Cayterer's been squirting tears in my ear over the phone. By the sound of his whining, somebody's done him wrong for one of his millions" (40). And his speech represents the ease and familiarity with which he relates to others. Robin, put off by his dad's chatting up their client in "The Nails in Mr. Cayterer," notes that this kind of casual language represents "...survivals of Indian council fire and bushman community hut, [and] might have been dispensed with in favor of modern conciseness and clarity" (43).

Indeed, language lies at the heart of the Robin Thin stories. Before readers arrive at Robin's observations about his father's speech, Hammett immerses them in the narrator's self-indulgent, meandering style. Robin Thin doesn't write (or, one assumes, think in) short, direct, simple sentences. For example, at the beginning of "The Nails in Mr. Cayterer" readers get this sentence:

> Now I do not like deception, no matter how mild, but neither did I
> like having Papa quarrel with me, and more forcible, if not actually
> greater, than my abhorrence of duplicity was Papa's antipathy to my
> poetry, a prejudice which, I may be excused from believing, owned
> much of its vigor to the fact that he had never read, so far as I knew,
> a single line of my work [40].

Hammett purposely made his narrator go on and on: the average sentence
on the first two pages of "The Nails in Mr. Cayterer" is 44 words long and
Hammett stretched one out to 81 and another to 101 words. This is a far
cry from the Continental Op stories where the average sentence length
struggles to reach double digits. In addition to purposely making Robin
Thin's utterances lengthy and loaded with parenthetical stop-overs, Hammett also stressed his diction in "The Nails in Mr. Cayterer" by contrast-
ing it with the earthy speech of the father as well as with the slang and
casual diction of Cayterer's soldier of fortune nephew, Ford Nugent, who
notes that Robin doesn't fit the usual detective image: "I never saw one
that looked, acted, and talked less like one" (55). In "A Man Named Thin"
he continued the contrast of Robin's speech with his father's and added
the cop talk of Sergeant Hooley ("some bird come in here ... put Mr. Barn-
able and his help under the gun, took 'em for what was in the safe, and
blew out..." [336]) as well as that copper's mockery of Robin's speech: "I
had engaged him in conversation hithertofore, an elusively derisive expression — as if, with intent to annoy, he pretended to find in me, in my least
word or act, something amusing" (336).

In spite of Robin's notation that his dad's speech lacks "conciseness
and clarity," so does his own. In both Robin Thin stories Hammett used
the narrator's language both to contrast him with the kind of world of
crime and detection Hammett had depicted in the Continental Op stories
and to create the image of a prissy, naïve, insecure young man. In spite of
seeing himself as an avant-garde poet, on top of his old-fashioned diction
and syntax, Hammett portrayed Robin Thin as conventional and conservative. In "The Nails in Mr. Cayterer," for example, one of Robin's first
observations has to do with his approval of Cayterer's traditional office
furnishings as opposed to "the rigid angularity and hard shininess that
make modern commercial furnishings so hideous" (41). More significant
than his taste in furniture, Hammett gave Robin Thin conservative notions
about social relationships. Thus, Miss Brenham, Cayterer's businesslike
secretary, impresses Robin and he disapproves of his father's casual relationship with his secretary, Miss Queenan, especially when he interrupts
his father and her reading the funny papers in the office instead of working on detective business. Indeed, Hammett made Robin a character who

generally disapproves of (or perhaps does not understand) fun and spon-
taneity, the kinds of things found in his father and in Ford Nugent, of
whom Robin says "I found him a rather irresponsible, not to say foolish,
young man whose conversation was purely facetious" (57). In both of the
Robin Thin stories what Hammett does is present an insecure and timid
hero whose narration concentrates more on describing his father (hence
his repeated references to his dad as "papa") and on apologetic asides to
the readers than it does on describing crime and detection. Yet Hammett
also made Robin Thin a likable young man. A lot of this comes from the
hero's naïveté. In both of the Robin Thin stories the hero stumbles into
embarrassing social situations: in "The Nails in Mr. Cayterer" he is dragged
along to Nugent's wedding and in "A Man Named Thin" he becomes the
butt of Sergeant Hooley's sarcastic humor. In both cases he is puzzled
rather than uncomfortable or angry. Thus, in response to Sergeant Hooley's "I don't mind letting you in on the dirt, as we used to say at dear old
Harvard," Robin muses that

> I am not privy to the quirk in Sergeant Hooley's mind which
> makes attendance at this particular university constitute, for him,
> a humorous situation; nor can I perceive why he should find so
> much pleasure in mentioning that famous seat of learning to me
> who, as I have often taken the trouble to explain to him, attended
> an altogether different university [336].

Hammett, then, portrayed his hero as one with so little knowledge
of the real world of people and events that Thin's behavior in these situations evoked an air of charm rather than foolishness. It's not only that
about Robin that saves him for the readers. Robin Thin is an ace detective. While he may not like it, he is in the detective business—in "A Man
Named Thin," in fact, his pop mentions that he has been teaching Robin
to be a detective for ten years. Hammett took some pains in both of the
stories to set up the Thins in a real detective business. They have an office
suite, they have former clients, they keep an archive of newspaper clip-
pings about crime and criminals, and, in "The Nails in Mr. Cayterer," they
employ other "operatives"—in that story, a shadow man. Unlike the Continental Op stories, Hammett made the Robin Thin tales along the lines
of conventional detective stories of the mid–1920s with collections of enigmatic clues and situations followed by a surprise ending. And Robin Thin
makes a surprise ending happen. He has the knack of occasionally asking
the right question — as he does in "The Nails of Mr. Cayterer" when he
asks whether Cayterer wrote the extortion letters himself. And he is an
exceptionally acute observer of motives and of facts. At the end of each of

the stories, even though he is blissfully ignorant of many things, Robin effortlessly tosses off the solution to the crime problems. And that was Hammett's point; just as Robin fusses over how to properly express "incongruity in a lighter vein" (335) in the final couplet of his sonnet in "A Man Named Thin," Hammett expressed incongruity by making a naïve and prissy poet into the star detective in these two stories.

"THE ASSISTANT MURDERER"

The month after Hammett published the first Robin Thin story he introduced a completely different kind of detective in "The Assistant Murderer" (*Black Mask*, February 1926). He made this new detective, Alexander Rush, radically different from the Continental Op and the Thin family detectives. Not only is the new detective hero a different kind of character, but in "The Assistant Murderer" Hammett tried out what was for his detective stories a new kind of narration: it is told in the third person. After "The Assistant Murderer" Hammett's next take on the private eye and the detective story would be with Sam Spade in *The Maltese Falcon*. That makes this story significant.

The principal character difference in "The Assistant Murderer" is that the hero isn't quite respectable. In all of his other early detective stories Hammett went to some pains to depict private detective agencies as legitimate, respectable enterprises. The Continental Detective Agency, patterned on the Pinkertons, to be sure was an upstanding, efficient, purposeful, established, successful business dedicated to law enforcement. And the same values attach to the Thins' agency: it's two generations old, it has staff, it has established clients, and both the police and the public accept the agency as a valuable adjunct to society. Not only were Hammett's earlier detective agencies legitimate and efficient, they also possessed a communal, even familial, aspect. The Op lives as much at the shop as he does at his home, he expresses warm feelings for his colleagues, and a paternal figure presides over the Continental Agency. With the Thin stories, it's not just a father figure who runs the detective business but an actual father, and Hammett portrayed the atmosphere of the Thin agency as casual and attractive. None of this carries over to "The Assistant Murderer."

Alexander Rush has no operatives and no secretary. "The Assistant Murderer" begins with a concentrated look at Rush's seedy, minimal office. This could serve as the archetype for countless private eyes' offices in the decades to follow. Everything in the office comes from a secondhand store. The carpet is old and ratty; the bookcase rickety and mostly empty; the coatrack teeters under a minimal burden; the chairs are old and don't match; and the desk is scarred and littered with papers and cigar ashes and butts. Amid the furnishings, readers see Rush's black derby and his feet on the surface of the battered and chaotic desk. Hardly the offices of the Continental Detective Agency, Rush's office is what most people expect of a private detective: a disreputable mess. Hammett topped off this recitation of squalor in Rush's office with the fact that, although it was "an ugly office — the proprietor was uglier" (483). Throughout "The Assistant Murderer" the narration hammers readers with the fact that Alec Rush is not an attractive man: on almost every page we read that he is "ugly." It happens 26 times in the story. Here is the initial description of the hero:

> His head was squatly pear-shaped. Excessively heavy, wide, blunt at the jaw, it narrowed as it rose to the close-cropped, erect grizzled hair that sprouted above a low, slanting forehead. His complexion was of a rich darkish red, his skin tough in texture and rounded over thick cushions of fat. These fundamental inelegancies were by no means all his ugliness. Things had been done to his features [483].

It's not just his appearance that is off-putting. Hammett made for him an equivocally shady history. Unlike the other Hammett private eyes, Alec Rush is an ex-policeman, fired from the police force for something or somethings that may — or may not — have been heinous. Hammett is purposely vague about this and suggests both that Rush's departure from the force was politically motivated ("I can talk about politics, and being made the goat...." [487]) and that it was legitimate ("They didn't chuck you off the force for forgetting to hang up your stocking" [499]).

Among detective agencies, then, Alec Rush's one-man shop specializes in bottom-feeding. He says as much to his client: "Then you ran across my name, remembered I was chucked out of the department a couple of years ago. 'There's my man,' you said to yourself, 'a baby who won't be so choicy!'" [487]. The surface details make Rush seem to be brutal, uncouth, and unprincipled. In spite of this, he is none of them. Opposed to his appearance, the man has charm: "There was kindliness in Alec Rush's smile, and it was not easily resisted" (485) and in spite of his grotesqueness, his eyes give out "jovial friendliness." Not only that, he's also a crack detective.

In "The Assistant Murderer" Hammett goes to some pains to show Rush as a knowledgeable, efficient detective. The foundation of Rush's detection — like the foundation of much of the Op's detection — rests on shadowing suspects. Thus, Hammett emphasizes the details of shadowing.

These boil down to space and time. In the story readers can sense space by following the action on a street map of Baltimore as Rush follows people on foot and in his car (something of an innovation for Hammett's detectives) up and down named streets like Charles Street and Mount Royal Avenue. Shadowing, moreover, involves both space and time, and Hammett emphasized the burden of time on the watcher. When Rush waits for Hubert Landow, the narration marks off the hours and classifies office workers according to the time they leave for work. Throughout the story, then, Hammett's third detective hero spends most of his time following a variety of people through the streets of Baltimore. But there is more to being a detective than this kind of essential routine. Just as it is emphasized in the Op stories, "The Assistant Murderer" makes the point that detectives need to cooperate with one another and with the police. Minnie, a woman store detective, plays a significant role in the story. Rush has a convivial relationship with her and they cooperate in tracking one of the suspects to her apartment and, with the help of a policeman, in arresting her. Finally, Hammett makes Rush an ideal detective by endowing him with values about fairness and justice. He is not the thug his looks suggest that he is, and Hammett underlines this at the end of the story when the criminal attempts to buy off the hero and Rush replies, "Don't let my looks and my record kid you" (515).

Like that sentiment, Hammett tried out a number of things in "The Assistant Murderer" that he would later use to greater effect in *The Maltese Falcon*. The one thing that he did not use was the basis for the plot in the short story. Unlike the Op stories that deal with real criminals and (mostly) real crimes, the plot of "The Assistant Murderer" rests on a severely outmoded motif carried over from the 19th-century sensation novel — the stolen inheritance. It is the same motif he used in "Laughing Masks." It didn't work there and, unfortunately, it doesn't work here.

Western Stories

The editors and publishers of *The Black Mask* tinkered a good bit with it to make the magazine more appealing (and more profitable). They did cosmetic things, like dropping the "The" from the title, making their pulp *Black Mask*. More substantially, they tinkered with the contents. Stories of spiritualism, for instance, that were advertised in the first issue got dropped and westerns were added in the hopes of attracting still more readers. This, for Hammett, was a fortuitous addition because he had background of his own upon which he could draw — his time as a Pinkerton in Montana. It's hardly a surprise, then, that both of his westerns take place in that state.

"THE MAN WHO KILLED DAN ODAMS"

Coming out in the January 1924 issue of *The Black Mask*, "The Man Who Killed Dan Odams" tells the tale of a killer's escape from the jail in Jingo, Montana. The fact that he's a killer is never in doubt: he is simply "the man who killed Dan Odams" throughout the text and Hammett even hints at his criminal nature when he describes the man's eyes: "their animality emphasized by the absence of lashes" (70). Indeed, in the last third of the story the man talks about killing Dan Odams. The first third of the narrative covers the killer's jailbreak and the rigors of his escape through a rain-drenched Montana countryside. He becomes "a grotesque statue modeled of mud" (73). After eluding capture he finds a run-down farm occupied only by a woman and a young boy. Forcing his way into their modest house, the man who killed Dan Odams finds a kind of welcome; although the woman is taciturn, she tends the bleeding wound he received when he killed Dan Odams, feeds him, and supplies him with clothes from her husband (who, she says, has gone away). And she gives some signs that the welcome could become warmer: when the man awakens after one night in the cabin he finds that she has cleaned and tidied the cabin, put on a worn but fresh and clean dress, brushed and arranged her hair, and busied herself with domestic chores. In all, the cabin and the woman both look pretty good, warm and welcoming. It even seems that she has sent her son out in the rain to watch for pursuers—the man believes that he sees the boy in the distance watching. In Hammett's typical early fashion, however, all of this is a ruse. What the man sees is a dummy the woman has sewn. The boy has gone for help and two of the man's pursuers burst into the cabin and shoot him dead. The woman was Dan Odams's widow.

"The Man Who Killed Dan Odams" gives no signs of the kind of style that Hammett would fashion for his later stories. The narrative descriptions, such as the following, are overwritten and stilted.

> Then he climbed a hill and sprawled on the soggy ground, his lashless red eyes on the country through which he had come: rolling hills of black and green and gray, where wet soil, young grass, and dirty snow divided dominion — the triple rule trespassed here and there by the sepia ribbon of country road winding into and out of sight [70–71].

The narration throughout is heavy-handed and the repeated description of the main character as "the man who killed Dan Odams" becomes tiresome and too obvious. The story, however, does carry the principal marks of Hammett's early fiction. The main one is the fundamental irony of the piece. The circumstance that leads the killer to the home of his victim shows the workings of either a just universe or a sadistic one. The story first suggests, and heavily at that, that the main character has a criminal nature, that his killing (not, significantly, murder) of Dan Odams was a brutal act, and that the widow's vengeance at the close demonstrates proper justice. On the other hand, in the final parts of the story Hammett presents an alternate view. The man claims that he is more victim than villain: "I killed a fellow in Jingo last week... It was fair shooting... But he belonged to Jingo and I don'.... And I ain't figuring on being took back there and hung" (75). And in the final lines of the story the man who killed Dan Odams, with his dying words, magnanimously commends Dan Odams's widow for her actions: "'Good Girl,' he said clearly — and died." (78). Was he a criminal or a victim? In typical fashion Hammett leaves the question open ended.

"Afraid of a Gun"

The second, and last, of Hammett's western stories, "Afraid of a Gun" came out in the March 1924 issue of *The Black Mask*. Like "The Man Who Killed Dan Odams," it takes place in Montana, in a little bump in the road called Dime. "Afraid of a Gun" tells the tale of Owen Sack, a milquetoast man who has been chased all over the world — Australia, South America, etc. — by his own fears. Ever since a cockney sailor threatened him with a gun in a Baltimore dive in his youth, Sack has had a pathological fear of guns:

> [H]e hadn't been a coward, except where guns were concerned; but he had run too often; and that fear, growing, had spread like the seepage from some cancerous growth, until, little by little, he had changed from a man of reasonable courage with one morbid fear to a man of no courage at all [230].

By accident Sack runs afoul of a thuggish and violent family of bootleggers who used the Kootenai River to smuggle liquor into the United States from Canada. He may (or may not) have betrayed them to prohibition agents. The head of the rum-running clan, Rip Yust ("barrel-bodied, slope-shouldered, thick limbed" [227]), was inclined to give Sack the benefit of the doubt, but Sack's leaving town to avoid violence convinces Yust of the little man's guilt and Yust shoots him. Only slightly wounded, Sack loses his fear of firearms, borrows one from a storekeeper and empties it into the rumrunner. But the tale does not end with this vindication of the little man versus the bully, courage prompted by stress, crime versus domesticity. Freed from his fear of guns, Sack becomes obsessed with them and vows to hunt down and shoot everyone who has ever wronged him. And then he dies of the wound he received in the recent shootout with Yust.

Like "The Man Who Killed Dan Odams," this piece emphasizes the double interpretation of western fundamentals: justice and courage. In "Afraid of a Gun," Owen Sack acquires the courage to confront his oppressor, and the timid little guy beats the bully. The problem is that during and after that change he goes squirrelly. During the shootout, "he chanted his silly chant, and fired, fired, fired... [sic] Once something tugged at one of his shoulders, and once at his arm — above where he had felt the burn — but he did not even wonder what it was" (234). After the shoot-out and Sack's raving about gunning down everyone who has even intimidated him, the town doctor talks to him "like he was a child to be humored, or a drunk" (235). When Sack is not afraid of guns he is just as loopy as he was when he was afraid of them. And, once more, Hammett turns the tables both in terms of the action (the main character dies) and in terms of readers' interpretation of the characters.

Westerns are the smallest category of popular fiction that Hammett tried his hand at. They, no doubt, grew from his mining his own experiences for saleable material. As noted earlier, he had spent some time in Montana as a Pinkerton and his wife, Jose, was from Montana and had returned there during one of Hammett's severe bouts of tuberculosis. Especially in the first of the westerns, Hammett spent more time on scene setting and description than in his other stories. There is, as well, a more elemental quality to the characters and their actions than in the other kinds of stories: "The Man Who Killed Dan Odams" is about vengeance and "Afraid of a Gun" is about cowardice. These are manly things, except that in these stories it is a woman who achieves a vengeance, a vengeance that may not be justice; and confidence in the face of a six-gun isn't courage but craziness. These stories present justice and valor as equivocal things and employ the same irony found in his other kinds of fiction. Interestingly, Hammett makes no mention in them of the labor strife that infected Montana during his visit there as a Pinkerton and which he would use as background for *The Red Harvest*. It was, perhaps, too sensitive and controversial a subject for a writer in the pulps to undertake.

Literary Pieces and Reviews

BLACK MASK LETTERS

Hammett's first piece, "The Road Home," appeared in *The Black Mask* in December 1922. Six months later, in the same number that held his criminal piece "The Vicious Circle," *The Black Mask* published Hammett's first letter to the editor. It's odd in that it is signed S. D. Hammett but comments on a story printed under his pseudonym Peter Collinson. Over the next three years *The Black Mask* would print a number of Hammett's letters to the editor. Most of them were in 1924 — in the 1 January, 1 March (two letters), 15 March, June, August, and November issues. During that same period Hammett's fiction was becoming a staple of the magazine: *The Black Mask* featured eleven of his stories that year — three in January, one in February, two in March, two in April, and one each in June, September, and November. His last letter came in the June 1925 number of the magazine. In 1925 it appears that Hammett shifted his commentary (as opposed to his fiction) from *The Black Mask* to other magazine outlets.

Hammett's letters to *The Black Mask* reveal his desire to convince readers that his stories accurately reflect the reality of the world of crime and detection — even if some of the pieces are not, strictly speaking, detective stories. First of all, he repeatedly tells readers that while he has chosen to be a writer (an important fact for Hammett) he has also been a real detective.

> In the years during which I tried my hand at "private detecting" ... [15 June 1923, 21].

> Back — and it's only a couple of years back — in the days before I decided that there was more fun in writing about manhunting than in the hunting... [March 1, 1924, 25].

> An enigmatic want-ad took me into the employ of Pinkerton's National Detective Agency. And I stuck at that until early in 1922... [November, 1924, 27].

After this he emphasizes that his former profession provided the knowledge and experiences that he included in his stories. The March 1, 1924, letter calls attention to the "four rules for shadowing" from "The Zigzags of Treachery" and cites personal experiences to further validate them. And Hammett used the letters as a forum to debate issues involved with fingerprinting (i.e., whether prints can be forged). The letters also make the point that Hammett based characters in his stories on people he knew or had encountered: Owen Sack from "Afraid of a Gun" came from a boyhood acquaintance; Creda Dexter in "The Tenth Clew" was based on a real person.

The letters answered Hammett's desire to reinforce his credentials for accuracy in his *Black Mask* stories. Their tone is something else. First of all, it's defensive because in most cases in his letters to the editor Hammett is explaining or elaborating or defending something in one of his stories—characters, motives, methods of detection, etc. The tone, however, is hearty, casual, and familiar. His first letter (June 15, 1923), for example, begins with "I have been out of town for a couple of weeks—I have to go up in the hills to see some real snow at least once each winter…" (21). The March 1, 1924, letter begins with "I'll have another story riding your way in a day or two…" (24). He also aims at frankness and self-deprecation—as in the mini-biography Hammett provides in his November 1924 letter:

> After a fraction of a year in high school—Baltimore Polytechnic Institute—I became the unsatisfactory and unsatisfied employee of various railroads, stock brokers, machine manufacturers, canners, and the like. Usually I was fired [27].

This self-deprecation, as Layman notes (26), sometimes slips over into disingenuousness, as with Hammett's response to his editor's rejection of two of his stories.

> The trouble is that this sleuth of mine has degenerated into a meal ticket. I liked him at first and used to enjoy putting him through his tricks; but recently I've fallen into the habit of bringing him out and running him around whenever the landlord, or the butcher, or the grocer shows signs of nervousness… There are some men who can write like that, but I am not one of them [26].

But it seems that Hammett was one of those men: he scrubbed up the pieces Cody didn't like and had them published and he went on using the Continental Op as his meal ticket for several years. Finally, one of the most interesting aspects of the tone Hammett adopts for *The Black Mask* letters is that it is not literary. There are no allusions to literary bigwigs past or present. There is no talk about prose style. Mostly Hammett writes about characters' motivations—his own characters and, in his November 1925 letter to Phil Cody, about those of other writers. In that same letter—the only place in *The Black Mask* letters where Hammett comments on literature—his focus is on storytelling and he uses the most superficial method as the basis for his judgment: "…if you like Race Williams, this is a good story; if you don't it isn't" (29).

Over the course of *The Black Mask* letters one can see Hammett moving from amateur writer to enthusiastic practitioner to an increasingly distant professional more interested in the money than the enterprise. In his November 1925 letter to Phil Cody, the last one in the series, Hammett includes a witty reminder that he has sold *The Black Mask* only first serial rights and not all rights to "The Gutting of Couffignal" (28).

"In Defence [sic] of the Sex Story"

The outlet and timing of "In Defence [sic] of the Sex Story" both say something about Hammett's progress as a writer. First, the piece reflects that he did not present himself exclusively as a crime story or a detective story writer as of June 1924: he presents a balanced portfolio of six sex stories and "nine or ten stories in which not a single feminine name appeared" (7–8). It also shows that Hammett was working hard at learning how to become a writer by reading *The Writer's Digest*, the subtitle of which was "A Monthly Magazine for Writers of Short Stories, Photoplays, Poems, Popular Songs, Etc." Finally, unlike his letters to *The Black Mask*, in "In Defence" Hammett self-consciously cites Anatole France and Jack London as well as Shakespeare's *Henry VIII* and *Measure for Measure* to support his argument about fiction concerning relationships.

Mr. Hergesheimer's Scenario

In November 1924 Hammett's 65-word letter to the editor appeared in *Forum*. Not a how-to-journal like *The Writer's Digest*, *Forum* was a standard and serious journal, one that published essays on history, culture, aesthetics, and literary criticism along with poems, short stories, and serial novels. The subject of the letter is Joseph Hergesheimer's new novel *Balisand* (published by Knopf and sold for $2.50). Now entirely forgotten, at the time Hergesheimer was one of the most popular writers in the United States. In his letter Hammett makes the point that *Balisand* is a pictorial novel, "a dream dear to writers for the screen: … a story that could be produced exactly as written" (720). Interestingly, Hammett's taking up Hergesheimer as a subject for discussion was foreshadowed by Mencken's praise of that writer in the pages of *The Smart Set*. Thus, in his omnibus review of recent novels in 1922, Mencken writes that

> as Anatole France lately remarked, nearly all first-rate writers write "bad French"—or "bad English." Joseph Conrad does, Henry James

did. Dickens did. Shakespeare did. Thus Hergesheimer need not repine. He is sinful, but in good company. He writes English that is "bad," but also English that is curiously musical, fluent, chromatic, various, and lovely [138].

It is tantalizing to speculate on influences here: Hammett several times cites Anatole France as a model writer and critic; he surely likes Hergesheimer's works; and in his *Forum* letter he follows Mencken's ironic approach to criticism. Thus, Hammett ends his brief appraisal of *Balisand* with "*Balisand* is a moving picture, but even as literature it is not terrible" (720).

In 1924, at the same time that he was writing sex stories, westerns, criminal stories, and had moved the Continental Op from short stories to novelettes in the pulps, Hammett was also beginning to pay attention to writing as literature as well as to writing as a source of income. His letter to *Forum* on Hergesheimer was only one of his efforts to make his voice heard as a serious critic — these included both "Genius Made Easy" in *Forum* and a letter on Upton Sinclair's *Mammonart: An Essay on Economics,* which was rejected by that journal (Layman, *Letters,* 28). Hammett would speak of the Continental Op as his meal ticket, but in his interest in journals like *Forum* he casts a different light on his view of himself as a writer. They didn't pay for letters to the editor.

"VAMPING SAMSON"

In May 1925 Hammett got some recognition as a serious writer, not a genre hack, when *The Editor* published his "Vamping Samson." It was part of "a series of Autobiographical Letters on the Genesis, Conception, Development, and Writing of Fiction, Poems, and Articles Published in Current Periodicals" (41). "Vamping Samson" presents Hammett's reflections on his story "Ber-Bulu" (published in *Sunset Magazine* two months earlier in March 1925). One of the most important parts of "Vamping Samson" is the short autobiography that concludes the piece. In it Hammett goes beyond the brief and flippant account he provided *The Black Mask* in the November 1924 number and he says some important things about himself and his career as a writer. He praises Mencken and Nathan, notes his experience as a Pinkerton, admits that he had a hard time "getting the hang" of how to write detective stories, and works in the fact that while *Black Mask* stories have paid his bills he has written other kinds of fiction.

My first sale and appearance in print was … in *The Smart Set* under the editorship of Messrs. Nathan and Mencken, though it is conceivable they don't boast of the discovery.

...about half of the fiction I have written has had to do with crime, though, curiously, I was some time getting the hang of the detective story. And while, with the connivance of *The Black Mask*, that type of story has paid most of my rent and grocery bills during the past two years, I have sold at least one or two specimens of most other types... [42–43].

Before this generous and sober assessment of his career, Hammett writes a candid account of the writing of "Ber-Bulu." It begins with the admission that writing the account wasn't easy: "This is my second attempt to respond to THE EDITOR'S inquiry... I tore up the first one..." (41). When he gets down to it, almost all of Hammett's comments about the genesis of the story concentrate on the ingredients of the plot. He notes that the characters are stereotypes—"a giant whose weakness was hidden behind his hair... a Moro, and Moros are, if a people may be put in a few words, superstitious pirates, fighters, gamblers, and lovers of rough humor; and ... a shallow Malay girl who was desired by both men" (42). The whole thing was an updating of the biblical story of Samson, and once he had thought up the way to alter the original characters to fit "...nothing remained but the writing" (42). And that wasn't that hard: Hammett tells readers that the whole thing took him three days, which was unusual for him as his usual time for turning out a story was three weeks. The writing of "Ber-Bulu," Hammett says, wasn't hard, but in several places in "Vamping Samson" he mentions that he is not quite sure of how successful writing happens. In the first paragraph he writes that he tore up his first draft of the piece because it explained "...clearly if not truthfully, and was especially logical in dealing with things in the story that were done haphazardly, or, at best, intuitively" (41). And near the end of his description of the process of composition he adds that he simply cannot say how he put ideas and words together: "I can tell no more than anyone can about any story" (42). The remarkable thing about "Vamping Samson," then, is not its contents but its tone. For the first time in print Hammett writes about himself as a writer — not as an authority on crime or human nature as he had done for *The Black Mask* audience. It's still an advertisement: he ends the piece with a list of the magazines in which his fiction has appeared. Nonetheless, its overall approach is conscientious, serious, and modest as opposed to the sly, self-effacing comments he used in his earlier pieces about himself and his writing.

"GENIUS MADE EASY"

While his letter about Upton Sinclair never made it into print, *Forum* printed Hammett's letter about Mary Austin's nonfiction book *Everyman's*

Genius in its "Opinions About Books" section (July 1925). Here Hammett is back in his *Smart Set* form. *Everyman's Genius* provides a Jungian answer to how creativity works: "Genius, she premises, is the power to use the inherited racial experience stored in the deep-self. Individual experience constitutes the immediate-self, the seat of talent, which shapes the product of the deep-self" [316].

As a reader, Hammett thinks that Austin has some legitimate points: "Mrs. Austin has some sound things to say about the mechanics of the creative mind, on auto-suggestion, auto-prayer, and meditation" (316). And he notes their practical application: "These things, consciously or not, are the accustomed tools of him [sic] who tries to focus his mind in its entirety on any subject" (316). It is interesting to speculate that his reading of a book on the creative process may be a carryover from his thoughts about his own writing, explored in "Vamping Samson" three months earlier. Unlike that article in *The Editor*, however, in his final quip in his letter about Mary Austin's book, Hammett returned to his irony-loaded *Smart Set* style: "Although much of her evidence is trivial and logic is not in her, Mrs. Austin achieves a certain convincingness by sheer weight of humorless sincerity" (317).

"THE ADVERTISEMENT IS LITERATURE"

In 1926 Hammett began working for Albert S. Samuels Jewelry as advertising manager. He apparently found the work to be congenial; he wrote far less fiction during 1926 — no doubt because his check from Samuels covered his bills. And he began to think of himself not just as a writer but as an ad man. Thus, before he had worked a full year for Samuels, Hammett published an essay entitled "The Advertisement Is Literature" in the San Francisco–based journal *Western Advertising: A Magazine for the Buyer and Seller of Advertising Published Monthly by Ramsey Oppenheim*. It is the October 1926 issue's lead article.

"The Advertisement Is Literature" begins by glancing at the notion of creativity Hammett had discussed in his last two nonfiction pieces ("Vamping Samson" and "Genius Made Easy"): "Every writer who brings an idea to a blank sheet of paper is faced with the same primary task. He must set his idea on paper in such a form that it will have the effect he desires on those who read it. The more competent he is, the more stubbornly he will insist that the idea set down shall be his idea and not merely something like it" (35). After this, Hammett, backing himself up by alluding to "Goethe, Carlyle, Croce, Spingarn, [and] Mencken," argues that the proof of literary value is in a work's success. And using this test, "the bookkeeping department" gives a ready and easy answer: good ads affect readers, therefore they accomplish the same end as any literary work. Disregarding whether literature should have any philosophical, ethical, or moral purpose, Hammett moves on to style. He begins by rejecting "...disproportionately florid, [and] the gaudy" language and establishes efficiency as the standard for style:

> The needlessly involved sentence, the clouded image, are not literary. They are anti-literary.... Anatole France, probably the tallest figure modern literature has raised, and the most bookish of men in the bargain, said: "The most beautiful sentence? The shortest." He condemned the semicolon, a hangover from the days of lengthy sentences, as not suited to an age of telephones and airplanes. He insisted that all unnecessary "which's" and "that's" must be carefully weeded out, as they would spoil the finest style [35].

One of the implications of this view is that, instead of fancy words and frilly phrases, literary language is that of the man in the street. However, Hammett states that "the language of the man in the street is seldom either clear or simple" (36). Common language, Hammett holds, is banal and derivative. Even if it occasionally possesses lucidity or color it inevitably comes from repeating words or phrases that "originated in the mind of some professional worker with words, and reached the street by way of book, magazine, newspaper, pulpit, platform, theater or radio" (36). In writing, creating "common speech" is very difficult. It comes from "skillfully editing, distorting, simplifying, coloring the national tongue, and not by reporting it verbatim" (36).

Obviously, Hammett never proves that advertisements are literature. He pretty much gets off that track after the first few lines of the essay. What the essay is about isn't advertisements; it's about Hammett's view of literature or, more properly, literary style. To add weight to what he has to say about style he brings in his list of blockbuster literary names—not only Goethe, Carlyle, Croce, Spingarn, Mencken, Conrad, Galsworthy and (his perennial favorite) Anatole France, but also Aristotle and, in the final paragraphs, Ring Lardner. The whole point of the essay lies in establishing rules for simple, clear, vernacular style — the kind he developed as he wrote the Continental Op stories. Just as importantly, however, is that Hammett couches his argument for this kind of style not in terms of genius or indefinable creative impulses but in terms of work. When he speaks of original language used by "the man in the street" he says that it inevitably originated "in the mind of some professional worker with words," and when he speaks of the difficulty of writing simple, clear and arresting language he holds that the writer must be possessed of "a high degree of skill."

THE SATURDAY REVIEW OF LITERATURE

Hammett began as a regular reviewer for *The Saturday Review of Literature* in January 1927, a position, Layman suggests, that may have come his way as a result of Captain Joseph Shaw's (the new editor of *Black Mask*) influence (79). Unsigned, *The Saturday Review* published five columns before the publication of the first installment of what would become *The Red Harvest* in *Black Mask*. Hammett's reviews appeared in January ("Poor Scotland Yard!"), March ("The Story of Scotland Yard"), April ("Guessers and Deducers"), May ("Current Murders"), and June ("The Lost Adventurer"). Some cover single works, and some are omnibus reviews, looking at several new books. All of the books are mysteries. Hammett was, for the time being, *The Saturday Review's* in-house expert on crime fiction and nonfiction. And he talks like an expert. In the established manner of experts, in "Guessers and Deducers" (April 1927) Hammett trots out authorities at the beginning of his review:

> There exists a considerable body of reasonably authoritative litera-
> ture on crime detection. Such Europeans as Gross and Niceforo have
> been done into English; Macnaughten, Anderson, and Thompson
> of Scotland Yard, our own Pinkerton, Burns, and Dougherty, have
> given their experiences. Post, Dilnot, Gollomb, and others have
> published articles on police methods both here and abroad [743].

This was his second statement on his *bona fides*. The first was in his omnibus review in January, "Poor Scotland Yard!" which begins with "In some years of working for private detective agencies in various cities..." (510).

With a couple of exceptions, nobody remembers any of the books Hammett reviewed in 1927. Readers should recognize the name S. S. Van Dine: Hammett reviewed the first Philo Vance novel, *The Benson Murder Case*. And maybe a few will remember the prolific J. S. Fletcher and Sidney Horler. But the other writers he reviewed—George Dilnot, Walter Gilkyson, William Johnson. Lynn Brock, and Olga Hartley—have been lost to obscurity long ago. And for Hammett it would be well-deserved obscurity. Most of the books he looked at he found to be ploddingly predictable. Lynn Brock's *The Kink* is "written according to one of the current recipes" (734); readers will find the plot in Olga Hartley's *The Maralet Murders* "an old friend" (510); "the dozen stories in 'Aurelius Smith—Detective' are as mechanical as the others" (734). When Hammett begins his plot summary of William Johnson's *The Affair in Duplex 9B* he writes an aside to his readers about the tiresome nature of the plotting: "'The Affair in Duplex 9B' is—don't stop me if you've heard this one before—about the wealthy rascal who was done in" (734). Hammett found Sidney Horler, a British thriller writer in the same school as Sapper and his Bulldog Drummond fantasies, to be ridiculous. In the reviews Hammett rarely says much about prose style. He does mention the stilted dialogue in *The Affair in Duplex 9B* (734) and of Van Dine's dialogue, he says, "This Philo Vance is in the Sherlock Holmes tradition and his conversational manner is that of a high school girl who has been studying the foreign words and phrases in the back of her dictionary" (510). But the main feature of Hammett's reviews isn't his consideration of the presence or absence of attractive or even competent characterization or of plotting or style. It's about accuracy.

Hammett's first review in *The Saturday Review of Literature* begins this way:

> In some years of working for private detective agencies in various cities I came across only one fellow sleuth who would confess that he read detective stories. "I eat 'em up," this one said without shame. "When I'm through my day's gum-shoeing I like to relax; I like to get my mind on something that's altogether different from the daily grind; so I read detective stories" [510].

Rather than using the experience of private detectives to skewer writers for inaccuracy, however, Hammett repeatedly turns to the police in his reviews. In the passage from "Guessers and Deducers" cited above in which Hammett lists books on police science, he finishes the paragraph with "There's little evidence that many copies were bought by writers of detective stories. That's too bad" (734). In the same review he notes that Lynn Brock doesn't even know that the cops can trace license plate numbers. And when it comes to his views on S. S. Van Dine, Hammett spends as much time critically examining the knowledge and methods of Policeman Heath and District Attorney Markham as he does the writer's pip-squeak hero. Underlying all of the reviews, moreover, rests Hammett's belief that, in spite of some inadequacies, the police in the United States and in Britain have developed practical methodologies and do an admirable job of crime detection. Hammett believes that an accurate picture of British police presents an image of "a uniformed force of very great efficiency; and a detective force mechanically nearer perfection than most others" (668). So, throughout the reviews, his most emphatic advice to writers is to first get to know about the police and police methods.

Summary

The metaphor of apprenticeship doesn't exactly work for writers because of the challenges of a protean and inexhaustible language. It works a bit better with storytellers where there is a voice to be developed and techniques to be tried and mastered. In the six years between 1922 and 1927 Hammett worked at becoming a writer. And there were two sides to what Hammett did during those years. One was his aspiration to join the world of literature and the other was his need to put food on the table. His entry into the writing world was no doubt motivated by enrolling in Munson's Business College in early 1922 with an eye toward becoming a newspaper reporter (Layman 28). He chose as his model the most famous newspaperman of the day, H. L. Mencken. It is very, very likely that Hammett remembered Mencken from his Baltimore days since they attended the same secondary school and Hammett worked across the street from the *Baltimore Sun* offices. Thus, Hammett's early pieces aspire to the clever, ironic, erudite sophistication cultivated by Mencken in *The Smart Set*. Hammett chose to satirize the relationships between the sexes and the stupidity of criminals. And he scoured the library for bits like those he assembled for "The Great Lovers." But if it was hard for Mencken and Nathan to make a living out of clever, ironic, erudite sophistication, it was impossible for Hammett. Throughout the 1920s he would continue to write bits for magazines concerned with high (or higher) culture, but to make a living he turned to other ventures and other venues. The first of these was "The Road Home" in the new pulp magazine, *The Black Mask*. The adventure story, however, never proved to be an altogether congenial form for him, at its best it required a knowledge of the exotic and a belief in a kind of hero and heroism that Hammett did not possess. And so he turned to sex and crime. By 1924 he was as well known for his stories about the relations between the sexes as he was for any of his other kinds of fiction: in "In Defence [sic] of the Sex Story," Hammett does not even mention that he wrote detective stories. In early 1923 Hammett began to look into his own experience for material. He wrote "The Sardonic Star of Tom Doody" because he knew about criminals and he wrote about being a private detective in "From the Memoirs of a Private Detective." At that point, however, he still possessed the *Smart Set* point of view and saw both crime and detection as subjects for satire. As he noted in "Vamping Samson," "I was some time getting the hang of the detective story." And that was the case because he did not approach his own experience as a serious subject until he wrote the first Continental Op story, "Arson Plus." Having tried out various forms, approaches, and styles, Hammett found his niche with the stories about the Op and he made writing about the Op his principal occupation during the rest of the 1920s. But the Op was not Hammett's exclusive concern. With "The Second Story Angel," "The Ruffian's Wife," and "Ber-Bulu," Hammett wrote first-class magazine fiction that used and reevaluated the criminal story, the sex story, and the adventure story. By the end of the decade, however, Hammett had been typecast as a detective story writer. And in the ironic manner of all of his early fiction, this was both good and, in the end, very bad.

2

Making the
Continental Op

In 1925 Hammett looked back at his three years' experience as a writer and admitted that "...about half of the fiction I have written has had to do with crime, though, curiously, I was some time getting the hang of the detective story" ("Vamping Samson," 43). He didn't set out to write detective stories. Married, out of a job, and chronically ill, in 1922 Hammett first saw writing as a way to make a living and as a way, to use the shibboleth of the 1990s, to gain self-esteem. He thought that writers were important people and he aspired to write his way into the set of smart, witty, erudite people whose views informed, entertained and inspired others. While that hope never left him, it had little to do with his success as a writer or the impact that he has had on the world of letters. Those came when he "got the hang of the detective story" and created the Continental Op.

Just as the stories about the Continental Op were a new and different kind of popular fiction in the 1920s, they were also something new and different for Hammett. They were different for him, first of all, because they were about a detective; even though being a detective was the only thing that Hammett really knew, he shied away from the subject when he began to write. Private detectives (and the police for that matter) were not something that he thought people would want to read about. The police didn't have a rosy reputation in American life or letters in the first quarter of the twentieth century. When the cops appear in Hammett's earliest fiction they are seedy, incompetent, corrupt, and unattractive. The same was true for non-agency private eyes. This being the case, before he invented the Continental Op, he wrote "From the Memoirs of a Private Detective," which presents the whole business of cops and detectives as pretty silly or stupid. As for the crooks, Hammett could hardly find anything in them to make them much in the way of antagonists: his experience had led him to know criminals as stupid, inept bunglers. When he wrote the Op stories, however, Hammett did something different: he wrote about solving crimes as a worthy, useful, complex, and interesting pursuit engaged in by intelligent individuals, and he presented criminals as smarter and luckier than losers like Tom Doody and Joe Shupe in his early fiction.

Writing about the Op also meant adopting a new attitude, toward readers and toward writing. In his earliest pieces, Hammett aimed at being ironic, satiric, and maybe even snide. His pre–Op pieces portray people individually and collectively as vain, ignorant, and buffoonish in a style intended to call attention to the writer's cleverness. Everything is ironic. Both sides of issues are wrong or silly or corrupt. The thing to admire is supposed to be the writer's aloof point of view and the deviously clever way in which his prose gets this across. None of this carries over into Hammett's stories about the Op. His style changes. The language of the uneducated as well as that of the underworld is no longer the subject for derision but simply a recording of the way that people speak. The sentence is no longer a way to show off but a way to accurately describe and explain worlds with which readers are unfamiliar. And Hammett eases up on the irony so evident in his early works. While there may be bits of comedy in the Op stories, like the slapstick opening scene of "Arson Plus," superficially there is nothing ironic or satiric about what happens in them: they rest on fundamentals like good versus evil, and justice versus crime. Whether by accident or design, however, in the Op stories Hammett recognized that if one is going to use them, the most fit subject for irony or satire is oneself. And that recognition helped him make a new kind of hero and a new kind of fiction.

Chronology and Development

Before "The Cleansing of Personville" (November 1927; also the first installment of *The Red Harvest*, 1928), Hammett wrote 24 stories about his anonymous agent of the Continental Detective Agency named the Continental Op. Beginning with "Arson Plus" in the October 1, 1923, issue and ending with "The Main Death" in the June 1927 issue, 23 of these pieces appeared in *The Black Mask*. *True Detective Stories* published the only non-*Black Mask* Op story, "Who Killed Bob Teal?" in its November 1924 issue. Chronologically, Hammett published five Op stories in 1923, nine in 1924, six in 1925, one in 1926, and three in 1927. As the series proceeded, Hammett wrote longer Op stories. Indeed, a change came about with "The Tenth Clew," published on January 1, 1924, as it was Hammett's first story to be featured on the cover of *The Black Mask*. It is significantly longer than any of the earlier Op stories and more than double the length of the earlier "Slippery Fingers," "It," and "Bodies Piled Up." With the exception of "One Hour" (April 1924), "Who Killed Bob Teal?" "Mike, Alec or Rufus" (January 1925), and "The Creeping Siamese" (March 1926), the Op stories after "The Tenth Clew" are longer pieces, or "novelettes," most of which follow the pattern of "The Tenth Clew" by including chapter divisions. In addition to writing mostly longer Op stories, before 1927 and his first novel, Hammett published two sets of paired, semiconnected stories featuring the Op: in 1924 "The House on Turk Street" (April 15, 1924) and "The Girl with the Silver Eyes" (June 1924); and in 1927 "The Big Knock-Over" (February, 1927) and "$106,000 Blood Money" (May 1927).

Making the Op

Everyone familiar with Hammett knows that the Op's name came from the Continental Building located at the corner of Calvert and Baltimore streets in Hammett's hometown of Baltimore, Maryland. Now at the end of a strip of nudie bars, in Hammett's day the Continental was an imposing edifice — a tall, steel-frame building, one of the few downtown structures to survive the great fire of Baltimore. It was a block away from the Western Union offices as well as from the *Baltimore Sun*, where H. L. Mencken sat around, writing and smoking stogies. Much is occasionally made of the fact that the architectural decoration above the building's main entrance includes two birds that may be falcons or may be eagles. The offices of the Pinkerton National Detective Agency were located in the Continental Building. Hammett worked there as a Pinkerton operative from 1915 until he joined the Army in 1918. The first prominent fact about the Op, then, is that he has no name other than his identification with a business. Hammett, following the practice of the Pinkertons, increased the anonymity of his hero by using the term "operative" as opposed to "agent" or "detective," both of which implied more identity and romance than the one he chose. If not identity, for Hammett "operative" at least distinguished the Op from the "private detective." In "The Zigzags of Treachery" the Op comments about public perception of private eyes and says that most people are "anxious to believe that a private detective is a double-dealing specialist who goes around with a cold deck in one pocket, a complete forger's outfit in another, and who counts that day lost in which he railroads no innocent to the hoosgow" (113). While in the first run of Op stories there are no private detectives mentioned per se, Hammett portrayed non-agency detectives as a sorry lot. In the first few Op stories readers meet a couple of them: "The Montgomery Hotel's regular detective had taken his last week's rake off from the hotel bootlegger in merchandise instead of cash, had drunk it down, had fallen asleep in the lobby, and had been fired" ("The Bodies Piled Up" 42); "At the Marquis Hotel I got hold of the house detective, who is a helpful chap so long as his hand is kept greased" ("Slippery Fingers" 27). And even in "The Creeping Siamese" the private cops don't measure up: "Pederson, the house copper, a blond-mustached ex-bartender who doesn't know any more about gum-shoeing than I do about saxophones" (523). Hammett, then, made his hero not a private detective but an employee of an agency that is essentially the Pinkerton National Detective Agency, the most effective national law enforcement body in the country at the time. The first fact about the Op, then, is that he worked in concert with others as an operative of a detective agency, and portraying that fact formed a significant part of Hammett's purpose in creating this new character.

The Continental Detective Agency

Near the beginning of "Arson Plus," Hammett notes that his hero is an employee of the Continental Detective Agency:

> I had been doing business with this fat sheriff of Sacramento County for four or five years—ever since I came to the Continental Detective Agency's San Francisco office [3].

Other than this identifying reference, the role of the agency in the Op's first appearance is sparse: Hammett mentions the Continental only in the wire the Op sends to the agency's Seattle office and his stopping by the San Francisco office to receive the Seattle reply. No names or descriptions appear connected with the Continental Detective Agency. In the second Op piece, "Slippery Fingers" (October 15, 1923), Hammett made a tentative move toward expanding the role of the agency in the series. Almost halfway through the narrative the Op goes to the agency's office to wait for telephone calls, and for the first time, Hammett brought in named operatives from the Continental Agency: "I had sent Dick Foley — he is the Agency's shadow ace — and Bob Teal — a youngster who will be a world-beater some day — over to Clane's hotel" (28). In "Slippery Fingers," however, Hammett, does not describe Foley or Teal and neither of them has dialogue. As the Op stories progressed, however, he would use both characters to provide details, albeit small details, about the job of being a detective and of the workings of the Continental Detective Agency.

Hammett used Bob Teal in two stories after "Slippery Fingers" — "The Zigzags of Treachery" (March 1, 1924) and "Who Killed Bob Teal?" (November 1924). In the first of these stories Teal became a subordinate partner for the Op. They watch the principal suspect's residence together from rented rooms and exchange bits of mundane dialogue. In "The Zigzags of Treachery," Teal's action is limited to shadowing and watching on the Op's behalf, and Hammett provided little to characterize him other than that he is a named operative who helps the Op do a job. Rescuing Mrs. Estep, then, is not simply the Op's responsibility, but the agency's. Unlike the perfunctory role Teal played in the first two stories, Hammett used him for larger purposes in "Who Killed Bob Teal?" While he has been killed before the start of the story, Hammett provided readers with a relatively (for the Op) full description of Teal:

> I had been fond of Bob Teal — we all had. He had come to the Agency fresh from college two years before; and if ever a man had the makings of a crack detective in him, this slender, broad-shouldered lad had. Two years is little enough time in which to pick up the first principles of sleuthing, but Bob Teal, with his quick eye, cool nerve, balanced head, and whole-hearted interest in his work, was already well along the way to expertness. I had an almost fatherly interest in him, since I had given him most of his early training [262].

First of all, for the Op, and, by extension, for Hammett, Bob Teal possessed all of the requisites of the "world-beater" detective: he has the physique, the nerve, the commonsense, the dedication, as well as the capacity and willingness to learn and (significantly for Hammett who had only a meager education) the education necessary to be a first-rate sleuth. The passage, to be sure, also reflects on the Op's role in and attitude toward the Continental Detective Agency and its operatives. In addition to the ways in which "Who Killed Bob Teal?" reflects on the Op and on the character traits necessary to make the ideal detective, the story also reflects on the human solidarity of the agency. Thus, finding Teal's killer supersedes the normal operations of the agency, ratified at the beginning of the story when the head of the San Francisco office says, "I'm determined to find him [the killer] and convict him if I have to let all regular business go and put every man I have on the job for a year" [263].

Unlike Bob Teal, who Hammett used and disposed of after three stories, Dick Foley played an ongoing role in the Op stories, extending into both of the Op novels. In all, Dick Foley appeared in ten of the Op stories written before 1927: "Slippery Fingers," "The Bodies Piled Up" (December 1, 1923), "The Zigzags of Treachery" (March 1, 1924), "The Girl with the Silver Eyes" (June 1924), "The Scorched Face" (May 1925), "Dead Yellow Women" (November 1925), "The Gutting of Couffignal" (December 1925), "The Big Knock-over" (February 1927), "$106,000 Blood Money" (May 1927), and "The Main Death" (June 1927). While Hammett began to develop a unique dialogue style for Foley in "The Bodies Piled Up," he did not describe him until his fourth story appearance. Thus, in "The Girl with Silver Eyes," the Op tells the readers that Foley is "a little shrimp of a Canadian — there isn't a hundred and ten pounds of him — who is the smoothest shadow I've ever seen, and I've seen most of them" (168–69). And while Hammett had given an example of Foley's characteristic dialogue in his second appearance in the series, in "The Girl with Silver Eyes" he has the Op describe the way that Foley talks: "The little Canadian talks like a telegram when his peace of mind is disturbed, and just now he was decidedly peevish" (169).

As the stories progressed, Hammett continued to reprise the same theme about Dick Foley. In "Dead Yellow Women" the Op says that "the little Canadian talks like a thrifty man's telegram" (407), and in "The Big Knock-Over" he gives the longest mention of Foley's looks and speech:

> He was a swarthy little Canadian who stood nearly five feet in his high-heeled shoes, weighing a hundred pounds, minus, talked like a Scotchman's telegram, and could have shadowed a drop of water from the Golden Gate to Hongkong without ever losing sight of it [560].

Hammett's continued use of Foley as an ancillary character in the Op stories emphasizes the importance of surveillance in the agency's operations. On a personal level, however, through Foley, Hammett also worked in the point that shadowing is the least glamorous and fulfilling of a detective's duties. Thus, in "The Scorched Face" the Op reports Foley's singular outburst about the routine of his job versus the occasional action encountered in the detective business: "'I expected it,' Dick howled. 'Any time there's any fun I can count on being stuck off somewhere on a street corner!'" (380).

After Bob Teal and Dick Foley, the next character Hammett connected to the Continental Agency was the Old Man, introduced in the eighth Op story entitled "The Zigzags of Treachery." The Old Man, manager of the San Francisco office of the agency, appears in 9 of the 24 Op stories: "The Zigzags of Treachery," "The Girl with the Silver Eyes," "Who Killed Bob Teal?" "The Whosis Kid," "The Scorched Face," "Dead Yellow Women," "The Creeping Siamese," "The Big Knock-Over," and "$106,000 Blood Money." The Old Man's first appearance is a perfunctory one, included in order to demonstrate the utility of the Op's connection with the corporation — the Op calls up the Old Man and asks him to save him some time by detailing an operative to do a bit of routine research. Hammett doesn't do much more with the Old Man in "The Girl with the Silver Eyes." But in his next appearance, because of the significance of Bob Teal's murder to the Op and to the agency, Hammett included fuller descriptions of the character. The Op describes him as having an irritating habit of tapping his pencil on his desk, being fanatically devoted to the agency and its operatives, and possessing a mild voice and manner that masks any feelings he might have. In "Who Killed Bob Teal?" then, Hammett provided a hint at the Old Man's inner life along with a detail of idiosyncratic behavior (tapping the pencil) that he would transfer into later stories. None of this carried over to "The Whosis Kid" where the Old Man plays only a minor role with a reported interview connected to the case. In "The Scorched Face" Hammett returned to providing details about the character, introducing the fact that he really is old and again emphasizing the emotional side of the Old Man's character:

> The Old Man, with his gentle eyes behind gold spectacles and his mild smile, hiding the fact that fifty years of sleuthing had left him without any feelings at all on any subject. (Whitey Clayton used to say the Old Man could spit icicles in August) [371–72].

The reference to spitting icicles (no doubt a euphemism) would reappear in "The Big Knock-Over" and *The Red Harvest*. In "The Scorched Face," as in "The Whosis Kid," the Old Man provides assistance and information that help the Op solve the case in question. "Dead Yellow Women" begins in the Old Man's office and presents him as being in charge of the agency, interviewing a prospective client and assigning the Op to the case of Lillian Shan. At this point in the series references to the Old Man's inscrutability have become routine: "She looked at the Old Man, who smiled at her with his polite, meaningless smile — a mask through which you can read nothing" (398). In the much shorter story "The Creeping Siamese" Hammett once more emphasizes the Old Man's visible lack of emotion: "The Old Man's voice and smile were as pleasantly polite as if the corpse at his feet had been part of the pattern in the carpet. Fifty years of sleuthing have left him with no more emotion than a pawnbroker" (523). But he also added, for the first time, acknowledgment of his routine, detective-related skepticism: "Today is never Tuesday to the Old Man: it *seems* to be Tuesday" (523). Hammett reinforced this in "The Big Knock-Over": "…he was one of those cautious babies who'll look out the window at a cloudburst and say, 'It seems to be raining,' on the off chance that somebody's pouring water off the roof" (548).

In "The Big Knock-Over" the Op also gives the longest description of the Old Man: He's in his seventies and has been in the detective business for 50 years; he's tall, plump, and mustachioed; and he has a "baby pink" face and "mild blue eyes." He wears glasses without rims and looks like he could be anyone's grandfather. But these appearances are deceiving: he has "no more warmth in him than a hangman's rope" and his long exposure to crime and the detective business "emptied him of everything except brains."

> We who worked under him were proud of his cold-bloodedness. We used to boast that he could spit icicles in July, and we called him Pontius Pilate among ourselves, because he smiled politely when he sent us out to be crucified on suicidal jobs [543].

In the Old Man's final appearance before the reported references to him in *The Red Harvest*, Hammett gave him a small measure of something like emotion:

> The Old Man nodded his grandfatherly face and smiled, but for the first time in the years I had known him I knew what he was thinking. He was thinking that if Jack had come through alive we would have had the nasty choice between letting him go free or giving the Agency a black-eye by advertising that one of our operatives was a crook.
>   I threw away my cigarette and stood up. The Old Man stood also, and he held out a hand to me.
>   "Thank you," he said ["$106,000 Blood Money" 634].

That emotion, however, connects him to devotion to the agency and not to the operatives he sent out "to be crucified on suicidal jobs."

Just as Hammett expanded readers' views of the Continental Detective Agency by increasingly introducing the Old Man in the stories after "The Whosis Kid," he also introduced other characters who help to provide a somewhat larger view of the workings of a private detective agency.

In "The Whosis Kid" he introduced Tommy Howd, the agency's "freckled and snub-nosed office boy." Tommy plays a small role in "The Whosis Kid" where the Op recognizes and appreciates boyhood fantasies about detective work Hammett mentions him again in "The Creeping Siamese" and "$106,000 Blood Money." Along with the office boy, Hammett introduced Fiske, the agency's night man in "Dead Yellow Women," "The Big Knock-Over," and "The Main Death." Hammett makes Fiske into an obsessive and persistent teller of old and stale jokes: "I smoked, pretended to listen to Fiske's report on all the jokes that were at the Orpheum that week" ["Dead Yellow Women" 401].

The only other significant continuing Continental character is Jack Counihan who appears in "The Big Knock-Over" and "$106,000 Blood Money." Hammett portrayed him, while physically similar, as an anti-version of Bob Teal. The son of an affluent family whose father makes him get a job in spite of his belief "that squeezing through a college graduation was enough work for one lifetime," Counihan approaches being a detective as a lark: "He thought gumshoeing would be fun.... He was jingle-brained, of course, and needed holding, but I would rather work with him than with a lot of old-timers I knew" ("The Big Knock-Over" 548–49). By the time he introduced Counihan, Hammett had become more fascinated with the makeup of his characters' dialogue, so he created a unique diction for Counihan. Educated, athletic, and smart, Counihan presents an object lesson in being a detective. He lacks seriousness as well as devotion to duty and to the job, both of which he betrays in "$106,000 Blood Money" because he has not developed the defenses against emotions that Hammett portrays as essential traits of the Op and of the Old Man.

In the 24 Op stories before *The Red Harvest* Hammett introduced a few other incidental operatives of the agency. Gorman and Hooper from the Los Angeles office make cameo appearances in "The Golden Horseshoe" (November 1924). Porter, an employee in the San Francisco office, checks up the Op's expense account in "The Creeping Siamese." The not-very-smart Andy MacElroy ("a big boulder of a man ... with no more imagination than an adding machine" [615]) makes two brief appearances in "$106,000 Blood Money." And Mickey Linehan, who Hammett would use in *The Red Harvest*, plays minor, largely mute, roles in "The Big Knock-Over," "$106,000 Blood Money," and "The Main Death."

In the stories written before 1927 Hammett introduced eleven named employees of the agency and included some nameless functionaries who work for the agency in San Francisco and in other cities across the country. Fourteen of the 24 Op stories have named Continental employees in them. Ten stories make no mention of individual Continental agents:

"Arson Plus," "Crooked Souls," "It," "The Tenth Clew," "Nightshots," "The House on Turk Street," "One Hour," "Women, Politics and Murder," "Mike, Alec or Rufus," and "Corkscrew." These are mostly early or short pieces. Indeed, introducing personnel from the agency, developing their characters, and using them to help to define the Op was one, but only one, of the ways in which Hammett made his short fiction into "novelettes."

In addition to his development of characters connected with the agency in the Op stories before 1927, Hammett inserted details, albeit few of them, describing the San Francisco office and some of the agency's policies. To be sure, Hammett had little inclination to describe locales, and the action of the Op stories is at least peripatetic. In most of the stories, therefore, the office simply serves as a place for the Op to receive wires or phone calls from other operatives or to look up records—an activity that Hammett made more specific later in the series, moving from the Op reading generic reports to supplying specific case-file numbers. Several stories in the series begin at the San Francisco office—"Dead Yellow Women," "The Creeping Siamese," and "$106,000 Blood Money"—but most of the stories begin at clients' houses or, in the case of "The Zigzags of Treachery" and "The Golden Horseshoe," in the office of lawyer Vance Richmond. While Hammett frequently gave street locations for events taking place in San Francisco, it was not until the twenty-second of the 24 stories that he included the location of the San Francisco office: "The Continental Detective Agency's San Francisco office is located in a Market Street office building" ("The Big Knock-Over" 542). While "Dead Yellow Women" begins at the agency's offices, Hammett gives no details of the location, size, or furnishings. Two stories later, in "The Creeping Siamese," readers learn that the agency is not on the ground floor (it is accessible by an apparently automatic elevator), and that the front office contains the cashier's desk, the office boy's desk and a rail dividing the office. Most of the stories involving the Old Man give him an office and in "The Main Death" Hammett noted for the first time that the Op had his own office, something conspicuously absent in the earlier stories. Inferentially, there is a records room, as the Op sends Tommy Howd off to request records from a file clerk in "$106,000 Blood Money." On the whole, however, readers know very little detail about the offices of the Continental Detective Agency other than that they exist and function—which, for Hammett's purposes, may be all that they need to know.

For Hammett's purposes readers also needed to know a few of the agency's policies: (1) the agency does not do divorce work (see "The Main Death"); (2) neither the Agency nor its employees accepts reward money (see "Women, Politics and Murder" and "$106,000 Blood Money"); (3) the agency operates in a fiscally responsible, perhaps even frugal, manner (see the Op's complaints about expense account rules in "The Creeping Siamese" and "The Big Knock-Over"); and (4) the agency is a business ("In the normal course of business, the Agency's bookkeeping department sent Gallaway a bill for my services" ["Nightshots" 93]).

That Hammett chose to make the Continental Detective Agency a conspicuous part of his early series of detective stories carries with it a number of significances. First of all, it obviously plays a large role in the character of his hero. Lacking a name, the corporate identification forms a significant part of the hero's identity. When the Op has the occasion to introduce himself, he identifies himself either with a pseudonym or as an operative of the Continental Agency. While Hammett does mention the Op's apartment — most conspicuously in "$106,000 Blood Money" — he spends far, far more time at the office than he does at his home. Although during the course of the stories the Op seems to function as a free agent, ultimately he is not one: he is assigned to cases by his employer; he must go through channels; he must write up reports. Indeed, in a number of cases the Op works for people he dislikes, distrusts, or thinks are downright squirrelly — see, respectively, "Nightshots," "It," and "The Girl with the Silver Eyes." While the Op's relationship with the Continental Detective Agency may emphasize that he is an employee of the corporation, Hammett also occasionally describes the Op's relationship with others in the agency by using family metaphors. The Op tells readers of his "fatherly" interest in Bob Teal, and his relationship with Tommy, the office boy, if not paternal, is at least that of a sympathetic older brother. Equally as important as the agency's impact on the hero's character is the role the agency plays in Hammett's purpose in writing detective stories. Hammett recognized that his initial success as a writer depended almost exclusively on his own experience as a detective. A significant part of his purpose, then, in writing the Op stories was to let readers know how real detectives work. The Op stories, then, let readers know that real detectives do not work alone: they depend on others to do a host of routine jobs, from creating and maintaining records, to shadowing suspects, and even to collecting fees for services. In almost every story the Op depends on others in the agency — and in the agency's offices around the country — to supply him with crucial information that he cannot gather himself. Working for and with an organization was the way Hammett knew real detectives functioned, and conveying this fact to his readers was an important part of his motive in writing the Op stories. Creating details about the Continental Agency served one final purpose for Hammett. These details enabled him to keep on writing stories about the Op. By August 1924 Hammett wrote to Phil Cody, the editor of *The Black Mask*, and protested that he was conscious of the Op stories getting flat:

> The trouble is that this sleuth of mine has degenerated into a meal-ticket. I liked him at first and used to enjoy putting him through his tricks; but recently I've fallen into the habit of bringing him out and running him around whenever the landlord, or the butcher, or the grocer shows signs of nervousness.
>
> There are men who can write like that, but I am not one of them. If I can stick to the stuff I want to write — the stuff I enjoy writing — I can make a go of it, but if I try to grind out a yarn because I think there is a market for it, I flop [Layman, *Letters,* 191].

Around the time he wrote this to Cody, Hammett began, among other things, to develop more details about the Continental Detective Agency. In "Who Killed Bob Teal?" he expands the character of the Old Man; in "The Whosis Kid" he introduced Tommy Howd, the office boy; in "The Scorched Face" he gave Dick Foley a bit more personality than simply that of the shadow man; in "Dead Yellow Women" he introduced Fiske, the joke-telling night man; in "The Creeping Siamese" he invented Porter the agency cashier; and, beginning with "The Big Knock-Over," he used an expanded cast of Continental operatives. What the agency did for Hammett, then, was to enable him to keep on writing fiction about a character that he increasingly felt he had worn out.

How to Be a Detective

Giving the Op a corporate identity was only Hammett's first step in creating his new hero. The next step was to use him to show readers how real detectives do their jobs.

Before he began the Continental Op stories, Hammett occupied himself with trying to sell bits of ironic frippery like "The Great Lovers" to *The Smart Set*, seeking to make his mark writing sex stories about men and women making one another miserable, writing tales recounting the stupidity of criminals, and producing dribblets of exotic, romantic adventure like "The Road Home" for *The Black Mask*. Searching for a subject that would get him into print, he published "From the Memoirs of a Private Detective" in the March 1923 issue of *The Smart Set*. This is a collection of 29 entries of a few sentences each that cite people, events, and maxims reflecting the experience of a private detective. The majority of them are ironic, even sarcastic, and intended to be wryly humorous. For example, entry 8 is "I was once falsely accused of perjury and had to perjure myself to escape arrest" (906). Ten of the "Memoirs" entries (3, 10, 11, 12, 17, 18, 20, 25, 27, 29) make serious observations about crime or the real experience of a detective. Of these, six (3, 10, 12, 17, 18, and 25) reflect on the nature and practices of criminals: number 12, for instance, is " I have never known a man capable of turning out first-rate work in a trade, a profession or an art, who was a professional criminal" (907). Of the remaining four entries, two are about fingerprints (11 and 18) and two are about public perceptions of crime and its detection; thus, number 27 contrasts the detective of fiction and the real world, and number 29 concludes the "Memoirs" by telling readers "that the law-breaker is invariably soon[er] or late[r] apprehended is probably the least challenged of extant myths" (909). In "Memoirs of a Private Detective" Hammett used his experience as a Pinkerton as a means of entertaining an urbane and sophisticated audience, mixing in a few serious comments on the real world of the working detective.

With the Op stories Hammett realized that his experiences with the Pinkertons were more than a way of entertaining, they were his meal ticket; as well as providing him with the raw material for the narratives, his work as a Pinkerton validated his stories about detectives and legitimized them for readers in a way that the stories of other writers could not be validated or made legitimate. His experiences as a detective could get him into print and get him paid. Frequently, therefore, when Hammett used his own voice during the early period, he fit in the fact that he had been a real detective. It's there in his first letter (June 15, 1923) to *The Black Mask*: "In the years during which I tried my hand at 'private detecting'" (21). He concludes "Vamping Samson" in the May 1925 issue of *The Editor* by saying, "I spent some years sleuthing around the country in the employ of the Pinkerton's National Detective Agency" (43). And even late in the 1920s, when Hammett had gained enough of a literary reputation to write for *The Saturday Review of Literature*, he mentioned his Pinkerton experience: his January 15, 1927, review begins with "In some years of working for private detective agencies in various cities" (510). Indeed, in "A Man Named Thin," written in the mid–1920s but not published until it appeared in *Ellery Queen's Mystery Magazine*, the private detective's boss (and father) says,

> "But why ... pick on poetry? Aren't there plenty of other things to write about? Why, Robin, you could write some good serious articles about our work, articles that could tell the public the truth about it and at the same time give us some advertising" [333].

One wonders whether Hammett said this kind of thing to himself or whether someone else said it to him.

At any rate, for Hammett, the Op stories became at first an extension of "From the Memoirs of a Private Detective" but written with a serious purpose and for a different audience — an audience interested in reading about crime and detectives as well as their adventures instead of perusing the urbane contents of *The Smart Set*. The use of the Op's first-person narration, something new for Hammett (before "Arson Plus," his only other first-person narration was in "From the Memoirs of a Private Detective"), went a long way toward establishing the illusion of firsthand accounts of actual experience. And the narratives themselves, of course, pretend to be the recounting of real cases. In "Who Killed Bob Teal?" in fact, the Op, in an uncharacteristically clumsy manner, makes this plain to the readers:

> Those who remember this affair will know that the city, the detective agency, and the people involved all had names different from the ones I have given them. But they will know also that I have kept the facts true [264].

Passages like this, of course, are standard devices of the detective story going all the way back to Poe and to Doyle — recall that the second collection of Doyle's short stories was entitled *The Memoirs of Sherlock Holmes*. But Hammett did not stop there.

Hammett went beyond the traditional techniques for creating the illusion that readers are encountering real crime and real detectives. And the principal means he used to do this was by inserting in the Op stories nuggets of encapsulated observations about real detectives and how they work. These fall into several categories. First of all, throughout the stories, the Op inserts generic observations about "the detective business":

> And a good motto for the detective business is, "When in doubt — shadow 'em" ["Zigzags of Treachery" 91].

> I had had people try to frame me before — no detective stays in business long without having it happen — but I had never got used to it ["Women, Politics and Murder" 210].

> An investigation in Monterey had established reasonably — which is about as well as anything is ever established in the detective business — that the girls had not been there recently ["Scorched Face" 361].

> I wasn't any too sure he hadn't slipped me. I didn't know that he lived in this place I was watching…. However, in the detective business pessimistic guesses of that sort are always bothering you, if you let them ["Whosis Kid" 313].

> The idea in this detective business is to catch crooks, not to put on heroics ["Whosis Kid" 347].

The Op also includes comments that demonstrate detective knowledge gained from years of professional experience. Thus, on the ransom note and the ways of criminals in "Crooked Souls," the Op's narrative observes that it was "A peculiar note in several ways. They are usually written with a great pretense of partial illiterateness. Almost always there's an attempt to lead suspicion astray" (39). At the end of the same story, the Op says that "three bullets would have been in my fat carcass if I hadn't learned years ago to stand to one side of strange doors when making uninvited calls" (49).

Twice in "The Girl with Silver Eyes," the Op makes the same kind of statement, passing on and generalizing the detective knowledge gained from his years of experience:

> I went to the office of this transfer company, and found a friendly clerk on duty. (A detective, if he is wise, takes pains to make and keep as many friends as possible among transfer company, express company and railroad employees) [155].

> ...I went up to the Chronicle office and searched the files for weather conditions during the past month, making a memorandum of four dates upon which it had rained steadily day and night. I carried my memorandum to the offices of the three largest taxicab companies. That was a trick that had worked well for me before" ["Silver Eyes" 159].

In addition to these inserted capsules of his collected detective wisdom, the Op includes passages that describe details of detective work that he specifically addresses to "you" (the reader). Thus, in "Arson Plus," the Op tells readers that

> tracking baggage is no trick at all, if you have the dates and check numbers to begin with...and twenty five minutes in a baggage room at the Ferry and half an hour in the office of a transfer company gave me my answer [14].

In "The Zigzags of Treachery" he tells about shadowing:

> There are four rules for shadowing: Keep behind your subject as much as possible; never try to hide from him; act in a natural manner no matter what happens; and never meet his eye [92].

And in "Mike, Alec or Rufus" he gives readers a lesson on the reliability of witnesses:

An identification of the sort the janitor was giving isn't worth a damn one way or the other. Even positive and immediate identifications aren't always the goods. A lot of people who don't know any better — and some who do, or should — have given circumstantial evidence a bad name. It is misleading sometimes. But for genuine, undiluted, pre-war untrustworthiness, it can't come within gunshot of human testimony. Take any man you like — unless he is the one in a hundred thousand with a mind trained to keep things straight, and not always even then — get him excited, show him something, give him a few hours to think it over and talk it over, and then ask him about it. It's dollars to doughnuts that you'll have a hard time finding any connection between what he saw and what he says he saw [246].

In terms of content, Hammett's inserted observations about detection range from macro to micro. On the macro side, the Op comments about business practice and policies:

The two great bugaboos for a reputable detective agency are the persons who bring in a crooked plan or a piece of divorce work all dressed up in the garb of a legitimate operation ["Silver Eyes" 149–50].

Of all the work that comes to a private detective (except divorce work, which the Continental Detective Agency doesn't handle) I like weddings as little as any ["Gutting of Couffignal" 450].

On the micro side there are the passages above about how to shadow, the fallibility of witnesses, the methods of kidnappers, the methods of tracing luggage, as well as others. In "The Zigzags of Treachery," he includes a passage on shooting, and in "The Tenth Clew" there is the following passage on the most effective way to question suspects: "One of the things that every detective knows is that it's often easy to get information — even a confession — out of a feeble nature simply by putting your face close to his and talking in a loud tone" (72–73).

Perhaps the most telling of the Op's observations about being a detective reflects on the mundane and routine nature. These observations begin in one of the earlier stories, "The Bodies Piled Up," with "We now dropped that angle and settled down to the detail-studying, patience-taxing grind of picking up the murderer's trail. From any crime to its author there is a trail" (49). This continued through "One Hour": "Ninety-nine percent of detective work is a patient collecting of details — and your details must be got as nearly first-hand as possible, regardless of who else has worked the territory before you" (253). And the Op describes his struggle with mundanity in "Dead Yellow Women": "I chewed on my plug of tobacco—a substitute for cigarettes—and tried to count up the hours of my life I'd spent like this, sitting or standing around waiting for something to happen" (420).

Interestingly enough, Hammett's expert observations about crime and detectives stand at both ends of the first series of Op stories. "From the Memoirs of a Private Detective" comes before "Arson Plus," and a two-part series named "Suggestions for Detective Story Writers" from the *New York Evening Post* in 1930 came after Hammett had left off writing about the Op and turned to writing about Sam Spade in *The Maltese Falcon*. While "Memoirs" dwells largely on the comic side of being a detective, the series known as "Suggestions to Detective Story Writers" is technical and serious. In it Hammett included 24 entries about ballistics, fingerprints, shadowing, injuries, and the titles and jurisdictions of law enforcement personnel. His lead into the lists of facts in "Suggestions" is that, in an attempt to be accurate, "detective story writers could afford to speak to policemen now and then" (910). The change in tone from "Memoirs" to "Suggestions" says a great deal about Hammett's development as a writer. He came to take himself and what he had to say seriously. And this happened because he started to write about the Continental Op.

The Police

One of the other significant points Hammett wanted to make in the Op stories was that private detectives—or good ones at least—do not work alone. They work with the cops. In his earliest fiction Hammett isn't very nice to the police. His first cop is "the fat man under the stiff straw hat" with folds of fat on his "burly neck" and his partner had a "protruding lower lip [that] overlapped the upper in a smile that tempered derision with indulgence" ("The Sardonic Star of Tom Doody" 32). Four months after "The Sardonic Star of Tom Doody," Hammett brought in his second policeman character, Detective Murray, in "The Joke on Eloise Morey": "A heavy middle-aged man with a florid face and a bellicose black moustache came in. He did not think it necessary to remove his hat, but his manner was polite enough, in a stolid way." (75)

In addition to Murray, in the same story, Hammett introduces a police chief with a comb-over: "a little fat man with a sparse handful of white hair spread over a broad pink scalp" (76). In both "Tom Doody" and "Eloise Morey," the cops are not only disagreeable looking, but they also arrest the wrong person. There's the same bungling injustice in "The Green

Elephant," but, then, the cops who accidentally stumble on Joe Shupe have been reprimanded for laziness, incompetence, or both. Taking these three stories by themselves, things didn't look too good for the cops in Hammett's works. He demonstrated in them the same attitude toward policemen that one can find in most other period fiction about crime. Readers can see this especially in Cassidy in "The Second Story Angel" who embodies most of the conventional clichés about cops: he's Irish, he's big, he's intimidating, he's corrupt, and one can spot him as a copper from a mile away — even though he may not be one. But with the Op stories Hammett changed the way he portrayed cops dramatically, because he knew better.

Hammett's first story about the Continental Op begins not at a client's residence or in the offices of the Continental Detective Agency, but in a sheriff's office: "I had been doing business with this fat sheriff of Sacramento County for four or five years — ever since I came to the Continental Detective Agency's San Francisco office" ("Arson Plus," 3). At the opening of "Arson Plus" the Op and Sheriff Jim Tarr sit around smoking cigars and trading a few wisecracks and Hammett brings in a bit of Keystone Kops slapstick when all of Tarr's deputies come stumbling into his office. In this first story, however, Hammett also introduced Deputy Sheriff McClump. In spite of McClump's name and his comic introduction in "Arson Plus," Hammett tells readers that with this rural deputy there is more than meets the eye: "Mac's too lazy to express an opinion, or even form one, unless he's driven to it; but that doesn't mean they aren't worth listening to, if you can get them" (11). Indeed, McClump functions as the Op's partner to a far greater extent than any of the Continental operatives Hammett would create later in the series. He not only accompanies the Op in all of his interviews in Sacramento County, but it is also McClump who shoots the fleeing villain at the close of the story.

In the second Op story, "Slippery Fingers," Hammett centers the action in San Francisco and introduces readers to what would become in the later stories a parade of San Francisco cops: "At the city detective bureau I hunted up the police sleuths who had been assigned to the murder: Marty O'Hara and George Dean. It didn't take them long to tell me what they knew about it" (24). O'Hara and Dean take part in the initial questioning of suspect Joseph Clane and serve as witnesses to the Op's accidental discovery of the deception upon which the entire crime (and story) rested. O'Hara plays a less prominent role in the story than Dean does; he acts while Dean talks. Hammett, however, brought O'Hara back in "The Bodies Piled Up" where he and Dean question Ansley's partner and Develyn's employees. Significantly, the Op swaps ideas with them, and he uses the pronoun "we" to refer to the conduct of the background investigations in the case. While in "Slippery Fingers" and "The Bodies Piled Up" Hammett treats O'Hara and Dean collectively, he brought George Dean back into the Op series to serve a somewhat different purpose a year after "The Bodies Piled Up."

In "Who Killed Bob Teal?" the Op runs across Detective Dean early in his investigation: "I saw a big, hulking man going up the apartment house steps, and recognized him as George Dean.... Dean isn't a bad sort, but he isn't so satisfactory to work with as some of the others; that is, you can never be sure he isn't holding out some important detail ... which doesn't make for teamwork" (265). The Op's criticism of Dean — along with the implied physical contrast between the Op and the "hulking" Dean — manifests a couple of important points about the Op and what he does, and it makes the point that doing detective work is both objective and anonymous, and that it is a collective activity.

In "Slippery Fingers," Hammett also introduced his first police expert: Phels, the department's fingerprint man. While Phels first appears to be an arrogant "expert" in this story, at the very end Hammett makes him into a stereotyped comic scientist: "When I left the bureau ten minutes later Farr [the forger] and Phels were sitting knee to knee, jabbering away at each other as only a couple of birds who are cuckoo on the same subject can" (34). Hammett brought Phels back into the series in "The Bodies Piled Up" in order to make a point about his own interest in fingerprints: "Phels was unable to get prints from either their necks or their collars" (44). He would reiterate this forensic point in 1930 in his *Crime Wave* column in the *New York Evening Post*: "Finger-prints of any value to the police are seldom found on anybody's skin" (911). And at the end of the initial Op series, in 1927, Hammett brought Phels back for a walk-on role in "The Main Death." In addition to Phels, Hammett invented two other police experts in the last story of the series, "The Main Death": Lewis from the identification department and an anonymous handwriting expert. While few of Hammett's stories turn on forensic details, his introduction of these police experts once more emphasizes the communal or collaborative nature of real detective work as opposed to the polymath fictional detective from the Sherlock Holmes tradition who knows everything and how to do everything.

In the third Op story, "Crooked Souls," Hammett introduced a trio of cops named Thode, Lusk, and O'Gar.

> Then I reached the police detectives who were working on the case —
> O'Gar and Thode — by telephone, and went down to the Hall of Justice to meet them. Lusk, a post office inspector, was also there. We turned the job around and around, looking at it from every angle, but not getting very far [38].

In "Crooked Souls" Hammett does little to delineate these characters. But he did make them continuing characters. He returned to Detective Bill Thode in "Dead Yellow Women" where he is a member of the Chinatown detail and "who talks the language some" (432). Lusk, the postal inspector, reenters the Op canon in "The Golden Horseshoe" where their friendship permits the Op to edge around the rules:

> Post office inspectors are all tied up with rules and regulations that forbid their giving assistance to private detectives except on certain criminal matters. But a friendly inspector doesn't have to put you through the third degree. You lie to him — so that he will have an alibi in case there's a kick-back — and whether he thinks you're lying doesn't matter [222].

While Lusk and Thode continue only as very minor characters, the third cop introduced in "Crooked Souls" is arguably one of the most important characters in the Op stories.

The third member of the trio, O'Gar, appears in seven of the Op stories before *The Red Harvest*: "Crooked Souls," "The Tenth Clew," "The Zigzags of Treachery," "Women, Politics and Murder," "The Golden Horseshoe," "The Creeping Siamese," and "The Big Knock-Over." While he served as a minor character in "Crooked Souls," Hammett gave him a major role in his first "novelette," "The Tenth Clew." In that story Hammett created the description of O'Gar that he would repeat with variations in later pieces:

> O'Gar — a bullet-headed detective sergeant who dresses like the village constable in a movie, wide-brimmed black hat and all, but who isn't to be put out of the reckoning on that account — was in charge of the investigation. He and I had worked on two or three jobs together before, and hit it off excellently [53].

In a real sense, O'Gar and the Op act as partners and as friends throughout "The Tenth Clew." They talk together, they eat together, they interview suspects together, and they puzzle over the enigmatic evidence together. They even share the same kind of wisecracking relationship implicit in that between the Op and McClump in the first Op story, "Arson Plus," illustrated in "The Tenth Clew" by O'Gar's reply, "You have a lot of fun, don't you?" to the Op's description of having been slugged and dumped in the bay to drown (78). Significantly, Hammett created for O'Gar a characteristic diction, a choice of words, moreover, that rubbed off on the Op: "The Creda Dexter I had talked to — a sleek kitten, as O'Gar had put it" (73). But more on this later. In "The Zigzags of Treachery"

Hammett adds to his embellishment of the character that O'Gar is in charge of the San Francisco Police Department's Homicide Detail (a body of eight men, readers later learn in "The Golden Horseshoe"). And in "Women, Politics and Murder" he adds more physical detail to his description of O'Gar:

> In the detectives' assembly-room I found O'Gar, the detective-sergeant in charge of the Homicide Detail: a squat man of fifty who went in for wide-brimmed hats of the movie-sheriff sort, but whose little blue eyes and bullet-head weren't handicapped by the trick headgear" [101].

While he does appear in "The Big Knock-Over," O'Gar's major roles in the Op stories occur in "The Tenth Clew," "The Zigzags of Treachery," "Women, Politics and Murder," "The Golden Horseshoe," and "The Creeping Siamese." In each of these stories he acts as the Op's partner and friend — roles no other continuing character fills. O'Gar's character and the relationship that Hammett created between him and the Op, moreover, have real bearing on the fundamental nature of Hammett's Continental Detective Agency operative.

After his initial development of O'Gar in "The Tenth Clew," Hammett returned to the McClump pattern he used in his first story. Thus, in "Night Shots," he introduced Deputy Sheriff Shad, the law in the rural setting of the story. Shad is a competent and conscientious country lawman who has a ready understanding of the facts of the case and with whom the Op enjoys a relaxed and collegial relationship. As with McClump, Hammett chose to individualize Shad through the use of nonstandard, lower-class diction. He did the same in "The Scorched Face" with Deputy Abner Paget, a character upon whose expertise, not the way he talks, the Op depends when he is forced to investigate circumstances in the country. Like their country counterparts, Coffee and Kelly, the San Francisco Police patrolmen who play notable roles in "One Hour" and "Women, Politics and Murder," both use nonstandard English, a fact that serves as no impediment or even comment on their intelligence or competence. This fact alone makes Hammett's Op stories a landmark — or an oddity — in the ways in which American fiction has treated ordinary police officers.

Between "The Tenth Clew" and "The Scorched Face" Hammett not only introduced ordinary patrolmen, he also brought in two new, named San Francisco detectives, Lieutenant McTighe in "Women, Politics and Murder" and Bill Garren in "Mike, Alec or Rufus," as well as Detective Lew Maher of the Boston Police Department. With McTighe Hammett brought in the issue of political influence on law enforcement — a theme that would become prominent in later hard-boiled fiction. As Hammett presents him, however, McTighe is not an unattractive figure:

> I knew McTighe, and we were on pretty good terms, but I wasn't an influence in local politics, and Tennant was. I don't mean that McTighe would have knowingly helped Tennant frame me; but with me stacked up against the assistant city engineer, I knew who would get the benefit of any doubt there might be ["Women, Politics and Murder" 208].

While he exists in "Mike, Alec or Rufus" to help demonstrate the Op's acumen, Detective Garren, of the pawnshop detail "isn't a bad bimbo, but he hasn't any meekness" (244). Detective Lew Maher from "The Whosis Kid" makes a brief appearance in which the Op records a bit of their shop talk about crimes and criminals.

Chronologically, after briefly mentioning the Boston policeman, Hammett created another more fully developed police character: Pat Reddy in "The Scorched Face." In that story he brought together fragments of McClump, the Op's warm relationship with Bob Teal, O'Gar's wisecracks, as well as the implications of the role of economic or political influence on law enforcement he developed with his picture of McTighe in "Women, Politics and Murder." Chapter IV of "The Scorched Face" opens with an uncharacteristically long passage describing then-patrolman Reddy arresting Althea Wallach for a parking violation and for rudeness to a police officer, followed by a description of how he dealt with her millionaire coffee baron father:

> He took her over to the station and dumped her in a cell.
> Old Wallach, so the story goes, showed up the next morning with a head full of steam and half the lawyers in San Francisco. But Pat made the charge stick.... Old Wallach did everything but take a punch at Pat in the corridor afterward. Pat grinned his sleepy grin at the coffee importer, and drawled:
> "You better lay off me — or I'll stop drinking your coffee" [365–66].

Three days after this contretemps the couple that met over a parking violation gets married, a ceremony at which the Op — by accident, he says — serves as a witness. Thus, the Op has more than professional connections with Reddy — as he also had with Bob Teal. Just as with Bob Teal, Hammett included the ideal qualities of a private detective, and with Pat Reddy, he also enumerated the ideal qualities of the police officer: observance of the law, immunity from the power of money and influence, and devotion to duty. To these Hammett added a droll sense of humor, proletarian habits and tastes, along with a natural inclination to insouciance. In the climax of "The Scorched Face," the Op and Reddy become comrades in arms, saving each other's lives in the battle at the headquarters of Hador's cult. And the Op's final actions in that story spring from both his obligation to save the reputation of his client's daughter and his desire to save Pat Reddy's marriage.

After "The Scorched Face" Hammett gave cops a rest for a few stories. There are no lawmen, except the deputized Op, in "Corkscrew"; he brought Detective Bill Thode from "Crooked Souls" back for a brief appearance in "Dead Yellow Women"; and Sergeant Roche of the Harbor Police comes in to "The Gutting of Couffignal" only to help with the cleanup. After that, Hammett wrote an Op and O'Gar story, "The Creeping Siamese." He then developed a cast of cop characters for the last three stories in the series: "The Big Knock-Over," "$106,000 Blood Money," and "The Main Death." In "The Big Knock-Over" Hammett mentions Detectives Bender, Hunt, Tully, and Reeder, who play small roles along with Hammett's old favorite, O'Gar. In that story, however, O'Gar plays only a minor role, and Hammett chose to develop the character of Lieutenant Duff, who appears in both "The Big Knock-Over" and $106,000 Blood Money." In "The Big Knock-Over" he gave Duff a dramatic entry when he comes into the detectives' room, shouts "Allez Oop," and collects his troops (and the Op) because "there's a thing worth looking at in Filmore" (554). Hammett also gave Duff a large measure of imperturbability ("Duff shrugged his thick shoulders and stepped over bodies to get to the telephone" [556]) as well as a cynical sense of humor ("A few more tricks like this … and we'll all be out of jobs. There won't be any grifters left to protect the tax-payers from" [555]). Additionally, Duff, like O'Gar, trades wisecracks with the Op. At the end of "The Big Knock-Over," he surveys Nancy Regan and says to the Op, "That's how your Agency evens up.…The she employees make up for the looks of the he's" (590).

The last set of police detectives Hammett introduced in the run of Op stories leading to *The Red Harvest* was the team of Hacken and Begg from "The Main Death":

> The captain told me Hacken and Begg were handling the job. I
> caught them between leaving the detectives' assembly room. Begg
> was a freckled heavyweight, as friendly as a Saint Bernard puppy, but
> less intelligent. Lanky detective-sergeant Hacken, not so playful, car-
> ried the team's brains behind his worried hatchet face" [636].

At the beginning of "The Main Death" they share information, ideas, and frustrations with the Op in the same way that O'Gar does in the earlier stories. With Hacken and Begg, Hammett had created 29 named law enforcement officials—sheriffs and their deputies, police department experts, police managers from captain to lieutenant to sergeant, detectives, and beat patrolmen. And almost all of them have names. Eight police characters appear in more than one of the early Op stories, with O'Gar topping the list with seven appearances. Along with this proliferation of policemen, Hammett described their workplace, the San Francisco Hall of Justice on Kearney Street, with as many details as he supplied for the headquarters of the Continental Detective Agency. Indeed, in the last story in the series, Hammett went out of his way to provide bits of technically unnecessary descriptive detail about the policemen's workplace. He tells readers about the detectives' assembly room:

> While we talked we had gone into the assembly room, with its school-room arrangement of desks and benches. Half a dozen police detectives were scattered among them, doing reports ["The Main Death" 636].

And, somewhat extraordinarily, he tells readers the telephone number of police headquarters: Davenport 20.

Collectively, Hammett paid more attention to policemen than to the Op's coworkers from the Continental Detective Agency. Cop characters appear in 21 of the 24 early Op stories as opposed to 14 stories in which Hammett introduced other characters from the Continental Agency. And he made policemen significant characters, more significant than the private eyes from the Continental. With the exception of the Old Man, all of Hammett's Continental characters are factotums or gofers, characters who do things for the Op largely because he cannot be in two places at once and because he needs others to provide information for him that he cannot access himself. None of them acts as a partner for the Op. Indeed, with Dick Foley, the most frequently mentioned subsidiary character in the series, Hammett stripped him of all attributes, successively manipulating his speech until it lacks pronouns and articles and consists of only the barest essentials to convey information. Of the two characters from the agency closest to the Op, for whom he expresses almost paternal concern, Bob Teal and Jack Counihan, one is killed and the other betrays him. This is simply not the case with Hammett's police characters. With several police characters, McClump being the first of them, Hammett makes a point of having the Op comment on their intelligence. This extends even to Patrolman Kelly in "Women, Politics and Murder." Unlike his interactions with agency ops (excepting the Old Man), with a number of cops, the Op sits down and chews over facts and theories about the crime at hand. And he does this in a manner far different than the way in which he converses with the inscrutable Old Man. This kind of relationship begins with Deputy McClump in "Arson Plus" and extends into the ways in which the Op relates to Detectives O'Gar and Reddy in later stories. The Op and his police partners share not only the intellectual challenge of solving cases, but they also share what should be viewed as one kind of close male relationship, the kind that relies on wisecracks and wit as accompaniment and ratification of friendship. This shows up, for example, in "The Tenth Clew" when the Op arrives at the police station to find the weary O'Gar puzzling over the assortment of clues that the case has generated: "What's all this? Souvenir of your wedding?" "Might as well be" (61–62).

And, for Hammett, increasingly, the Op and the police characters in the stories, as we will see later, share the way in which they talk.

In treating policemen the way he did in the Op stories of the 1920s, Hammett did something significantly different from what other crime writers were doing and what he himself had done in his early portraits of the police. He treated police officers with respect at a time when they received very little. Police officers certainly received little respect in nineteenth-century detective fiction where they were principally portrayed as slow or dim-witted lower-class impediments to the genius detective. And there is a lot of evidence from the beginning of the twentieth century that added corruption to the accepted notions about incompetence. The Wickersham Commission (1931–32), for instance, discovered that in the United States

> "official lawlessness" by police, judges, magistrates, and others in the criminal justice system was widespread in many jurisdictions, including major cities. It investigated illegal arrests, bribery, entrapment, coercion of witnesses, fabrication of evidence, "third degree" practices, police brutality, and illegal wiretapping [www.lexisnexis .com/academic/2upa/Aj/WickershamComm].

William Nolan, in *Dashiell Hammett: A Casebook,* quotes Herb Caen's picture of San Francisco when Hammett arrived there in the 1920s:

> The Hall of Justice was dirty and reeked of evil. The criminal lawyers were young and hungry and used every shyster trick....The City Hall, the D.A. and the cops ran the town as though they owned it.... [39].

Omitting the first sentence, William Marling in *Dashiell Hammett* repeats the same passage (12). This kind of corrupt city and this kind of predatory police force and the theme of the private detective versus a malign authority would become a feature of hard-boiled fiction, such as Chandler's Bay

City stories. But that was later. It is demonstrably and emphatically not the way in which Hammett treated policemen in the Op stories of the 1920s.

While the Op may not like a few of the cops with whom he interacts in the stories of the 1920s (as he does not like Detective Dean) and while some of them are not overly bright, like Detective Blegg, Hammett does not make the Op observe, report, or comment on most of the common anti-police themes of those times. There simply are no cops on the take in the Op stories: no extortion, not even free cups of coffee. And while in "$106,000 Blood Money" the Op differentiates the Continental's policy on agents accepting reward money from the same policy of the police, Hammett does not introduce any police characters motivated by or receiving reward money anywhere in the series. Indeed, with the vignette about Pat Reddy's refusal to be swayed from duty by the influence of a millionaire's power, influence, and money, Hammett gives policemen the same incorruptibility that forms the basis of the Op's character. Although Hammett may attach the term "lazy" to both McClump and Pat Reddy, it reflects their casualness or imperturbability and has nothing to do with "cooping," sleeping or otherwise avoiding work, a practice identified by police reformers as early as Teddy Roosevelt. In point of fact, Hammett demonstrates the very opposite by showing many of his police characters as, if not workaholics, men dedicated to their jobs. In "Scorched Face" Pat Reddy may be one of the first policemen in fiction to be pulled out of bed in the middle of the night to fight crime. Rather than men practicing illegal or extralegal methods to obtain convictions, Hammett in "The Scorched Face" goes to the extent of comparing police practices with those of the Continental Detective Agency when the Op encourages Pat Reddy to accompany him in an illegal search and Reddy replies, "Have it your way. But if you get me smashed for searching a house without authority, you'll have to give me a job with your law-breaking agency" (380).

Hammett treats brutality, an issue connected to the police for as long as there have been police, somewhat more cavalierly. While he mentions brutality in passing in "The Whosis Kid" in connection with Duran, the house dick at the Marquis Hotel, police brutality becomes overt only in "The Big Knock-Over," a fact that, in itself, may be significant. There, the Op reports to the Old Man about the mayhem at the Hall of Justice where the cops are subjecting the thugs rounded up in the aftermath of an epic heist to the third degree. He flippantly notes that it's violent, but that no prisoners have been killed yet, and he also tells the Old Man that it's been effective, that the cops are making believers out of the crooks and some of them are talking. The Op also derides "newspaper writers who like to sob over what they call the third degree" (546). A page and a half after this statement, the Op tells readers that "I went back to the Hall and helped boil more prisoners in oil" (548). Hammett seems to be voicing a fairly common opinion of the period that brutality and the "third degree" might just be appropriate for certain classes or individuals—in this case, hardened criminals. At any rate, given the Op's statement about joining in on the fun, Hammett does not seem too opposed to properly applied police brutality. And in this passage he also sets up what would become a constant police story theme: the conflict between well-meaning but ignorant newspaper reporters and the police.

In "Women, Politics and Murder" and "The Big Knock-Over," Hammett brings in the issue of politics and police work. In the former, a San Francisco ward healer almost frames the Op, and the Op comments on the influence of politicians on police officers: "with me stacked up against the assistant city engineer, I knew who would get the benefit of any doubt there might be" (208). The Op acknowledges the reality of political influence but also focuses on the dilemma of an honest policeman confronted with that reality. In "The Big Knock-Over" Hammett looked at a different aspect of public policy and the problems of financing an adequate police force. In recounting the scenario of the big knockover to the Old Man, the Op presents what amounts to a defense of the police: this includes mention of the tactical and strategic problems the police face in protecting life and property in a large city, of the need for planning for emergencies, of the need for additional men and better equipment, and it also acknowledges that while taxpayers may complain about the cops' failures and focus on police corruption, they are not willing to pay for a sufficient and efficient police force. Here, and consistently through the Op stories before *Red Harvest,* Hammett makes police and policing significant themes. Rather than reflecting the city gone to seed and the police as a corrupt and sinister institution, Hammett showed them to be hard-working, honest, dedicated, overworked, law-abiding, and mostly likeable men engaged in the same cause as the hero of the series. Alongside Herb Caen's picture of San Francisco in the 1920s as a wide-open, lawless place, then, readers of Hammett need to take note that modern, enlightened policing began in the adjacent community of Berkeley through the leadership of Chief August Volmer, one of the most prominent and influential police reformers in the first part of the twentieth century. And readers, too, need to note that Hammett seems to have followed at least some of Volmer's accomplishments. He cites Volmer's work in his letter that appeared in *The Black Mask* on October 15, 1923, the same issue that contained "Slippery Fingers" and "Crooked Souls." Finally, the attitudes toward policemen and the police in the first run of Op stories reflect directly on Hammett's personal experience. Hammett never was just a private detective; he was a Pinkerton operative. And Pinkerton operatives cooperated with the police.

Learning a New Language

Hammett's creation of the Continental Agency and his descriptions of how detectives work in the real world made his Op stories different from other *Black Mask* fiction, but by themselves these reasons do not account for the popularity of the Op stories. One of the other things that accounts for their popularity was the characters' language. In the first series of Op stories Hammett remade himself in several ways. In writing them he learned to take his own experience as a detective seriously and moved from the aloof and ironic view he adopted for "From the Memoirs of a Private Detective" in *The Smart Set* to using both the business of detection and his audience's interest in crime, criminals, and detectives in the stories he wrote about the Op. Along with this, he needed to change his style to describe the world that he knew best and to convey a feeling for that world to a different audience.

At first when Hammett worked at making himself a writer he taught himself by reading library books and highbrow magazines. And here he was fortunate in that his aspirations to be a writer came at the time when H. L. Mencken and the advocacy of American English were the rage. Reflected in his early works especially, Hammett owed more than his first appearances in print to Mencken. He also owed him something in terms of style. During the 1920s whenever Hammett wrote about literary style, he advocated the same kind of directness and simplicity in style as Mencken did. Thus, in the midst of writing the Op stories, Hammett wrote a piece for *Western Advertising* in 1926 in which he preaches about simplicity of style.

> Another — perhaps the only other — point on which there is agreement is that clarity is the first and greatest of literary virtues. The needlessly involved sentence, the clouded image, are not literary. They are anti-literary. Joseph Conrad, whose work John Galsworthy pronounced "the only writing of the last twelve years that will enrich the English language to any extent" defined the writer's purpose as "above all else, to make you see." Anatole France, probably the tallest figure modern literature has raised, and the most bookish of men in the bargain, said: "The most beautiful sentence? The Shortest!" He condemned the semicolon, a hangover from the days

of lengthy sentences, as not suited to an age of telephones and
airplanes [35].

And in the Op stories Hammett heeds the following advice: "Hammett's
average sentence, in his early work, is 13 words long. Highly descriptive
passages run into flab at 15 words. Fight scenes are built of sentences aver-
aging eight words each, some only three or four words long" (Marling 44).
But the trouble is that Conrad, Galsworthy, and Anatole France didn't hang
out with cops and criminals and other Pinkerton operatives. And while
this gang, too, eschewed the lengthy sentence, they didn't talk like the
boulevardiers who read *The Smart Set*. So, if Hammett wanted to accurately portray and explore the part of his experience in which a new class
of readers was most interested, he had to do more than just write short,
clear sentences. He had, in the words of the same *Western Advertising* piece
(albeit directed toward a different end), "to talk to the man in the street
in his own language" (35) while still maintaining literary value — an ambi-
tion intricately tied in with Hammett's aspirations throughout his writing career.

From "Arson Plus" onward, Hammett worked at creating characters
and voices appropriate to the world in which the Op lived and worked.
One of the ways in which he did this from that first story onward was in
creating unique speech to particularize some of his characters. In "Arson
Plus," on the simplest and crudest level, Hammett brought in a stutterer:
"'I n-n-never s-saw Th-Thornburgh,' he said, 'and I n-n-never had any
m-mail for him.'" (10). Thankfully, there is but one more stutterer in the
Op stories in "$106,000 Blood Money." On this same simplistic level, in
the Op stories Hammett gave characters on clichéd accents. There is the
African American door guard in "The Scorched Face": "'Fore God, Fat
Shorty...you done hurt me!" (381). In "Dead Yellow Women" the incidental Chinese characters replace r's with l's: "No saavy. Mabe Closs stleet"
(410) and with Chang Li Ching he played with exaggerated Asian formal-
ity: "This old joker was spoofing me with an exaggeration — a burlesque —
of the well-known Chinese politeness" (414). Cipriano, "the bright-face
Filipino boy" is another accent character in "Dead Yellow Women." And
there is Maurois' Franglais ("I do not *comprehends ze anglais* ver' good")
in "The Whosis Kid" along with Inez's accent, which is "either Spanish or
Portuguese." In "The Gutting of Couffignal" there may be a Russian accent
with Ignati, but it's difficult to tell since he has so little dialogue in that
story. And in "Women, Politics and Murder" Hammett may have wanted
to give Patrolman Kelly an Irish brogue, but with only dropped g's characterizing his speech this is difficult to pin down. There is little difficulty,

however, in spotting the Western drawl of the characters in "Corkscrew": "'I'm bettin' you took your draw off'n th' top, too'" (255). In that same story there is also Nacio's Spanish/English and the Op says that one of the cowboys (who has only one line) speaks with a brogue. Hammett, then, used a sprinkling of characters who talk funny in the Op stories. Indeed, in the 1925 stories ("The Whosis Kid," "The Scorched Face," "Corkscrew," "Dead Yellow Women") accents regularly characterize both minor comic additives and principal characters.

Hammett most prominently called attention to the way his characters speak and, thereby, used speech to define a character with Dick Foley. Although Hammett introduced Foley in "Slippery Fingers," he did not give him dialogue until "The Bodies Piled Up." In that story the Op does not characterize Foley's speech — as he later does— but Hammett presents it as clipped, often omitting subjects in sentences. Thus, in "The Bodies Piled Up," Foley speaks like this:

> This Orrett baby is our meat…. Picked him up when he got his mail yesterday afternoon. Got another letter besides yours. Got an apart- ment on Van Ness Avenue. Took it the day after the killing, under the name of B. T. Quinn. Packing a gun under his left arm — there's sort of a bulge there. Just went home to bed [48].

Six stories later, in "The Girl with Silver Eyes," the Op for the first time characterizes Foley's speech: "The little Canadian talks like a telegram when his peace of mind is disturbed, and just now he was decidedly peev- ish. 'Took me two blocks. Shook me. Only taxi in sight'" (169). Here Foley has less dialogue, but the pattern of his syntax, insofar as one can tell from his few words, remains the same. Hammett stripped Foley's speech down even further than in his earlier appearances, omitting even more nonessen- tial parts of speech:

> "Beat it for phone. Called Hotel Irvington. Booth —couldn't get anything but number. Ought to be enough. Then Chinatown. Dived in cellar west side Waverly Place. Couldn't stick close enough to spot place. Afraid to take chance hanging around. How do you like it?" [407].

With Dick Foley, then, Hammett used atypical grammar and rhythm to create a character. Significantly, this means something in the larger context of the stories. By stripping down Foley's speech, Hammett made him an efficient source of information as a human telegram conveying to the Op what he needs to know — no more and no less. Often in Foley's speech he does not refer to himself: he has lost the use of his first-person pronouns.

This, no doubt, was a position that Hammett filled during his own days as a Pinkerton operative, impersonally reporting on subjects followed and information gleaned. Perhaps because Foley plays this role, in "The Scorched Face," Hammett also has him object to being simply a source of important but too often routine information. But it does him no good. While Hammett introduces Foley in all of the late stories and in "The Big Knock-Over" he tells readers that he "talked like a Scotchman's telegram," Foley remains a minor character kept in the shadows, and his speech reinforces this.

If with Dick Foley Hammett pared language down to the barest communication, with "jingle-brained" Jack Counihan he did the opposite. Take this passage from "The Big Knock-Over":

> "My faithful taxi and I cried *Yoicks* after them, and they brought
> us here, going into that house down the street in front of which one
> of their motors still stands. After half an hour or so I thought I'd
> better report, so, leaving my taxi around the corner — where it's still
> running up expenses — I went up to yon all-night caravansary and
> phoned Fiske. And when I came back, one of the cars was gone —
> and I, woe is me! — don't know who went in it" [557].

As opposed to the stripped-down language Hammett used to create Dick Foley, he filigreed up Jack Counihan's speech with bits of fancy and affected, exhibitionistic diction, diction presenting a pale imitation of that used by P. G. Wodehouse's harmless numbskulls. Indeed, Hammett made Counihan a character who cannot shut up, a linguistic trait that leads to his flirting and gets him knocked silly by Red later in "The Big Knock-Over" and that also has a connection with his betrayal in "$106,000 Blood Money."

Unlike the accent characters and the created speech of Dick Foley and Jack Counihan, from the beginning of the Op stories Hammett consistently employed nonstandard, "improper" usage as an element in building his characters. This begins with McClump in "Arson Plus." McClump, the bright deputy sheriff in that story, consistently says "ain't" and uses double negatives: "She was up yesterday, but there wasn't nothing she could do, and she couldn't tell us nothing much" (4). Hammett continued to use this kind of speech in connection with country cops. Thus, Deputy Sheriff Shad in "Nightshots" talks like McClump ("I didn't find nothing. There weren't no marks on the porch roof, but that don't mean nothing" [85]), and so does Deputy Paget in "The Scorched Face" ("course that don't mean nothin' much. All these guineas peddle vino" [371]). While Hammett used nonstandard English — characterized most prominently by "ain't," double negatives and improper verb configurations — to characterize countrymen, he also used it to characterize crooks or one kind of crook. This begins with Clane in "Slippery Fingers." In his first appearance, Hammett branded Clane by the way he speaks: "I wasn't noways sure I had ought to do it. I wasn't never sure in my mind but what maybe Henny done for that fellow Waldeman — he disappeared sudden-like" (26). After "Slippery Fingers," Hammett used double negatives and other instances of nonstandard English consistently as a distinguishing feature of characters at the bottom of the criminal food chain. He used it with the pathetic Boyd in "The Zigzags of Treachery" Hook, the troglodyte in "The House on Turk Street" says, "There ain't nothing else to it. I went in and stuck him up just now. I meant to wait till you come" (127). Porky, the stool pigeon in "The Girl with the Silver Eyes," speaks the same language: "He ain't got no hat; I figure he ain't going nowhere. But he must of gone through the house" (173). "John Ryan," the hophead at the beginning of "The Golden Horseshoe," tells the Op, "I don't want no trouble, an' it ain't nothin' to me. I didn't know there was nothin' wrong" (226). Both Billie, the giant numbskull, and the sociopathic Kid in "The Whosis Kid" use the same kind of language. Billie says, "The taxi driver didn't give me no help in the fight, but he was a right guy and knowed where his money would come from" (331) and the Kid says, "You seen me all right...but if my rod hadn't of got snagged in my flogger you wouldn't have seen nothing else" (340). Dummy Uhl, the stoolie in "Dead Yellow Women," and Beno, the newsie in "The Big Knock-Over," carry nonstandard English to the end of the series of Op stories.

But a couple of things occur with their speech as Hammett threads criminals through the Op stories. For one thing, he begins to introduce both slang and underworld argot into the speech of his lowbrow criminals. Hook in "The House on Turk Street," for instance, uses a few bits of underworld argot in his speech — "lay" for situation, and "knockoff" for kill. In "The Whosis Kid," however, Hammett made fuller use of this characterizing technique in making the Kid's speech a combination of nonstandard usage, slang, and gangster terms and phrases. Thus, the Kid says things like "he put two X's to me" for double cross, "rod" for pistol, "twisted" for manipulated, "ribs you up" for convinces, "plugs" for plug-uglies or inferior henchmen, "flop" for believe, "gum" for impede, etc. In addition to creating criminals' characters by giving them distinctive ways of speaking, in the Op stories, significantly, not all criminals speak alike. Indeed, Hammett made a point of distinguishing between criminal brain and brawn in "The House on Turk Street" where Hook, the brawn, uses incorrect language and Tai, the brains, uses punctiliously correct British English; and he uses the French-accented English of Maurois for the same kind of contrast in "The Whosis Kid." Beginning with Orrett in "The Bodies Piled Up" Hammett introduced a better class of criminal, some of whom are linked to the tradition of the master criminal — in fact, at the end of that story, Orrett tells the Op that he is one of two lieutenants of a "master mind." In addition to those connected to master criminals or underworld bosses like Papadopolis in "The Big Knock-Over" and "$106,000 Blood Money," Hammett, with "Crooked Souls," brought in the character of the confidence man. In "Crooked Souls" there is "Penny" Quayle ("a con man who had been active in the East" [48]; in "The Tenth Clew" the bad guy is "a con man" (81), and Jacob Ledwich in "The Zigzags of Treachery" is "an ex-bunco man" (93). Criminals though they may be, these kinds of characters tend to use correct, standard English. This is the case with the principal bad guys in all of the Op stories after "The Bodies Piled Up." The effects are various. One of them, as noted above, is Hammett's occasional leaning toward the master criminal story. Another one is the attempt to create a multi-layered underworld with differentiated upper and lower classes for those with brains or brawn. Also, the use of the confidence man as criminal focuses on duplicity, so Hammett uses language as a means of duping both victim and detectives. Finally, the language, particularly the diction, used by characters in the Op stories increasingly connects the criminals and the cops.

The patrolmen who occasionally appear in the Op stories use the same nonstandard English spoken by the thugs because they, too, are lower-class individuals: thus, Officer Coffee in "One Hour" says, "Half a dozen people had seen him hit, and one of 'em had got the license number of the car that done it.... There was two fellows in the car when it hit Newhouse" (252). McClump and the other rural lawmen, of course, speak the same brand of nonstandard English as the beat cops and the lower-class crooks. Hammett's police detectives, however, speak relatively correctly — using, in the early stories, the same kind of English found in the Op's narration and dialogue. The difference in emphasis starts with O'Gar's appearance in "The Tenth Clew." In that story O'Gar has several kinds of speech — the kind he uses with witnesses like Charles Grantvoort, the kind he uses when analyzing facts with the Op, and the kind he uses when he is excited. When the Op and O'Gar puzzle out the correct way to solve the crime, the policeman breaks out in slang: he uses "flimflammed" for cheated, "noodle" for head, and then says,

> "Maybe that ain't so foolish!...You might be right at that. Suppose you are — what then! That Dexter kitten didn't do it.... Her brother didn't do it.... And, besides, you don't croak a guy just because you think he's too old to marry your sister" [69].

And, most significantly, in this story, as noted above, the Op emphasizes O'Gar's use of slang in "The Tenth Clew" when he says to the reader that a bit of it has stuck in his head: "The Creda Dexter I had talked to—a sleek kitten, as O'Gar had put it" (73).

The Op, of course, plays two roles in the stories—that of the narrator and that of the participant in the action. As the narrator of a detective story in which conventions oblige him to provide facts for the readers, the Op's language is standard, semiformal English. Thus, in "Slippery Fingers," he uses this kind of language to describe the crime scene:

> I made a quick inspection of the house and grounds, not expecting to find anything; and I didn't. Half of the jobs that come to a private detective are like this one: three or four days—and often as many weeks—have passed since the crime was committed. The police work on the job until they are stumped, then the injured party calls in a private sleuth [23].

Readers could find this kind of description in any of the detective stories written during the 1920s. What makes the Op stories stand out is Hammett's introduction of slang into the Op's dialogue and narration. Thus, alongside passages like the crime scene cited above, from the very beginning Hammett sprinkled nonstandard diction into the Op's grammatically correct sentences. In "Arson Plus," therefore, the Op tells readers that "I was a lot more interested in finding the bird who struck the match than I was in feminine beauty. However, I smothered my grouch" (12): he uses slang terms for "person" (bird) and "irritability" (grouch) and embroiders "arsonist" (the bird who struck the match). Indeed, it is possible and perhaps useful to track the development of the Op stories through Hammett's use of slang in them. With each new story, he used slang more and more. A case in point is the contrast between his terminology for horses and horse racing in the second Op story, "Slippery Fingers," and the fourteenth, "The Golden Horseshoe." In the former piece the Op talks about Clane's interest in "racing meets," "horse racing," and his ownership of "near-horses." By "The Golden Horseshoe," however, he has adopted the American term "race track" and instead of horses he talks about "ponies," "dogs," and "bang-tails." In spite of the fact that Hammett published his first three *Black Mask* stories ("The Road Home," "Arson Plus," and "Slippery Fingers") under the name Peter Collinson, demonstrating his familiarity with and capacity for using criminal slang, not a lot of slang appears before "The Tenth Clew." Having already made the step of characterizing O'Gar partly through his use of slang in "The Tenth Clew," two stories later he called attention to slang in the Op's dialogue. In "The Zigzags of

Treachery" the Op impersonates an underworld character, Shine Wisher, in order to gain the confidence of Ledwich, the villain. Ledwich speaks grammatically correct English but often punctuates it with slang. Ledwich's "elbow" means law man, "city dick" means policeman, "scratcher" means forger, "salving" means playing along, "bled" means extorted, "loaded" means false, "sap" means fool, "roll" means money, etc. When the Op speaks as Shine Wisher he uses the same kind of language: he uses "job" for criminal action, "bird" for man, "squeeze" for intimidate, "stirring" for happening, "jack" for money, "burg" for town, "circulating" for being seen in public, "nailed" for caught, and a number of other bits of nonstandard diction. Most importantly, Hammett both marked the Op's use of slang in his dialogue, and he had him pause in his narration to explain etymology to his readers.

> "I have been dirtier." Dirty is Pacific Coast argot for prosperous [101].

and

> "An elbow, huh?" putting all the contempt he could in his voice; and somehow any synonym for detective seems able to hold a lot of contempt [110].

Additionally, in "The Zigzags of Treachery" slang not only appears in the Op's speech, but it also infiltrates the Op's narrative voice. It is connected with O'Gar: "The key turned on the inside, and an angry Mrs. Estep jerked the door open. O'Gar and I advanced, O'Gar flashing his 'buzzer'" (105). And it's also associated with Ledwich: "He offered me enough money to tide me over until I could get on my feet again. I told him I didn't need chicken feed so much as a chance to pick up some real jack" (109). Both passages have the elements of standard diction ("O'Gar and I advanced" and "enough money to tide me over") but police slang (buzzer = badge) and criminal slang (jack = money) have become part of the way that the Op talks not only to the characters but also to the readers.

As the Op stories proceed, Hammett provided a richardsnary (as he called it at the start of *The Red Harvest*) of slang. Crooks engage in "scratching," "the blind game," "the Richmond razzle dazzle," and "bunco" schemes; men are eggs, yeggs, lads, birds, geese, plug-uglies, chumps, gonnifs, grifters, ginks, mugs, palukas, lollipops, and bimbos; women are babies, molls, and twists. Law enforcement people are cops, coppers, bulls, sleuths, and gumshoes. There is the vag charge, highgrading, the big house, the cooler, the joint. Money is jack, cush, gravy, and spinach. Heroin is hop and cocaine is C. Handguns are gats and rods, and to shoot is to cap.

To "read and write" is to fight and "all over the Rand McNally" means everywhere. Events can be duck soup and things can be dinguses. Toward the end of the Op series, especially in "The Golden Horseshoe" and "The Big Knock-Over," Hammett's use of slang in characters' speech and in the narrator's voice accelerates.

While the Op may occasionally color his speech with slang when speaking to clients, slang comes in often when he is playing a role as a crim-inal—as he does, for instance, in "The Zigzags of Treachery and "The Golden Horseshoe"—and when he speaks to those closest to him (fellow ops and policemen). The former can be seen above in the Op's conversa-tions with Ledwich in "The Zigzags of Treachery." The latter can be seen in the same story when the Op talks to both O'Gar and Bob Teal. In their brief conversation in "The Zigzags of Treachery" both the Op and Teal use terms like "bird" and "mug" for criminal, "bruiser" for big, tough man, and "safe-ripper" for bank burglar. Indeed, as the stories proceed, Hammett even extends the Op's use of slang in his conversations with the Old Man. By the time of "The Big Knock-Over," the Op talks to the Old Man in the same language he uses with other cops and ops. In "Corkscrew," in fact, Hammett even commented on mixed diction. In that story the Op calls attention to Clio Landes's speech: "I couldn't find out what her grift was. She talked a blend of thieves' slang and high-school English, and didn't say much about herself" (283). Slang increasingly becomes part of many of Hammett's characters and especially part of the Op in all of his roles. It, however, does say something about him. It connects with who he is (or isn't), it helps to characterize his relationships, and it helps to convey his attitudes toward others, toward himself, and toward readers.

The diction in the Op stories adds to Hammett's portrait of the real world in which his detective operates—versus the unreal world of the con-temporary "highbrow" detective story. It has to do with the detective's understanding and mastery of the environment in which he operates and sometimes must function in disguise. This part of the Op's language comes from the traditional notion that the detective needs to understand thieves' cant, a conventional crime story motif that goes back at least as far as Robert Greene's Cony Catching pamphlets in the sixteenth century. And Hammett's readers participate in this tradition when the Op explains underworld terms to them as he does in examples cited earlier from "The Zigzags of Treachery." This was a change for Hammett. In his pre–Op sto-ries he used thieves' cant and gangster argot as a curiosity. Pieces like "The Green Elephant" and even "From the Memoirs of a Private Detective" show that Hammett viewed underworld language as a curiosity, the object, at best, of derision or condescension. All of this changes in the Op stories.

Slang in the Op stories, moreover, also serves as social commentary. Many of the lawmen Hammett introduced into the stories—from McClump to O'Gar—use slang, and occasionally speak ungrammatically. While this probably is an accurate depiction of the way real police officers spoke in the San Francisco of the 1920s, Hammett does not connect it with lack of ability, intelligence, or commitment to duty; in fact, he takes pains to point out that his cops—even foot patrolmen like Kelly in "Women, Politics and Murder"—are intelligent and able individuals. In that not only a cop but also the hero uses nonstandard English, then, Hammett set his experience working with real cops and real criminals up against both his earlier snobbishness about language and contemporary, highbrow writers who consistently portrayed police officers as lower class and stupid, and heroes as pedantic geniuses. He knew the language of the Op's world, came to accept it, and learned to portray it—often with great vigor and effect.

In the Op stories, however, slang is not without its problems. It connects to the Op's participation in a violent world, the tawdry reputation of private detectives (as opposed to Continental or Pinkerton operatives), and the Op's dealings with underworld characters. Good guys and bad guys speak the same kind of language. This brings up moral ambiguity. In the other *Black Mask* star writer, Carroll John Daly, the moral ambiguity is there on purpose. Daly makes a point of blurring the connections of his heroes. Are they good guys or are they bad guys? Daly started off the narration of "Three Gun Terry Mack" with the hero affirming that "I ain't a crook, and I ain't a dick" (*Black Mask Boys*, 43). While the Op is emphatically a cop, he and the other cops operate in the same world and use the same language spoken by the crooks. Because of this, the villains in the Op stories often think that the hero is as dishonest and venal as they are. They doubt and test the Op's moral purpose. When this happens, the Op responds with actions and words that define who he is, the same kind of thing that Sam Spade would do at the close of *The Maltese Falcon*. These passages of self-definition appear in "The Zigzags of Treachery," "The Girl with the Silver Eyes," and "The Gutting of Couffignal." Rather than ending these stories with the unraveling of the crime puzzle, Hammett organizes them so that they end in counterpoint between the Op and the criminal. In "The Girl with the Silver Eyes," the Op finishes the story with what Hammett wants to be a ruthless unmasking of the lies and distortions in Jeanne Delano's account of events but which is essentially an assertion of the Op's allegiance to reason, honesty, and fair play versus her sexual blandishments. Once again, in "The Gutting of Couffignal," Hammett presents the Op's extended statement of his nature and vocation as a detective, in the face of promises of both wealth and sex.

But the use of slang in the Op stories means more than portraying Hammett's version of the real world of crime and detectives and establishing the place of the hero in that world. Part of it also has to do with the elemental powers of language making. This forms one of the bases of the Op's character. One aspect of language making, deeply rooted in slang, is playing with words. This aspect of slang can be seen in Hammett's use of bits of alliterative rhyming slang like "read and write" for fight or his layering of slang expressions when the Whosis Kid uses "the two X's" to mean double cross. Indeed, characters playing with words occur in several stories. For example, in "$106,000 Blood Money," Tom Tom Carey conspicuously and perhaps consciously (he is, after all, hunting for him) turns the name of the villain, Papadopoulos, into "Papadoodle" and then the Op converts it into another part of speech with his "Papadopoulos-ward." Slang-based play with language, in fact, gives the Op's (and Hammett's) narration the vigor that lies at the heart of his prose — and all hard-boiled prose — at its best. Perhaps no better example of this can be found than in the Op's account of looking for Rathbone's baggage in "It": "From the trust company I went to the Ferry Building baggage rooms and cigared myself into a look at the records for the twenty-eighth" (48). Here, the detective's routine of passing out cigars to elicit the goodwill of those from whom he seeks help is compacted into a newly minted verb that conveys both the act and its context in a way that no other expression could. That he sometimes, but not always, could do this kind of thing is the reason that Chandler, in "The Simple Art of Murder," says that "Hammett's style at its worst was as formalized as a page of Marius the Epicurean; at its best it could say almost anything" (17).

Another way in which Hammett came to characterize the Op's world is through the wisecrack. The wisecrack has several functions. It serves as an affront or challenge to authority and it also works as a means of communicating with and creating a bond in a distinct community. As the language themes of the hard-boiled story evolved, by the mid–1930s the wisecrack became one of the patented characteristics of the hero's speech. In later hard-boiled fiction, however, the wisecrack largely functioned as the challenge and had much to do with the theme of the lone hero versus authority. While wisecracks that challenge authority exist in the first run of Op stories, Hammett uses most of them to reflect solidarity among members of a distinct community: the community of cops.

The Op stories begin with wisecracking. "Arson Plus" starts with Sheriff Jim Tarr commenting on the unusual quality of the cigar the Op has offered him ("Fifteen cents straight....You must want me to break a couple of laws for you this time" [3]) and the Op commenting on the significance of his brand of repartee: "I had never known him to miss an opening for a sour crack; but it didn't mean anything" (3). The wise-cracking in "Arson Plus" doesn't end with Jim Tarr spoofing the Op about passing out cigars and the quality of his usual smokes. Half a page later, following the Keystone Kops entrance of Tarr's deputies, the Op asks, "Are you carrying a bodyguard around with you?" (3). And in response to being informed that the "city slicker" wants to know all about the burning of Thornburgh's house, McClump says, "Ain't the Lord good to us?" (4). After the comic opening of "Arson Plus," Hammett used wisecracks spar-ingly in the Op stories. He did call attention to the wisecrack as a chal-lenge to authority in "The Scorched Face" when the Op emphasizes Pat Reddy's comeback to the Coffee czar's threats: "You better lay off me — or I'll stop drinking your coffee" (365). Most of the rest of the wisecracks in the stories, however, go back and forth between the Op and O'Gar: "What's all this? Souvenir of your wedding?" ("Tenth Clew" 62); "You have all the fun, don't you?" ("Tenth Clew" 78); "Maybe a regular detective like you — with a badge and everything—can find more" ("The Golden Horseshoe" 238); and "I don't think, ... I'm a police detective" ("Women, Politics and Murder" 195). There is also the Op's rejoinder to Pat Reddy's complaints about having to get up early: "I'll cry with you after a while" ("The Scorched Face" 380). After the first wisecrack in the canon, the Op says that Jim Tarr's crack doesn't mean anything, but in the Op stories they do mean something. First of all, wisecracks being uninhibited speech reflect on the relationship between the speaker and the listener. In only the case of Pat Reddy's coffee comment does the speaker present a challenge to the listener. The rest of the cracks cited above represent uninhibited speech among friends. They are a form of inventive wordplay based on mock irony or sarcasm directed to intimates or, in the case of O'Gar's "I don't think," directed toward oneself. It is significant, then, that the Op doesn't crack wise with clients or with criminals, just with friends in the stories before *The Red Harvest*. With the novel, this changes.

Making a Character

In addition to Hammett's new approach to language in the Continental Op stories, the success of these stories rests on developing not just a realistic detective but a new kind of hero. The biographies of Hammett all agree that he took the name of the Continental Building for his detective and that he based the Op in part on his boss at the Baltimore branch of the Pinkertons, James Wright. Here's what Nolan has to say about Wright:

The man responsible for Hammett's detective training was James Wright, a squat, street-tough little bullet of a man, already a legend in Pinkerton circles for his daring and expertise. He was the assistant manager of the Baltimore office....

Jimmy Wright — who later served as Hammett's model for the Continental Op — was rough on his men, but played what Hammett called a "straight game." He taught young Hammett the basic code of the agency: Never cheat your client. Never break a law that violates your integrity. Stay anonymous.... Never take physical risks unless absolutely necessary. And, above all, be objective; never become emotionally involved with the client or anyone else connected with a case [Nolan, *A Life,* 9].

SHORT AND FAT?

The Op regularly talks about himself as being short and fat. Hammett was 6' 1" and weighed, at his most robust, about 160 pounds when he wrote the Op stories, so almost everybody was short and fat to him. How short, then, is short, and how fat is fat? Characters in some of the stories mention the Op's length and breadth. Farr, the forger in "Slippery Fingers," says, "Then this little fat guy...came around to the hotel" (34); Dick Foley describes Cruder, the gangster, as "a little fat guy" and the Op replies that "I'm his size and build" in "The Bodies Piled Up" (49); Jeanne Delano in "The Girl with Silver Eyes" addresses the Op as "Little fat detective whose name I don't know" (187); when punched, one of the door guards at Hador's cult says, "Fore God, Fat Shorty ... you done hurt me!" ("Scorched Face" 381); in trying to estimate a bad guy's appearance, the landlady in "Who Killed Bob Teal?" compares his size to the Op and Detective George Dean: "He ain't as short as you and he ain't as tall as this fellow with you [Dean]...and he ain't as fat as neither of you" ("Bob Teal" 270). Hammett, though, does narrow down how short short is and how fat fat is. In "The Tenth Clew," the Op admits to his weight: "I threw my right fist at his face — threw it with every ounce of my 180 pounds behind it" (80). He confesses to a plumper "one hundred-and-eighty-some pounds" (467) in "The Gutting of Couffignal." In the matter of height, questioning a witness in "Mike, Alec or Rufus" elicits the following:

> "Short and thin and —"
> "How short?"
> "About your height, or maybe shorter."
> "About five feet five or six, say?" [238].

Hammett is hardly talking about midgets and morbid obesity here. Indeed, even current height/weight tables make the Op only 15 or 20 pounds overweight. And in that it's clear that the Op carries "hard fat," he would not be labeled as being very roly poly, even today. Hammett, moreover, did give readers really fat characters, and it's the Op as narrator who calls attention to their girth as he does in "One Hour" when he describes Chrostwaite as "a big balloon of a man" (250). And in the matter of height the Op is not all that short. Other characters are short: the Op calls the five-foot-tall Dick Foley a "shrimp" and refers to Chinese servants as "runts" in "Dead Yellow Women." The Op at 5'5" or 5'6" would have been about average for men in the 1920s.

The short and fat connection, then, had to do with something else. James Wright's build had something to do with it. Perhaps, just perhaps, it was also an adjunct to the Op's generally avuncular demeanor at the agency and in the Hall of Justice — the friendly fat guy motif. Part of the motive for all of the attention called to the Op's height and weight also came from Hammett's desire to step into the detective story with an unusual character — as opposed to the he-man hero familiar to readers of *The Black Mask* and other pulps. In his repertoire of detectives he used to get into print in the 1920s, after all, Hammett offered an ugly detective and a poet detective. And for the same reason he invented the short, fat Op. Increasingly, however, Hammett did not simply write realistic detective stories. As the Op stories proceeded, he included more and more underworld characters and involved his hero in more and more violent action. Except when using the David/Goliath formula — which Hammett does use in places like the Op's confrontation with the door guards in "The Scorched Face" — when it comes to violence, size does matter. And so in the stories after "The Tenth Clew," while still mentioning that the Op is short and fat, Hammett has it both ways: he has a short, fat anti-hero as well as a hero for whom he provides enough details that demonstrate that he is tall enough and meaty enough to handle the rough stuff.

For Hammett, however, the Op's size was more than a gimmick. It also was one of the means he used to provide glimpses into character. Throughout the stories not only do other characters talk about the Op's girth and height, but the Op himself also talks to the reader about them as well. In "Crooked Souls," the Op tells readers that "I carry a lot of weight these days, but I can still step a block or two in good time" (43) and "three bullets would have been in my fat carcass if I hadn't learned years ago to stand to one side of strange doors" (48); in "It" he says, "And I became uneasily aware of my bulk. I am thick through the waist, and there in the dark it seemed to me that my paunch must extend almost to the ceiling — a target no bullet could miss" (56–57); in "The Zigzags of Treachery" he tells readers that he was "trying to act like a fat little guy on an errand for his wife" (91); in "The Big Knock-Over" (where he identifies himself as "short and lumpy") he says that he was "doing my best to look like the little fat man I was" (569); in "The Girl with Silver Eyes" he begins his narrative with "I said I would, and, yawning, stretching and cussing Pangburn — whoever he was — got my fat body out of pajamas and into street clothes" (146); and, in his first meeting with the Russian princess, the Op notes that "she was tall. I am short and thick. I had to look up to see her face" ("The Gutting of Couffignal" 456). In all of these statements to the readers, Hammett aimed at presenting a semirealistic hero. The Op may be paunchy but he can still hoof it after the bad guys. There is some mundane realism in the Op's comments about feeling fat while struggling out of his pajamas — an event, no doubt, that resonates with any number of readers. A lot of the Op's statements about his size and shape, however, clearly contain hyperbole: the Op is simply not that short and fat. In size he is an average man — like the imagined readers of *The Black Mask*. While his size connects the Op with the average man, his comments about it portray an extraordinary person who is able to accept who he is in a balanced, good-humored and often self-parodying, ironic fashion.

THE BENEFITS OF AGE?

The other superficial anomaly the Hammett invented for his new hero was his age. Instead of being a young man, from the very first Op story the hero makes it clear to readers that he is "a busy middle-aged detective" ("Arson Plus" 12). In the rest of the first run of stories the Op occasionally mentions that he is no longer a young man. At the start of "The Golden Horseshoe," for example, the Op tells readers that there

> was a time ... I was a young sprout of twenty or so, newly attached to the Continental Detective Agency. But the 15 years that had slid by since then had dulled my appetite for rough stuff. I don't mean that I shuddered whenever I considered the possibility of some bird taking a poke at me; but I didn't call that day a total loss in which nobody tried to puncture my short, fat carcass [219].

In "The Big Knock-Over," the Op "was no fire-haired young rowdy. I was pushing forty, and I was twenty pounds overweight. I had the liking for ease that goes with that age and weight" (569). In addition to these direct references to the Op's age, Hammett bracketed him with, at one extreme, the Old Man, and at the other with Bob Teal and Jack Counihan, both of whom he labels as young men.

Hammett pushed the Op's age toward the half-century mark for the same reason he made him short and fat. He wanted his hero to be different from the typical hero of the detective story, pulp or otherwise. When he started to write the Op stories, though, Hammett was 29. A fat lot those in their twenties really know about pushing 40 — except perhaps in inaccurate nightmare visions. What Hammett knew about what he called middle age was that he could put it to good use in building his new detective hero. First of all, he used the Op's age to validate his expertise as a detective. The Op knows the trade and all of its tricks. In "Who Killed Bob Teal?" the Op touches on the fact that being a detective is something that involves a considerable apprenticeship: "Two years is little enough time in which to pick up the first principles of sleuthing" (262). Having been a detective for a long time means that the Op knows people. He is a familiar face at the Hall of Justice and maintains a friendship with the 50-year-old O'Gar. Indeed, "Arson Plus" begins with the fact that the Op has known Sheriff Jim Tarr and McClump for a number of years. He knows people and he has seen almost all that a detective can see: "I'm no sensitive plant, and I've looked at a lot of unlovely sights in my time" ("The Bodies Piled Up" 43). And he knows the faces of criminals— he, for example, recognizes Penny Quale when he passes him in the hall in "Crooked Souls" and after an eight-year gap he recognizes the Whosis Kid because a Boston detective told the Op to "put him on your list." The tricks of the detective trade, too, that the Op frequently shares with readers gain more credence from the fact that the Op has experience that only years can bring.

The other aspect of the Op's middle age that Hammett used in the stories is his less-than-enthusiastic attitude toward women and sex. It's not that Hammett was averse to writing about sex and relationships— indeed, many of his early non–Op pieces revolve around them and show the folly and irrationality of both women and men in relationships. But he aimed for something different in the Op stories, and he included middle age with that altered focus. In the first story, therefore, he coupled the Op's profession with his age as producing a mild indifference toward women: "I was a busy middle-aged detective…and I was a lot more interested in finding the bird who struck the match than I was in feminine beauty" (12).

It's not that the Op is beyond the pull of temptation: in "The Girl with the Silver Eyes" Jeanne Delano's sexual magnetism has an effect on him, but he can also put it into perspective with the dark side of her character and resist her sexual invitation. By the time of "The Gutting of Couffignal," however, the Op's calling makes him proof against sexual lures:

> "You speak only of money," she said. "I said you may have whatever you ask."

That was out. I don't know where these women get their ideas.
"You're all twisted up," I said brusquely, standing now.... "You
think I'm a man and you're a woman. That's wrong. I'm a manhunter and you're something that has been running in front of me.
There's nothing human about it" [479].

Hammett provided a summary of the Op's attitudes toward age, women
and sex in "The Whosis Kid":

I am neither young enough nor old enough to get feverish over every
woman who doesn't make me think being blind isn't so bad. I'm at
that middle point around forty where a man puts other feminine
qualities— amiability, for one — above beauty on his list [329].

Here, the Op voices the outlandish notion that middle age (or any age for
that matter) exempts men from sexual folly. Nonetheless, Hammett made
these attitudes (profession versus sex and the maturing effects of middle
age) part of the Op's character. But these were not the only reasons that
he made the Op standoffish about women. In "Women, Politics and Murder," while waiting for Mrs. Gilmore in her library, the Op passes the time
by skimming a book (something that happens again in "The Gutting of
Couffignal"): "I found a book and spent the next half-hour reading about
a sweet young she-chump and a big strong he-chump and all their troubles" (200). In other words, he reads a clichéd "sex story," one based on
naïve, deluded characters and the dilemmas they face in their relationship.
Hammett had written this kind of story himself and wanted to distance
his newer kind of fiction from his or anyone else's "sex stories." He didn't
want his new hero to make himself or be made a chump by anyone or anything.

Much has been made about the Op's carting Jeanne Delano off to jail
in "The Girl with the Silver Eyes" and shooting the princess at the end of
"The Gutting of Couffignal" as evidence of the Op's hard-boiled character. There is, however, a pronounced chivalric side to the Op, too. True,
there are plenty of rotten women in the Op stories. Audrey Gatewood is
one of the reasons the story is called "Crooked Souls." Creda Dexter, the
"sleek kitten" in "The Tenth Clew," has no conscience — "I don't believe
her enjoyment of her three-quarters of a million dollars is spoiled a bit by
what she did to Madden" (83). Jeanne Delano of "The House on Turk
Street" and "The Girl with Silver Eyes" embodies most of the worst traits
available. And the princess in "The Gutting of Couffignal" is anything but
a princess. Beginning with "Nightshots," however, Hammett interweaves
women into the stories who are victims, victims who attract the sympathy and protection of the Op. The Op protects the innocent nurse from

the killer's diseased fantasies in "Nightshots." In "The Zigzags of Treach-ery," despite being put off by Richmond's hysterical rhetoric and protes-tations about only doing a job, at a crucial point in the story, the Op realizes that saving Mrs. Estep's life was more important, and more pressing, than the finer points of the law. In "The Golden Horseshoe" at the beginning of the story the Op meets the wife looking for her missing husband and tells readers that he "liked Mrs. Ashcraft" (228) and further along in the narrative he advises Kewpie, the bar girl, to leave what will inevitably be a ruined and ruinous relationship. "The Scorched Face" turns on the Op's uncovering and destroying a cult that victimizes women and he expresses sympathy not only for the women directly involved in the action, but also for all of the anonymous victims whose lives had been threatened or ruined by Hador's evil. There is a Chinese slave girl and Lillian Shan in "Dead Yellow Women," both saved for better lives by the Op. Finally, the Op manipulates things in "The Main Death" to cover up Enid Gungen's infidelity and save her marriage. And the first run of Op stories has its own set of sympathetically portrayed women: Nancy Regan and Angel Grace. If the Op doesn't always save them, he wants to.

THE PROTECTIVE SHELL?

Several times during the first run of Op stories Hammett inserted comments about the necessity of protecting oneself from the chaos and horror that is the inevitable consequence of being a detective by, in essence, learning to forgo emotions and even optimism about human nature. The first one comes from attorney Vance Richmond in his pleas to the Op to save his client:

> You're a detective. This is an old story to you. You're more or less callous, I suppose, and skeptical of innocence in general ["The Zigzags of Treachery" (87)].

In "The Golden Horseshoe" the Op discourses on the same subject:

> You hear now and then of detectives who have not become callous, who have not lost what you might call the human touch. I feel sorry for them, and wonder why they don't chuck their jobs and find another line of work that wouldn't be so hard on the emotions. A sleuth who doesn't grow a tough shell is in for a gay life — day in and day out poking his nose into one kind of woe or another" [238–39].

To illustrate this point even further, late in the series Hammett made the Old Man the epitome of aloofness. Thus, in "The Scorched Face," the Op says that "fifty years of sleuthing had left him without any feelings at all on any subject (372), and he uses the same words with an added metaphor to describe the Old Man in "The Creeping Siamese": "Fifty years of sleuthing have left him with no more emotion than a pawnbroker" (523). Callous though Hammett may portray him, over the course of the stories the Old Man, in fact, is not without emotion. In "Who Killed Bob Teal?" the Op notes that "his voice was as mild as his smile, and gave no indication of the turmoil that was seething in his mind" (262). The emotion here may have to do with the Old Man's commitment to his operatives (just as at the end of "$106,000 Blood Money" when the Old Man again shows a splinter of emotion, it has to do with the agency), nonetheless he is not altogether an automaton. Neither is the Op. As noted above, he does display sympathy toward some of the innocent and suffering people with whom he comes into contact during his cases.

In a few instances the Op's demeanor can even be described as avuncular. In this Hammett portrays a basic tenet of detecting, private or public: finding information often depends on developing and maintaining the goodwill of those from whom one seeks it. The Op freely passes out cigars and hobnobs not only with cops but also with felons. In "The Big Knock-Over," for example, Paddy the Mex invites him to his table and introduces him as "the biggest hearted dick" in San Francisco whose kindness is as well known as his efficiency and fairness as an agent of the law. However, there is more to the Op's connections with people than this superficial bonhomie. The Op specifically says that he has a "fatherly" interest in fellow op Bob Teal. And the same relationship extends to Pat Reddy in "The Scorched Face" where attending Reddy's wedding may not have been as accidental as the Op claims, and where the Op manipulates events in the plot so as to save his friend's marriage. Hammett, then, did not altogether couple indifference to humanity with the Op's calling.

VIOLENCE?

Hammett also did not altogether couple adventure and violence with the job of being a detective. At the start of "The Gutting of Couffignal," the Op settles down with a book from the Hendrixson's library.

> The book was called *The Lord of the Sea*, and had to do with a strong, tough and violent fellow named Hogarth, whose modest plan was to hold the world in one hand. There were plots and counter-plots, kidnappings, murders, prison-breakings, forgeries and burglaries, diamonds as large as hats and floating forts as large as Couffignal. It sounds dizzy here, but it was as real as a dime [452].

This is not a made-up book. Hammett brought in a real thriller by M. P. Shiel, published in 1901. Apropos to *The Lord of the Sea*, Hammett began his January 15, 1927, review of a number of thrillers in *The Saturday Review of Literature* with the following:

> In some years of working for private detective agencies in various cities, I came across only one fellow sleuth who would confess that he read detective stories. "I eat 'em up," this one said without shame. "When I'm through my day's gum-shoeing I like to relax; I like to get my mind on something altogether different from the daily grind; so I read detective stories [510].

In the 1920s Hammett toyed with writing action/adventure stories, beginning with "The Road Home." By the time of "The Ruffian's Wife," however, he saw the adventure hero as little more than a sham and a "sneak thief." Hammett's original purpose in the Op stories, then, was to give an accurate (or more accurate) account of the "daily grind" of the detective and to delineate this character more accurately than had been done by British and American thriller writers.

One of the things that the "daily grind" of detective work means in the Op stories is the patient examination of evidence, and Hammett stressed this in the earliest Op stories. The Op's first outing, "Arson Plus," emphasizes the evidence of witnesses: the Op and McClump interview 17 people about the fire and the habits of the supposed victim. In "Slippery Fingers" Hammett brought in his fascination with the technicalities of fingerprints—a fascination evident from his letters to *The Black Mask* and his commentary in "Suggestions for Detective Story Writers." Throughout the stories the Op repeatedly says that patience and routine solve cases. There is one reference to this part of detective work as the "patience-taxing grind" in "The Bodies Piled Up" and another in the calculation in "One Hour" that "ninety-nine percent of detective work is a patient collecting of details" (253). Hammett summed up this part of the detective business in "The Zigzags of Treachery," when the Op says, "I am not what you'd call a brilliant thinker — such results as I get are usually the fruits of patience, industry, and unimaginative plugging, helped, now and then, maybe, by a little luck" (100).

This, however, smacks of being disingenuous. Looking at the way the Op solves crimes, when solving crimes is the focus of the story, often shows something other than the patient sifting of evidence. In "Arson Plus" the solution comes when "the pieces were beginning to fit together under my skull" (18) and those pieces have only a marginal connection with the collected testimony. In "Slippery Fingers," from early on the Op just knows that Clane is guilty and proof comes when the Op gets "mad clean through." The tenth clue in "The Tenth Clew" is the Op's recognition that puzzling over the collection of clues is a waste of time. Increasingly, moreover, the Op stories move away from the conventional detective story: the whodonit pattern of tantalizing but enigmatic clues followed by a surprise ending. Beginning with "The Bodies Piled Up" and continuing more emphatically with stories after Hammett began to write "novelettes," there are fewer traditional poser stories. "Nightshots," "Women, Politics and Murder," "Who Killed Bob Teal?" and "Mike, Alec or Rufus," for instance, all present puzzles with surprise endings. After the first four stories ("Arson Plus," "Slippery Fingers," "Crooked Souls," and "It") however, fewer Op stories deal with domestic or accidental crimes, which are staples of conventional detective stories. In more and more of them, either the villains' identities are known early on or detective work — sifting clues— has little to do with identifying and catching them. "The House on Turk Street," "One Hour," "The Whosis Kid," "The Golden Horseshoe," and "The Big Knock-Over" all drop the Op into nests of thieves and he needs to find his way out of tough spots. Finding that way out, though, has little to do with chewing on the clues.

Setting the Op up as short, fat, and pushing 40 to make him different from he-man heroes, Hammett also added, if not an aversion to violent action, then a prudent avoidance of it. "The idea in this detective business is to catch crooks, not to put on heroics" ("Whosis Kid" 347). There is also the passage in "The Golden Horseshoe" cited earlier:

> But the 15 years that had slid by since then had dulled my appetite
> for rough stuff. I don't mean that I shuddered whenever I considered
> the possibility of some bird taking a poke at me; but I didn't call that
> day a total loss in which nobody tried to puncture my short, fat
> carcass [219].

In the earliest stories the Op engages in little or no violence and violence itself plays only a minimal role in the plots. In "Arson Plus," it's McClump who shoots the fleeing bad guy; there's a struggle or two but no real violence in "Slippery Fingers"; and in "Crooked Souls," Penny Quayle wrestles the gun out of Audrey Gatewood's hands without the Op's intervention. After "Crooked Souls," however, the Op is involved in violence — gunplay or fistfights— in all of the stories except "Nightshots," "The Creeping Siamese," and "The Main Death."

When fistfights happen without other forms of violence they occur at significant moments. "The Tenth Clew," "Women, Politics and Murder," and "Mike, Alec, or Rufus" all end with the Op rearing back and slugging someone. And this makes a point. Sometimes it is cathartic as when the Op slugs Tennant at the end of "Women, Politics and Murder" or in "The Tenth Clew" when "I threw my right fist at his face — threw it with every ounce of my 180 pounds behind it, reinforced by the memory of every second I had spent in the water, and every throb of my battered head" (80). And sometimes violence proves guilt as when the thugs attack the Op in "One Hour," or when the Op punches the cross-dresser in "Mike, Alec, or Rufus" to demonstrate with finality the correctness of his solution to the case.

As the stories proceed, gunplay becomes more common than fisticuffs. After "The Bodies Piled Up" shots are fired in "It," "The Zigzags of Treachery," "The House on Turk Street," "The Girl with Silver Eyes," "Who Killed Bob Teal?" "The Golden Horseshoe," "The Whosis Kid," "The Scorched Face," "Corkscrew," "Dead Yellow Women," "The Gutting of Couffignal," "The Big Knock-Over," and "$106,000 Blood Money." The earlier stories tend to minimize the Op's involvement with violence. In "The Bodies Piled Up," for instance, he is an observer at the climactic shoot-out between Orrett and Cudner. In "It," "Who Killed Bob Teal?" "The Zigzags of Treachery," and "The Golden Horseshoe" the Op disarms people who are shooting at him. Indeed, in "The Zigzags of Treachery" Hammett made much of the Op shooting the gun out of Ledwich's hand. Starting with "The House on Turk Street" and then consistently after "The Whosis Kid" Hammett was inclined to bring more violence and general mayhem into the Op stories. As a preliminary, in "The Girl with Silver Eyes" the Op is knifed by a gangster and kills another in a gunfight. But the action picks up in "The Whosis Kid" where there are fistfights, knifings, gunfire, and a shoot-out between the Op and the Kid. In "Scorched Face" the Op and Pat Reddy battle through a whole house of thugs intent on maiming or killing them. The same kind of thing occurs in "Dead Yellow Women" and "The Big Knock-Over." "Corkscrew," fundamentally a Western story, features out-and-out warfare, and "The Gutting of Couffignal" does the same thing but with a Bay Area setting.

Part of the use of mayhem and mass violence in the stories rests on the Op's use of chaos as something that will result in order. Whereas in the early stories violence is incidental, increasingly Hammett plotted not just violence but mass violence into the Op stories: the falling out of double-crossing crooks in "The House on Turk Street"; the confusion of the Op fighting gangsters at the roadhouse in "The Girl with the Silver Eyes"; the fights between a second batch of double crossing crooks in "The Whosis Kid"; the chaotic free-for-all in "The Scorched Face"; the tussle with anonymous Chinese in "Dead Yellow Women"; the donnybrook at

Larrouy's in "The Big Knock-Over." In several of these the Op contends with masses of anonymous baddies intent on doing him harm. His involvement in these fracases, however, is not altogether incidental or gratuitous. It's one of his methods. Far from puzzle solving or ratiocination, in "The Whosis Kid" the Op explains the uses of violence and chaos:

> Something was going to happen in these rooms.... Few men *get* killed. Most of those who meet sudden ends *get themselves killed.* I've had twenty years of experience at dodging that. I can count on being one of the survivors of whatever blow-up there is. And I hope to take most of the other survivors for a ride [339, emphasis in original].

And so it happens that at the end of the story the Op comes out on top and all the thieves and murderers lie dead. The melee at the end of "The Scorched Face" gives the Op and Pat Reddy access to the secrets of Hador's cult and the solution to the case; the struggle in the dark at Lillian Shan's house in "Dead Yellow Women" reveals the smuggling operations that lie at the center of the crimes; the fight at Larrouy's in "The Big Knock-over" leads the Op to the masterminds behind the big knock-over. Chaos and mass violence open the way for the solution.

The Op comes into contact with a variety of violent people in these stories. One kind is the cretin — simian thugs like Hook in "The House on Turk Street" and Porgy in "The Big Knock-Over." There are also criminal psychopaths like the Whosis Kid: natural born killers. Sentimentalists, too, are confronted by the Op: love motivates Porky Grout in "The Girl with Silver Eyes" and Billie in "The Whosis Kid." And there are also a few characters like Red and Big Flora in "The Big Knock-Over" whose acceptance of and capacity for violence Hammett portrayed as awesome and even impressive.

The Op's capacity for violence as well as his acceptance and understanding of it, however, is quite different. First of all, the Op doesn't engage in gratuitous violence and says in a number of places that it is something he would rather avoid. Violence, however, serves him as something he has come to understand. It is something that sorts things out. While evil may be self-destructive, it often needs a nudge to make that so. In the domestic stories that nudge comes in the form of the detective discovering the flaw in the illusion created by the criminal or by the criminal's overreaching. Thus, stories like "Arson Plus" turn on the Op discovering the flaw in the criminal's artifice, and those like "It" show the villain's downfall caused by doing too much to deflect suspicion. In the Op's gangster stories, however, the push that propels evil to destroy itself comes from the detective helping the criminals turn on one another. In the largest sense, then, all of the Op stories are providential.

The Op stories are, after all, detective stories and the traditional function of detective stories is to uncover crime and assert the inevitability of justice. While in the shorter Op pieces the hero does this using traditional means— interviews, tracing clues, etc.— in stories like "The House on Turk Street" and "The Whosis Kid" Hammett plotted justice resulting from chaos and violence. In two well-known passages from "The Big Knock-Over," Hammett, incidentally or not, connected the Op's participation in violence with providence. The first is the choreography passage in which the Op repeats "swing right, swing left, kick" and emphasizes that in doing the dance of violence, "God will see there's always a mug there for your gun or blackjack to sock, a belly for your foot" (570).

The second is the Op's somewhat tongue-in-cheek fantasy of the afterlife "in heaven where I could enjoy myself forever and ever socking folks who had been rough on me down below" (587). While it would be easy to make too much of these remarks, they do, nonetheless, say something about providence. Opposed to the Op's earlier view in "The Whosis Kid" that "few men *get* killed. Most of those who meet sudden ends *get themselves killed*," in "The Big Knock-Over" it's providence, one assumes, that guides actions so that one will not "get themselves killed"— a pretty high statistical possibility when one jumps into a melee of brass knuckles, knives, and bullets. The second passage is an ironic, off-the-cuff remark about retribution. It, to be sure, is the fantasy of the oppressed: that some day, some way, the tables will be turned. As such it connects with the Op as the short and fat "average" man. But it is also the Op's ironic comment about himself. The events leading up to the Op capturing the criminals at the end of "The Big Knock-Over" hardly demonstrate a conventional view of virtue. The Op, after all, has just shot a man in the back— something worse than "stealing a crutch from a cripple" (something, incidentally, that he technically does not do in "The Gutting of Couffignal")— in order to discover the criminals' hide-out. If the Op's slugging bad guys with a piece of pipe demonstrates anything then, it demonstrates the efficacy of stirring up the bad guys so that they precipitate their own downfall.

In the End

In "The Simple Art of Murder" Raymond Chandler talks about Hammett as a means of introducing his own definition of the hard-boiled hero. While Chandler credits him with inventing the hard-boiled story, he has his doubts about whether Hammett consciously set about to change the pattern and course of mystery fiction:

> I doubt that Hammett had any deliberate artistic aims whatever; he was trying to make a living by writing something he had firsthand information about. He made some of it up; all writers do; but it had a basis in fact; it was made up out of real things [16].

Looking at Hammett's work before 1927, it's pretty clear that in the macro sense Hammett had no "artistic aims" regarding remaking the detective story. Writing detective stories, in fact, was something he resisted in his first year as a writer. It then became something that "curiously" took him a while to get the hang of. Once he began writing the Op stories, however, he pretty clearly had "artistic aims." These aims are evident in Hammett's conscious development of narrative and dialogue. They're also evident in his intent to portray cops and ops. And they're evident in his creation of the shaping and re-shaping of the Continental Op character.

3

The Op Novels

The Red Harvest

The Red Harvest is comprised of four pieces originally published in *Black Mask*: "The Cleansing of Personville" (November 1927), "Crime Wanted — Male or Female" (December 1927), "Dynamite" (January 1928), and "The 19th Murder" (February 1928). Together, the four stories total 98 pages. After the last part of the serial appeared in *Black Mask* Hammett sent the typescript to Alfred Knopf in New York, hoping that it would become a book instead of an accumulation of pulp stories. The rest is a familiar history. Blanche Knopf happened on the manuscript, liked it, accepted it for publication, and Harry C. Block of Knopf took on the job of doing the editorial work that made the *Black Mask* stories into *The Red Harvest*.

ORIGINS

The usual background given for *The Red Harvest* begins with recognition of Hammett's familiarity with its setting in Montana. Hammett knew something about the place. For one thing, his wife, Jose, was from Anaconda, Montana, and she retreated there with their daughter during one of Hammett's serious bouts with TB. Before *The Red Harvest* he had written two stories set in Jose's home state — "The Man Who Killed Dan Odams" and "Afraid of a Gun." Neither of these stories, however, has much to do with the Montana of *The Red Harvest*: they cover elemental western virtues and vices, and they take place in very small towns like those one sees in the typical western movie. *The Red Harvest* takes place not in frontier towns like those in Hammett's two short stories but in a city of 40,000 inhabitants (a fact mentioned twice in the novel), whose existence depends on copper mining. Hammett, it turns out, knew more about Montana than its scenery and its linkage with the Old West; he knew something about the history of copper mining in Montana. In 1917, as a Pinkerton operative, Hammett had been sent to Anaconda to work for the copper mine owners and against the striking miners (*Hammett, A Life on the Edge*, 14). Because of this bit of biography, everyone who discusses *The Red Harvest* begins their discussions of the origins of the story with a brief description of the protracted struggle that lasted from 1912 until 1920 between miners organized by the International Workers of the World and the mining companies. The owners, through the use of money, power, and brute force, won, and the miners, heading into the Depression, lost. Critics make much of this. Marling, for example, says that the labor strife in Montana "attracted Hammett's interest because it permitted a more complete rendering of the Hobbesian society" (49). Whether or not Hobbesian society meant anything to him, Hammett had been on the scene of this dispute in Montana, which was one of the nasty, brutal, and not-so-short labor struggles of the first quarter of the twentieth century.

Clearly *The Red Harvest* starts off with Montana and labor troubles before and after World War I. The Op first hears of Personville in "the Big Ship" in Butte, Montana, and his first view of the city centers on its copper mining industry. The Op mentions the brick stacks of the copper smelters silhouetted against the surrounding mountains that had "yellow-smoked" the town and its surroundings into a "uniform dinginess." Not much in the way of architectural beauty to begin with (he calls it an "ugly city"), the Op finishes his initial description of Personville by noting that the pollution of the copper mines had made an ugly city even uglier. One of the first people he meets in Personville is Bill Quint, a union organizer for the "Wobblies" sent to the town from the union headquarters in Chicago. Hammett puts in the I.W.W. password line from the song "Joe Hill" ("He's not going to die any more"), and the Op and Quint go to a speakeasy where the Op gets "the low-down" on what has happened in Personville. Thus, on the fifth page of the novel Hammett gives a lengthy summary of Bill Quint's history lesson. It's about the strife between the copper miners and Elihu's Personville Mining Company that began during World War I. Then, when the miners had the upper hand, they demanded better working conditions, which Old Elihu grudgingly gave them. But in 1921 when the copper business got bad he reneged on his agreements and brought back the bad old days. The miners called in help from the Chicago headquarters of the I.W.W. and got Bill Quint who recommended sabotage instead of strikes as the most effective means of combating the owner's high-handed action, but, ignoring this advice, the miners went on strike. "Old Elihu hired gunmen, strike-breakers, national guardsmen and even parts of the regular army" (7) to break up the strike, and in the end of the bloody confrontations, "organized labor in Personville was a used firecracker" (7).

All of this business about Montana mining and labor strife, while Hammett gives it emphasis in the opening of the novel, has very little impact on what happens in *The Red Harvest*. Bill Quint disappears as a character after one appearance and is mentioned subsequently only in passing as one of Dinah Brand's conquests and as a very dubious suspect in her murder. Insider trading of mining stock gets brief reference as part of Dinah Brand's diversified portfolio. And as for miners, they get less than cursory treatment and appear only in the crowd scene in the first chapter of *The Red Harvest*:

> There were men from the mines and smelters in their working clothes, gaudy boys from pool rooms and dance halls, sleek men with slick pale faces, men with the dull look of respectable husbands, a few just as respectable and dull women, and some ladies of the night [5].

From Hammett's only survey of Personville's inhabitants it doesn't look like the miners (or the "dull" middle-class people for that matter) are going to attract much attention in the rest of the story. And they don't. The members of underworld crew — not the miners or the union men — look like they are going to be the ticket. And they are.

While the Montana background had something to do with the origin of *The Red Harvest*, Hammett used it because the idea of a community wracked with unrest and violence fit in with one of the patterns he had used in his earlier fiction. While it is not something that occurs in the Op's San Francisco stories, Hammett had used the notion of cleansing a corrupt city in two of his short stories. The first of these was "Nightmare Town" (December 1924), in which the hero innocently arrives at Izzard, Arizona, a town run by a criminal syndicate and entirely peopled by criminals. Without the hero's intervention, the criminals fall upon one another and the story ends with the entire destruction of Izzard, which is set on fire by feuding factions. The second of these pre–*Red Harvest* pieces is "Corkscrew," published in September 1925. Like "Nightmare Town," this story takes place in Arizona: Corkscrew, Arizona. When the Op arrives, sent by the Continental Detective Agency and made deputy sheriff by the local authorities, one of the local bar flies announces, "Ladiesh an' gentsh...th' time has come for yuh t' give up y'r evil ways an' get out y'r knittin'. Th' law hash come to Orilla County" (252). As the Op then explains, because of the prevalence of smuggling and because he had recently "knocked over" a smuggling operation, "the Orilla County people thought I could do the same thing for them down here. So hither I come to make this part of Arizona ladylike" (271). The story, however, isn't so much about its stated purpose — bringing law and order to Corkscrew — as it is a compendium of popular story bits: there's a whodunit, a glance at the Op as dude in the Old West, and there are feuding factions, Mexican bandits, overzealous cowboys, and illegal immigrants.

In these two early stories Hammett centered on small communities in the Southwest. As in *The Red Harvest*, both of them focus on the wholly corrupt locale and employ the motif of cleansing. Nolan suggests that Hammett's source for the town-cleaning fable in *The Red Harvest* and, by implication, the two early stories, was Allan Pinkerton's book *The Model Town and the Detectives* (*A Life* 75). Published in 1876, the link between this ghosted piece of Pinkerton promotion and Hammett's novel, however, seems somewhat problematic. Rather than depending on Pinkerton, "Nightmare Town" echoes the biblical account of the destruction of Sodom and Gomorrah, the completely degenerate place whose final destruction depends on God's hand and not the hero's acts. "Corkscrew," alternately, uses the western story idea of the lawman arriving to root out bad men and pacify the lawless inhabitants.

Just as what has happened in Personville in *The Red Harvest* is the result of a wide-ranging conspiracy, the corruption of both Izzard and Corkscrew stems from criminal conspiracies — moonshining in Izzard and smuggling in Corkscrew — and in all cases this affects all of the towns' other institutions, especially law enforcement. Interestingly, Hammett never deals with the issue of for whom the hero ultimately cleans up the towns — other than the imprecise mention of "the Orilla County people." *The Red Harvest* ignores (and maybe even disparages) average citizens; in "Nightmare Town" there are no average citizens; and in "Corkscrew" the Op associates more with and has more sympathy for the rowdies in the town than for the "better" element. In the latter story Hammett shows the preacher-schoolmarm-decent citizen crowd in Corkscrew as a nest of prudes and bluenoses. In each of these cases Hammett focuses on and engenders admiration for unconventional characters on the edge of society rather than for society itself. With these inclinations about motive and characters as well as with his Montana background, when he started "The

Cleansing of Personville," Hammett already had some of the basic elements of the fable. Putting those elements together moved him forward, but he first had to get rid of the more overt elements of the Old West he had used in the early cleansing stories, and he had to find a credible way to focus on cleaning up Personville without them.

Abandoning the overt western elements of the earlier pieces along with bulking up the size of the town, while necessary, caused problems that Hammett chose to ignore. For one thing, the size and population of Personville in *The Red Harvest* seems too small for the grand scale of the action. Hammett's 40,000 inhabitants form a poor economic base for organized crime: subtract a third of the population as children, factor out half of the rest as women, and add in that the remaining male population is comprised largely of workers who had just suffered through a protracted strike and lost, and one winds up with an environment that would hardly provide a fertile field for organized crime. On top of this, taking *The Red Harvest* out of the Old West meant Hammett could not attach to his hero the archetype of the new sheriff come to rid the town of its outlaws.

While the pattern of the new sheriff coming to town in "Corkscrew" showed one way and the feud among villains in "Nightmare Town" another way of actively cleaning up a corrupted locale, in *The Red Harvest* Hammett added a different character motif and theme that he had evolved in the course of writing the Op stories. Between the two early cleansing stories he began to broaden the focus of his *Black Mask* stories about the Op. With "The House on Turk Street" (April 1924), Hammett began to edge away from creating domestic crime problems for the Op to solve and began to add stories in which the Op encounters professional criminals and organized crime. Since the importance of clues and problem solving diminishes in this kind of story, Hammett devised a different way for the Op to deal with the issue of good versus evil. He made the Op an agent provocateur rather than a conventional detective. As opposed to simply exposing or arresting or killing the antagonists, he stirs things up and turns the bad people loose on each another. The Op even talks about this as his methodology in "The Whosis Kid" when he is confronted by multiple factions of sociopaths:

> I wasn't altogether dissatisfied with the shape things were taking. Something was going to happen in these rooms. But I wasn't friendly enough to any present to care especially what happened to whom. For myself, I counted on coming through all in one piece. Few men *get* killed. Most of those who meet sudden ends *get themselves killed.* I've had twenty years of experience at dodging that. I can count on

being one of the survivors of whatever blow-up there is. And I hope
to take most of the other survivors for a ride [339, emphasis in
original].

This is something he transported quite directly to *The Red Harvest*. In the
novel Hammett has the Op repeat and refine his earlier definition of his
methods to Dinah Brand:

Plans are all right sometimes.... And sometimes just stirring things
up is all right — if you're tough enough to survive, and keep your
eyes open so you'll see what you want when it comes to the top [57].

And so in *The Red Harvest* he depicted a town as corrupt as Izzard from
"Nightmare Town," used the hero as the agent of reforming the town by
ridding it of bad people from "Corkscrew," and he carried over to it the
Op's predilection for creating chaos so that order can emerge from it.

In addition to these recycled and remade elements of his earlier
fiction, Hammett also quite literally carried over to *The Red Harvest* the
Continental Detective Agency and its personnel that he had invented for
his short stories. As staples in *The Black Mask* they both ensured his read-
ership and were easier to use than creating a new context for a new hero
from scratch. But in *The Red Harvest* neither the Continental nor its operatives are what they were in the short stories. When he wrote the early *Black
Mask* Op stories, for various reasons, Hammett invented the Old Man,
Dick Foley, and Mickey Linehan as subsidiary characters of varying importance. Introduced in "The Zigzags of Treachery," the Old Man, manager
of the San Francisco branch of the Continental Detective Agency, appeared
in nine of the Op stories before *The Red Harvest*. He does not appear in
the novel but the Op and the other Continental operatives mention him
at several junctures during the action of *The Red Harvest*. In chapter 15,
when the other Continental operatives arrive in Personville, the Op
describes the Old Man to the readers. Here, Hammett simply cribs the
description of the Old Man he had used in "The Big Knock-Over" with
the allusion to Pontius Pilate and ops being sent out to be "crucified" on
"suicidal jobs" along with the euphemism about spitting icicles in July in
contrast to his appearance as a kindly, polite, understanding old duffer.
One of the main functions of the Old Man in *The Red Harvest* lies in the
significance of his repeated demands for reports from his operatives in
Personville and the Op's dilatory response to those demands. This is something new.

In the stories leading up to *The Red Harvest* the agency's rules play
only a minuscule role and have no real impact on what the Op does. The

principal function of the agency in the earlier Op stories is to provide clients and to supply the hero with information he cannot obtain himself. In *The Red Harvest* Hammett was still interested enough in the Continental Agency to provide brief glimpses into its operating procedures. He reiterates the agency's policy against doing divorce work and, for the first time, notes in the Op's bantering with Dinah Brand that the agency pays for information. While in the *Black Mask* stories the Op may grumble about his expense account and in several instances he is sent to work for people he does not like very much, he largely has a free hand in doing what he does. And what the Op does in those stories occasionally encompasses illegal acts—in the later stories he shoots people and commits illegal searches and seizures. Indeed, Policeman Pat Reedy calls attention to the agency's cavalier attitude toward the law in "The Scorched Face": he calls the Continental a "law breaking agency." It is not unusual in the early Op stories, either, to have the hero consort with criminals and there is never any agency comment on this as being unusual. Things become more punctilious in *The Red Harvest* and a lot of this connects with the Old Man. He begins in the novel as the efficient, demanding administrator. This comes in tangentially with the Op's bullying of Elihu Willsson into signing a contract and paying a retainer to the Continental Agency and this is the same kind of thing that happens in the short stories. The Old Man's reiterated requests for reports, however, have to do with the law and the legitimacy of the Op's actions in Personville. The Op repeatedly putting off reporting to his boss, then, indicates pretty strongly that he knows that the Old Man will disapprove of his actions. By implication this makes the Old Man represent not simply agency rules but also the law and it emphasizes the Op's consciousness of the fact that his actions can be construed as and probably are quite illegal. It's something that never bothered him before. Even though in the novel invoking the Old Man's name holds the Op's actions up against law and legitimate detection, the Old Man, nonetheless, also represents rules and law that ultimately are flexible and understanding. The novel ends with these sentences: "I might just as well saved the labor and sweat I had put into trying to make my reports harmless. They didn't fool the Old Man. He gave me merry hell" (142). But that "merry hell" didn't involve being fired.

In addition to the Old Man, Hammett brought back Continental operative Dick Foley from the *Black Mask* stories. The character in *The Red Harvest* has the same name, but Dick Foley in the novel seems a very different character. Hammett described Foley several times in the Op stories. Chronologically the closest description of the Continental's shadow man occurs in "The Big Knock-Over":

> He was a swarthy little Canadian who stood nearly five feet in his
> high-heeled shoes, weighing a hundred pounds, minus, talked like a
> Scotchman's telegram, and could have shadowed a drop of water
> from the Golden Gate to Hongkong [sic] without ever losing sight of
> it [560].

The Op describes him affectionately and with admiration here and elsewhere in the stories. The externals remain the same but the tone is different
when the Op introduces Foley in *The Red Harvest*. Instead of being a
"swarthy little Canadian" he is a "boy-sized Canadian." The narrative
replaces "swarthy" with a description of Foley as being ferret-faced and
irritable. On top of that, he's now something of a fop: "He wore high heels
to increase his height, perfumed his handkerchiefs and saved all the words
he could" (77).

Gone is the Op's admiration for Foley's talent as a shadow man; here
he becomes unattractive, irritable, and foppish. Foley has lost the sense of
intimacy with the Op that in some measure he possesses in the stories. In
addition to serving simply as a watcher whose watching, because of the
Op's instructions, has no impact on the outcome of the action, Dick Foley
leaves the Op when it looks like the Op murdered Dinah Brand: "He
seemed to think I'd killed Dinah Brand. He was getting on my nerves with
it" (136). And in this respect he connects with the other elements in the
novel that set up the Continental Agency as a model of legitimate and legal
operations and adds to the coloring of the Op as something of a loner and
a rogue operative. This is very different from the earlier stories.

The last of the three Continental carryovers from the *Black Mask* stories is Mickey Linehan. Linehan appears in the last three Op stories before
"The Cleansing of Personville." In them he's a very minor character, little more than a name attached to an insignificant agency operative. He has
little dialogue and Hammett does not describe him in the early stories. In
The Red Harvest he does.

> Mickey Linehan was a big slob with sagging shoulders and a shape-
> less body that seemed to be coming apart at all its joints. His ears
> stood out like red wings, and his round, red face usually wore the
> meaningless smirk of a half-wit [77].

Of the two agency operatives sent to Personville to help out the Op, Linehan gets the most play. Hammett derived him in part from the earlier character of Fiske, the Continental's joke-telling night man. Starting with the
description of Linehan as being funny looking, he, like Dick Foley, doesn't
have much to do with the plot — he follows people and comes up with little to help the Op. But at least he has dialogue. Unlike the telegraphic

Foley, Linehan talks. And Hammett spiced his speech with wisecracks, all of which occur in conversations with the Op. Linehan also stays with the Op even when it appears that he may have killed Dinah Brand, and at the end of the novel he is the one to whom the Op entrusts the final tidying up of affairs in Personville. Indeed, insofar as the Op has uninhibited relationships with anyone in the novel, one of them is the minuscule connection he has with this coworker from the Continental Detective Agency.

In addition to using Continental Detective Agency characters he had invented for the Op stories in *Black Mask* to people *The Red Harvest*, Hammett turned to another of his early pieces as the source for two significant characters in the novel: Dinah Brand and Dan Rolff. The Op's first view of Dinah Brand hardly summons up images of the femme fatale. He describes her as big: she's taller than the Op (about 5'8"), has broad shoulders, and muscular legs, as well as full breasts and round hips. And, like the woman in "Esther Entertains," age is catching up with her, apparent in the lines around her mouth and eyes. And she's sort of a slob. The Op notes that she not only needs to comb her hair but she also needs a haircut, that she can't put her lipstick on straight, and, in addition to the run in her stocking, that she is popping out of her clothes. Whenever she appears in the novel there's something wrong with her dress or her grooming. In Chief Noonan's words, she's "a soiled dove...a de luxe hustler, a big-league gold-digger" (16). One of her former conquests, however, tells the Op that part of her allure is that "she's so thoroughly mercenary, so frankly greedy, that there's nothing disagreeable about it" (19). Her live-in companion, Dan Rolff, emaciated by tuberculosis, is "a thin man with a tired face that had no color in it" (21), with an "educated man's" voice. Even though he consistently points out her slovenly appearance and greed in his narration, the Op is fascinated by Dinah Brand and he is also the only person to display any understanding or compassion toward Dan Rolff. Hammett found the models for both of these characters in one of his bleakest early stories, "Holiday."

As seen earlier, "Holiday" centers on Paul Hetherwick's search for diversion from his life as a tuberculosis patient at a veterans' hospital. Women play a particularly significant role in Hetherwick's day's activities and in his thoughts. During the course of the story Hetherwick comes across three women: one has "the most beautiful face he had ever seen," one is a pretty red-haired girl whose company brings him "a certain definite delight," and one is a bar girl "a sub-harlot...holding out false promises of her monstrous body to bring about that stimulation of traffic in liquor for which she was employed" (116). Although two of the women present images of beauty and freshness, Hetherwick thinks most about the bar girl: he feels that given a certain turn of temper, there would be a savage, ghoulish joy in her" (118).

Part of the substance of "Holiday," then, is a tuberculosis patient thinking about women and choosing a forthright, slatternly woman who is capable of "savage ghoulish joy" versus, presumably, what may be the empty promises of ethereal beauty or domesticity. Hammett, then, took the consumptive Paul Hetherwick's frustrated longings and made them into the ideals and frustrated love of Dan Rolff and prettied up the bar girl (somewhat) and made her into Dinah Brand, the only individual in *The Red Harvest* in whom the Op finds honesty in her "utter coarseness" and who experiences "savage ghoulish joy" in her companionship.

THE POLICE

Of all the evils that beset Personville, throughout the novel Hammett focuses most on the corruption of the town's police department. On the first page of *The Red Harvest* Hammett briefly plays around with under-world argot, establishes the theme of civic corruption, provides a quick glimpse of the local scenery, and, before he gets the plot of Donald Willsson's murder underway, he describes the local constabulary:

> The first policeman I saw needed a shave. The second had a couple of buttons off his shabby uniform. The third stood in the center of the city's main intersection...directing traffic, with a cigar in one corner of his mouth. After that I stopped checking them up [3].

After reading the 24 Continental Op stories that precede *The Red Harvest*, this is something very new for Hammett. Without exception, the Op stories before Hammett's first novel present the police at every level as honest, hard-working, diligent, law-abiding, mostly intelligent, responsible men. This is decidedly not the case in *The Red Harvest*. The Op's initial impression of the cops in Personville serves as a prelude to Hammett's presentation in *The Red Harvest* of a police force possessed of every vice associated with the profession. Starting off with slovenliness, the Op catalogues them during the course of the novel. It's not just the uniformed cops in Personville who are unkempt; Hammett reinforces the appearance of Personville's police force during the raid on Whisper's headquarters when the Op says, "I didn't think much of them — a shabby, shifty-eyed crew without enthusiasm" (34). Not only slovenly, the Personville cops are also insubordinate: a number of times during the course of the book individual officers refuse to follow their chief's orders and are openly disrespectful to him at a time when the introduction of military organization and order were seen as the bedrock of police reform. The Personville cops repeatedly engage in police brutality: there is "the wrecking crew" in the basement of the police station and Hammett shows suspects being beaten in the station offices. This, to be sure, pales in comparison to the trumped-up, warrantless raids and the massive use of shotguns and machine guns during those raids, all when police brutality, for the first time in U.S. history, became the subject of public examination and outrage. And they're crooked, too: the Personville cops are susceptible to bribery. Hammett shows this most forcefully during the raid when Whisper buys off the policemen surrounding his hideout and tells Jerry, who will do the actual payoff, not to pay any of the cops more than they are used to being paid for colluding with the criminals. The second crime puzzle in *The Red Harvest*—Tim Noonan's death—pivots on one of the witnesses bribing a police officer.

But they're not just crooked—the Personville cops actively collude with criminals on a large scale. Thus, the police raid on the Cedar Hill Inn clears way for Reno's robbery of the First National Bank, and criminals pop in and out of the town jail as if it were a hotel. The bane of labor strife during the early twentieth century, the Personville cops use "specials" (deputized civilians) to guarantee order. Thus, late in the novel Pete the Finn's thugs become auxiliary police officers to maintain "order" in the town. Perhaps worst of all, the Personville cops are a law unto themselves: the quartet of Personville powers that Bill Quint names for the Op at the beginning of the novel includes Noonan, the chief of police. Finally, the crooked Personville cops are neither very smart nor very efficient. While he may possess a degree of low cunning, Personville's police chief isn't very smart either.

Of the four bad men responsible for the day-to-day corruption of Personville mentioned in the first chapter, Hammett pays the most attention to and devotes the most space to Noonan, the police chief. Readers should note that Chief Noonan appears in more scenes of *The Red Harvest* than any other character except the Op: he features in ten chapters (3, 5, 6, 7, 12, 14, 15, 16, 18, and 19) and his death is reported in chapter 20. Dinah Brand, while she has more dialogue than Noonan, appears in eight chapters; Reno Starkey in six; Whisper Thayler in five; and Elihu Willsson, the critics' favorite, is in five chapters. Interestingly enough, readers never get a chance to make up their own minds about the chief during the course of the novel: Bill Quint's summary of what's wrong with Personville labels Noonan as corrupt before he even enters the novel. As had been standard operating procedure for the Op in all of the early stories, soon after arriving in Personville he visits the police station to present his credentials and establish his bona fides. In chapter 3 the Op meets the chief who he describes as a fat man with a "jovial face" who welcomes him with a hand-shake and proffers him a cigar (the first of many). Throughout the rest of the novel Hammett never misses a chance to mention the chief's obesity. When the Op and the chief interview Mrs. Willsson, the chief has "beefy" paws and a smile that "made funny lines and humps in his fat face" (17). One of the goons at Whisper's place calls Noonan a "lard can" (35). He has a fist the size of a cantaloupe. Enough said on that matter. On top of being fat, Noonan has flamboyantly unctuous manners. Every time he appears Hammett inserts the word "fine" into his dialogue.

And in the manner of a politician (or of the Op in the early stories for that matter) he is forever passing out cigars: even when he visits Elihu Willsson's bedroom to check out the intruder who lies dead at the foot of the invalid's bed, Noonan produces cigars for the Op and for bedridden old Elihu. In the first half of the novel, Noonan maintains a cordial atti-tude toward the Op while he tries twice to have him killed — once at Whis-per's headquarters and once in the Op's hotel room. The assassination attempts, one assumes, are the chief's efforts to prevent the discovery of his corruption and to keep anyone else from representing law in Person-ville, but this is never stated in the novel. After the Op digs into the his-tory of his brother's murder, however, Noonan's attitude shifts. Noonan begins to treat the Op as a confidante. He first opens up to the Op about the political and personal pressure put on him as chief of police: "Just because a man's chief of police doesn't mean he's chief...Don't make any difference if I think you're a right guy. I got to play with them that play with me" (66).

Two-thirds of the way through the novel, Noonan falls apart. In chap-ter 18 the Op tells readers that Noonan "wasn't looking well," and that "his face was gray, flabby, damp, like fresh putty" (96). When invited to view the scene of Lew Yard's murder, Noonan tells the Op that "I'm getting sick of this killing. It's getting to me." (95). Finally, when the Op urges him to hunt down Whisper, Noonan has become so "sick of this butchering" that he can no longer stand to witness or contemplate the violence he has helped to become epidemic in Personville. Already a broken man, Noonan goes to the peace conference at the Willssons' and the Op sacrifices him to his enemies. Ending more pathetic than evil, Noonan is killed offstage in the chapter after that.

THE AXIS OF EVIL

If with Chief Noonan Hammett developed a fairly full sketch of the effects of graft and corruption on an individual, few aspects of *The Red*

Harvest show Hammett's inexperience as a novelist as plainly as the depiction and deployment of the other men who have poisoned Personville.

In setting the scene in the first chapter of the novel Hammett ends Bill Quint's synopsis of the history of Personville with a catalogue of the principal bad men in the burg: there is the bootlegger Pete the Finn (probably "the strongest of them"); pawnbroker, loan shark, and bail bondsman Lew Yard; gambler Max Thayler; and fatso Noonan who "just about helps Elihu run his city" (8). So the quintet of Pete the Finn, Lew Yard, Whisper Thayler, Noonan, and Elihu stands at the beginning of the novel as the Op's prospective opposition. Only this was more than Hammett could handle. Two of the principal bad guys shrink into negligible characters. Pete the Finn ("probably the strongest") appears in only two late chapters (chapters 19 and 25) where Hammett describes him ("The bootlegger was a big-boned man of fifty with a completely bald head. His forehead was small, his jaws enormous — wide, heavy, bulging with muscle" [97]), gives him a skimpy nine lines of dialogue, and then kills him off. Lew Yard suffers a more ignominious fate. He is mentioned less frequently than the Finn and his murder is not even shown, it's reported. Granted, Whisper and Elihu Willsson play significant roles in the book, but, oddly enough, even though Hammett had bad guys aplenty at the beginning of *The Red Harvest*, he neglected to do much with two of them and then introduced a new bad guy, Reno, and made him the most significant character in the last third of the book.

Among the bad guys, throughout the novel Hammett uses Elihu Willsson as the most prominent continuing character. Commentators like to make a lot out of this and see the portrait of Elihu as precursor of the political views Hammett voiced later in his life. Maybe it was, but maybe it was also Hammett's use of a character he had in stock — the arrogant millionaire. In "Crooked Souls" Hammett invented a despicable rich guy in war profiteer Harvey Gatewood. While the source of it is clearly tainted, in the early Op story Gatewood's defining fault isn't exactly his money, it's his high-handed and imperious manner, and his belief that he can and should control everything, a bias in the story that is undermined by the headstrong actions of his daughter. Gatewood became the base for the portrait of Elihu Willsson in *The Red Harvest*. On top of that Hammett added semi-senility, a lack of morality, cash-fueled political muscle, and the brand of deviousness and independence available only to the affluent. In his fiction up to and even beyond *The Red Harvest*, however, Hammett was not universally opposed to rich people. In "The Girl with the Silver Eyes," for instance, Roy Axford, a millionaire "who had his finger in at least half of the big business enterprises on the Pacific Coast" (150), receives sympathetic treatment. And even though their son is goofy, the wealthy Collinsons in *The Dain Curse* are an understanding and generous bunch. During the period when he began writing novels, Hammett, one might recall, had thrown himself into his job of promoting Samuels Jewelry, hardly the meeting place of the proletariat.

Hammett introduces Elihu in a chapter entitled "The Czar of Personville"—the only other times he refers to things Russian are in "Laughing Masks" and "The Gutting of Couffignal" where Russian aristocrats are portrayed as arrogant, cruel, and brutal to their servants. Because it wasn't his inclination, there's no scene setting to contrast Elihu's wealth and power with the tawdriness and squalor of the town he controls, but Hammett gave him an atypically detailed physical description when he enters the story. In it he stresses the roundness of Elihu's head ("the old man's head was small and almost perfectly round"), the predatory look in his eyes (hidden behind bushy brows but with the potential to "jump out and grab something"), and the old man's remaining menace suggested by his "meaty shoulders," and the Op's summary comment that "he wasn't the sort of man whose pocket you'd pick unless you had a lot of confidence in your fingers" (10). Besides the emphasis on age (which continues every time Hammett describes him), this description draws attention to a combination of physical power, sickness, and the geometric anomaly of his almost perfectly round head—a fact that may (or may not) connect with the second of the Op's laudanum-induced dreams later in *The Red Harvest*. The next most salient fact about him is that Elihu is an irascible old man and when the Op describes his conversations with him he consistently notes that Elihu "yells" or "bellows" or "shouts." He is always belligerent and confrontational in his approaches to relationships that are by implication connected to wealth and power and the tenuous hold Elihu has on them at the beginning of the novel. Elihu's hectoring has an impact on the Op, and the way he responds to the old man's lack of manners and abuse helps to establish an attitude and tone very different from that of the early Op stories. Wise to who and what Elihu Willsson is, the Op has countermoves for the old man's attempts to manipulate him and control his actions. While during his second meeting with Elihu, the Op specifically realizes that he is dealing with a sick and frightened old man who is trying—just as Dan Rolff tries—to maintain his dignity as a man, nonetheless he also realizes that Elihu—loudmouth, braggart, and bully—is going to win in the end. Thus, in their last encounter, the Op tells Elihu that now that he has solved all of the town's problems "you'll have your city back, all nice and clean and ready to go to the dogs again" (134).

While Elihu Willsson and what he stands for serves as a subtheme to which Hammett returns periodically throughout *The Red Harvest*, the Op focuses successively on two other bad guys in the novel: Whisper and Reno. Max "Whisper" Thayler gets the first half of the book. Part of Hammett's conception of Thayler has more than a bit of the cinematic about it — a narrative quality he found praiseworthy in his early review of Hergesheimer's novel in 1924. Hammett repeatedly emphasizes the character's appearance: for example, "he looked like something displaying suits in a clothing store window" (71). And, of course, there's Whisper's voice. Both of these elements tend toward cinema as opposed to narrative. Underlying both the character's dress and his speech, however, resides Whisper's essential toughness. He has, the Op tells readers, a "thin hard mouth" (36), and "a pretty face ... yellow and tough as oak" (53). And when he is arrested for Tim Noonan's murder, "Whisper stood up under all they could give him. He would talk to his lawyer, he said, and to nobody else" (73). In his action, too, Hammett focuses on Whisper's decisive and dispassionate nature. The murder in the ring of Ike Bush for not keeping his commitment to throw the prizefight and Whisper's shooting one of his own men for menacing Dinah Brand demonstrate for Hammett an attitude that is both frightening but perhaps awesomely admirable.

Portraying Whisper as hard and tough — as opposed to the sinister but fumbling chief of police and the no-shows Lew Yard and Pete the Finn — is, no doubt, the reason that Hammett centered a good bit of the first half of the novel on him. The Op uses him first as a suspect in Donald Willsson's death and then as a suspect in Tim Noonan's murder. Starting with the smartest and toughest opponent shows something about the hero and it also serves as an example of the Op's situational manipulation of people and events in Personville in that in the first case he clears Whisper of the murder and in the second case he frames him for a murder the Op knows he did not commit. From the point of view of the bad people in Personville, the Op is unpredictable. And that's good.

Whisper plays a significant role in the first part of *The Red Harvest*, but after the midpoint Reno Starkey takes over. And the Op has a harder time with Reno than he does with Whisper. Reno enters the novel for the first time when Dinah Brand wants to go out for a good time in chapter 17. The Op and Dinah Brand encounter him as he escapes from people shooting at him at The Silver Arrow roadhouse. Reno is a far cry from the dapper and handsome Whisper; the Op describes him as having a humorless, stolid horse face. While readers don't know it at the time, Reno is one of the fruits of the Op's stirring things up in Personville. In the "Peace Conference" chapter Hammett later reveals that Reno was one of Lew Yard's gang who has taken advantage of the chaos and gone off on his own: "Reno was Yard's pup, but he didn't mind crossing up the head man" (99). Reno is much more in charge of events than the other bad guys in *The Red Harvest*. After having been saved by the Op and Dinah Brand from the contretemps at the Silver Arrow, Reno strands them in the boondocks where they run the risk of being shot by his enemies. Reno is the one to whom the Op turns when he needs an alibi for the time of Dinah Brand's murder, and Reno raids Pete the Finn's headquarters where he "called him [Pete] a lousy fish-eater and shot him four times in the face and body" (130). Reno, the Op learns in the last few pages of the novel, also killed Dinah Brand — a fact that the Op does not uncover with the same alacrity that he demonstrates in solving the murders of Donald Willsson and Tim Noonan. Hammett draws Reno as a much more thorough thug than Whisper or the other gangsters in the novel. Nonetheless, the end of the novel highlights Reno's courage:

> He meant to die as he had lived, inside the same tough shell. Talking could be torture, but he wouldn't stop on that account, not while anyone was there to see him. He was Reno Starkey who could take anything the world had without batting an eye, and he would play it that way to the end [141].

In addition to Noonan, Whisper, and Reno, Hammett gives passing notice to an assortment of minor gangsters during the course of the novel. There are clots of hangers-on attached to both Whisper and Reno. Of Reno's gang Hammett says little, other than that one of them who throws fire bombs at Pete the Finn's headquarters is named "Fat." At Whisper's headquarters, however, early in the novel, Hammett provides a snapshot of his followers. Mostly they're kids: most of Whisper's gang are "no more than twenty" and the Op describes them as boys, except for a chinless man of 30. Hammett describes the young men as "angular." They're all bored. This is the same group that appears at Dinah Brand's house after the Op has bamboozled Whisper over the fixed prizefight. The chinless hood is Jerry, Whisper's second in command who is killed by Reno in the bank robbery later in the novel. Brief though it may be, the description emphasizes idleness, youth, and, with Jerry, physical defects. The connection between youth and gangland "soldiers" comes in again when Pete the Finn announces that "I got one army of young fellows that know what to do on any end of a gun" (100). The motif of physical defects, moreover, comes up with all of the bad people in the novel: Noonan is fat, Thayler has something wrong with his throat, Jerry has no chin, Reno has a horse face, Pete the Finn has enormous jaws, and MacSwain has "bowed legs and a long sharp jaw, like a hog's" (46). It's tempting, here, to guess that Hammett is echoing Lombroso who included unusual jaws as one of the atavistic physical attributes of born criminals.

While there may be a bit of Lombroso in some of Hammett's portraits of criminals, he does present a more complex set of motivations for
criminal behavior with MacSwain, the perpetrator of the second murder
mystery in *The Red Harvest*. The first interpretation of MacSwain's character comes from Dinah Brand who links him securely to the "poisonville"
theme of the novel when she says that becoming a policeman corrupted
him: "He had been a pretty good guy, straight as ace-deuce-trey-four-five,
till he got on the force. Then he went the way of the rest of them" (59).

Later, however, when confessing to the Op, MacSwain brings back
the motivations Hammett had used in his sex stories when he attributes
his descent into criminality not to his being a cop but to the defects of
and failure of his marriage. Thus, when he confesses to the Op, MacSwain
talks about his wife's insatiable demands on him and his difficulty in meeting them ("Mostly what she wanted was tough on me") and how the pressures of his marriage and then his wife's abandonment of him changed him
("You can ask anybody if I wasn't a good guy before that" [75]). Just as in
his sex stories this inserted account of MacSwain's marriage shows disaster attending infidelity — after she has run off, Tim Noonan rejects Mac
Swain's wife who is then killed in a (probably purposeful) car accident and
the abandoned husband becomes a murderer. Hammett's examination of
MacSwain's motivation reiterates in an even more tawdry fashion the motivation behind the first murder in the book, committed by a passionately
romantic man who has been spurned by a cynical and mercurial woman.
While the stories of Albury's and MacSwain's passion comprise episodes
in *The Red Harvest*, Hammett also threads mini-portraits of Dan Rolff's
passion for Dinah Brand — of him as frustrated, betrayed, hopeless, and
pathetic — as a minor theme throughout the novel.

All told, there are an awful lot of bad people in *The Red Harvest* and,
as noted before, no examples of good people — those for whom the town
needs to be cleaned up. With the wholly corrupt town, the portrayal of
the Old Man as a distant and demanding authority, and the Op's flight from
Personville at the end of the action, the novel echoes the Sodom and
Gomorrah theme Hammett had used in "Nightmare Town." But in addition to showing the extirpation of evil it also has some things to say about
the nature of bad men. One of them, of course, is the thesis that evil is
self-destructive. In the western story the shoot-out between the hero and
villain marks the climax of the struggle between good and evil, but even
though there are echoes of the western in *The Red Harvest*, this doesn't
happen. While there is violence aplenty in the book, it does not end in a

shoot-out between the sheriff and the black hat villain: during the course of the novel the hero is forced to kill only two very minor, even incidental, bad guys (Big Nick in chapter 6 and the "red faced man" in chapter 13). The bad men in the novel eliminate one another. Indeed, the last scene of the book focuses on the results of the Whisper-Reno feud rather than the actions of an agent of justice. As noted above, Hammett also marks all of the bad men with physical defects—obesity, speech impediments, unusual facial features. In addition to this, *in extremis* some of the villains of the piece are downright pathetic. The narrative, for instance, shows the disintegration of Chief Noonan from backslapping prince of the city to broken man shambling off to his own death. In spite of this, the paradox of the novel lies in the fact that while Personville is run by corrupt men whose motives boil down to greed and power, some of them, nonetheless, provide examples of principled behavior, examples that are at once frightening and admirable. One of these acts is when Whisper shoots one of his own men for not following orders and for menacing Dinah Brand. The other, more important, example is the depiction of Reno's stoicism during his death throes, a scene that gains power because of its contrast with Hammett's earlier portrait of Myrtle Jennison's anguished, gruesome, and pathetic death in the hospital. Both Whisper and Reno present examples of phyrric chivalry and stoicism that form part of the code of the hardboiled hero.

Something Old, Something New

When Hammett began to write the serial that became *The Red Harvest* he had written 24 stories featuring the Continental Op. Over the course of those stories the Op changes, but the changes are subtle and gradual. To be sure, in *The Red Harvest* Hammett makes the Op the same short, fat, and middle-aged man he always was (or wasn't), but, as in the short stories, he mentions this only sporadically and, as seen in the earlier pieces, it signifies little more than the writer's distancing his hero from the conventional hero of contemporary detective stories. In the novel, however, the Op is more isolated and confrontational than he had been in the short stories. In the early Op stories one of Hammett's purposes was to portray the private (or agency) detective in a more accurate manner than the other detectives in popular fiction. One of the ways he did this was to supply readers with advice about how to be a detective—for example, how to shadow suspects, how to trace baggage, etc. As the Op stories continued, however, Hammett came to rely less and less on this kind of material and by the time of *The Red Harvest* the "how to be a detective" advice mostly disappeared from the Op's character. In terms of the standard crime problems in *The Red Harvest* (i.e., who killed Donald Willsson and Tim Noonan) Hammett shifts the Op's problem solving from an emphasis on process to an emphasis on the detective's brilliance. Thus, before the Op reveals the culprit in these crimes he teases characters (and readers) with announcements that he knows who the murderers are. This is different. The same kind of change holds true for the nature of the stories themselves: the earliest Op stories concentrate on largely domestic murder crime puzzles while the later ones move more and more into the world of organized crime or at least professional criminals. Because of this Hammett came to place increased emphasis on action as opposed to method as a means of solving problems. Additionally, the early Op stories make a point of showing the detective's working relationship with his agency colleagues and also with the police. In them, therefore, characters like Dick Foley, the Old Man, O'Gar, and Pat Reedy play meaningful roles in the Op's world. If not partners, he has colleagues with whom he shares a convivial relationship in his battle against crime. As seen above, however, all of this disappears in *The Red Harvest*. The Op's relationship to the Continental Detective Agency changes entirely in the novel, and the police in Personville present a radical departure from the cops in San Francisco as well as the small communities where the Op's employment had taken him in the short stories. Each one of these developments, then, alters the Op's relationship with his world as well as his relationship with his readers.

There are also several elements of the Op's character that are implicit in the short stories that become manifest in *The Red Harvest*. Perhaps the most prominent of these is that the novel is awash in booze. While Hammett mentions the Op drinking occasionally in the stories, in *The Red Harvest* he magnifies this a thousandfold. In the novel there are very few scenes during which the Op does not have at least a mild buzz on. He drinks by himself and he drinks with other people. Most notably, during every visit to Dinah Brand's house they break out the gin and lemons. And sitting around drinking inevitably leads to verbal sparring. Consequently another underdeveloped element in the short stories that Hammett magnifies in *The Red Harvest* was the wisecrack.

The wisecrack plays a significant role in the history of the development of the hard-boiled hero. It's one of the things that Raymond Chandler would later capitalize on. As noted earlier, the wisecrack serves several purposes: it demonstrates the speaker's linguistic agility, it ratifies the bond between individuals (usually men) in an exclusive and intimate group, and it acts as a challenge to authority. In all of its ramifications, the wisecrack is about attitude. In the early Op stories Hammett uses the wisecrack sparingly. On those occasions when the Op or someone else (usually O'Gar) cracks wise, Hammett uses the witticism for the first two purposes—to show facile language use and to illuminate the casually intimate relationship between the characters. In *The Red Harvest* this changes. For one thing, Hammett put into the novel a lot more wisecracks and expanded their uses. The Op cracks wise with Bill Quint in the opening scenes of the novel, and he and Mickey Linehan trade wry comments in the second half. It's a guy thing—an aspect of self-identification and of male bonding. But the wisecrack in *The Red Harvest* functions in new ways for Hammett. First of all, while in the Op stories the hero inevitably keeps his opinions to himself when confronted by difficult clients, in *The Red Harvest* the Op takes off the gloves with Elihu Willsson. During his first interview with the Czar of Poisonville the Op tells Elihu, "Don't be a chump," and includes both sarcasm and a wisecrack in response to the old man's bellowing when he says, "And if you don't yell maybe I'll be able to hear you anyway. My deafness is a lot better since I've been eating yeast" (11). Here, of course, the challenge to authority works as one of the ingredients both of the hero's bravado and of his integrity. In addition to the wisecrack as challenge, looking forward to *The Thin Man*, in *The Red Harvest* Hammett introduces trading wisecracks as an aspect of a particular kind of male-female relationship. The verbal give and take in the novel that goes on between the Op and Dinah Brand helps to delineate her character and their relationship. It may not quite be courtship, but it demonstrates that, like the Op, Dinah Brand is quick on the uptake, frank, and that verbally at least she is in the same league as the Op.

The entire matter of the Op's relationship with Dinah Brand, in fact, is something new. In the pre–*Red Harvest* stories Hammett makes sexuality an issue in several places—most notably in "The Girl with the Silver Eyes," "The Whosis Kid," and "The Gutting of Couffignal." Each of these stories revolves about organized crime and professional criminals. The women in these stories use the lure and promise of sex in attempts to influence the Op's actions—to divert him from his purpose as a detective. Jeanne Delano and the Russian princess both seek to buy their freedom with the promise of their bodies, and the woman in "The Whosis Kid" clings to the Op only because he offers protection from her gangster friends. In all examples the women possess exotic beauty and act as the aggressors. In *The Red Harvest*, some things about Dinah Brand are different. First of all, Dinah Brand is no exotic beauty. She is big and she's slovenly: "Dinah Brand opened the door for me. Her big ripe mouth was rouged evenly this evening, but her brown hair still needed trimming, was parted haphazardly, and there were spots down the front of her orange silk dress" (45).

Every time the Op meets her he highlights something wrong with her appearance. She is also loud, outspoken, cynical, and forthrightly mercenary. As the Albury subplot demonstrates, she maintains relationships only as long as her companion is able to pay his own and her own way. Hammett emphasizes Dinah Brand's lack of any principles beyond self-aggrandizement through the inserted comments of her live-in companion, Dan Rolff. While she is marginally attached to and strangely protective of Rolff, the educated consumptive's impotent upbraiding of her actions as disreputable, dishonorable, and "utterly filthy" have no effect upon her. Dinah Brand's pursuit of the Op, then, has nothing to do with romance or sex or domesticity: she maintains their relationship because she sees the Op and the Continental Detective Agency as a source of money. Like the miscellaneous gangsters in the novel and like old Elihu, her allegiance goes to those she perceives to be winners in the power struggles of Personville. Also, in an odd inversion, she becomes the suitor and the Op plays the role of the lover who enjoys the game of promising and then coyly withholding favors. As noted above, she is a new version of the honesty represented in the slatternly and openly commercial bar girl from Hammett's early story "Holiday." She also reflects the refinement of that story's theme that appears in "The Whosis Kid" when the Op says,

> I am neither young enough nor old enough to get feverish over every woman who doesn't make me think being blind isn't so bad. I'm at that middle point around forty where a man puts other feminine qualities— amiability, for one — above beauty on his list [329].

In *The Red Harvest* that amiability manifests itself not in the pursuit of a relationship but in the pleasures of witty verbal combat enhanced by the effects of constant semi-inebriation.

Perhaps the most central new element in the Op's character in *The Red Harvest* is his response to violence. It is often remarked that *The Red Harvest* chronicles a remarkable amount of violence — Hammett himself calls attention to this with devices like entitling a chapter "The Seventeenth Murder." Blanche Knopf and editor Harry C. Block both felt that the novel contained too much mayhem, and Block worked to tone it down as he edited the *Black Mask* serial into the Knopf publication (Layman 91). In some ways the increased violence in *The Red Harvest* is a natural development of the short stories, which include more shooting and fistfights as the series progresses. It should be noted, however, that while the plot of *The Red Harvest* moves from murder to murder, a significant portion of the violence in the novel happens offstage. The murders of Donald Willsson and Tim Noonan; the killing of Jerry, Lew Yard, and Noonan in the middle of the book; and the action leading to the deaths of Whisper, Reno, and Dan Rolff at the end of the book all occur away from the readers' view. Significantly, the Op does not directly participate in much of the violence in the novel: he commits only two of the multitude of killings in the book and these two— policeman Nick and Whisper's henchman — happen early in the novel and are clearly acts of self-defense. Much more often the Op acts as a witness to acts of wholesale and wanton slaughter like the raid on the bootlegger's roadhouse, and Reno's gang's strike on Pete the Finn's headquarters. Just as in a number of earlier stories like "The Scorched Face," "Dead Yellow Women," and "The Big Knock Over," in *The Red Harvest* Hammett focuses on the brawl rather than gunplay to demonstrate the Op's toughness and to distinguish him from the gentleman detective of conventional mystery fiction. This occurs, to some extent, in the tussle with MacSwain, but more pointedly in the melee at Dinah Brand's house in chapter 13 where the Op punches, kicks, head butts, and thinks about biting Jerry when his opponent collapses. As in the short stories, then, the kind of work the Op does here is not for gentlemen. The Op fights dirty because in his world it is the only way to survive. It is not, then, the violence in the novel, per se, that makes Op's character different in *The Red Harvest*. It's the way that he responds to the violence that makes his character different from the hero of the short stories.

THE FRUIT OF THE POISONED TREE

One of the central themes of *The Red Harvest* lies in the Op's motives for being in Personville and for doing what he does. Throughout the course of the novel these change. At the beginning of *The Red Harvest* the Op arrives in Personville to undertake an unspecified job for Donald Willsson — this, no doubt, was to involve the exposure of graft and corruption in the town to be published in Willsson's newspaper. In the context of America in the 1920s, revelations about civic graft and corruption were a usual part of newspapers' missions and it was not unheard-of to have private detectives undertake investigative work for them. In *The Red Harvest*, however, since Willsson is murdered in the first chapter of the book Willsson's intentions are only implicit. Later in the novel, in fact, whether Donald Willsson would have published facts that indicted his father is open to question. At any rate, Willsson's murder changes things and in his first interview with old Elihu, the Op makes no mention of his original job and changes his mission to uncovering Donald Willsson's murder and doing it right. When Elihu begins his rant about his daughter-in-law's character and presumptive guilt, the Op reminds him that accusations and arrests need to be based on evidence. He then broadens out the list of suspects for Donald's murder to include Elihu's political friends and enemies: "the other angle has got to be looked into too— the political end" (12). Overlooked here is the fact that the Op is totally wrong — politics, reform or otherwise, had nothing to do with Willsson's murder — and the Op's initial insertion of himself into the civic well-being of Personville is either gratuitous or based on the detective's honoring the intent of the dead man's abortive contract with the agency, even though Hammett never specifies the terms of that contract. But Hammett does nothing with these implications. Nevertheless, in the matter of looking into Donald Willsson's murder the Op does stress the importance of evidence and legitimate, legal action.

In chapter 5 Hammett finally puts the cleansing of Personville on a legitimate footing for the first time. Here, moreover, in his answer to Elihu's ranting, the Op punctures his hyperbole and overblown rhetoric and uses hardheaded, business terms to describe his prospective role in Personville's affairs: the Op talks about the possibility of taking on the Personville job as long as it's appropriate ("in my line"), fairly honest, and fairly compensated. Just as he had confronted Elihu with the need to base accusations on evidence in the matter of his son's murder, shortly after this exchange the Op makes it clear that the arrangement with the Continental Agency and himself will be based upon principles (presumably those of law and justice) rather than upon persons. Once more there are commercial terms as well as the Op's insistence that whatever he does in the town must be exempt from politics, thereby underlining his intent to be objective, fair, and evenhanded.

Three chapters later, however, the Op's attitude changes. In chapter 8 he no longer talks about his role in Personville being a contractual one or one simply based on law, objectivity or justice. What happens in Personville now carries with it for the Op both the personal satisfaction of revenge and the gratification of fun and games; as Elihu did in his earlier outburst, the Op "gets poetic" with the prospect of using Elihu's money to get back at everyone who had been making his life difficult in Personville: "I'm going to use it opening up Poisonville from Adam's apple to ankles" (43).

The next time the Op speaks of his purpose in Personville, however, he returns to talking about it in terms of evidence and legal processes. When he explains his methods to Dinah Brand he talks about running an ad in the paper ("Crime Wanted — Male or Female") and rolls out his notion about the inevitability of the corruption of Personville collapsing upon itself. Nonetheless, during this conversation the Op returns to talking about legal process and about finding and using evidence. Further, he continues to speak of Elihu as "my client" and emphasizes his business relationship with affairs in Personville, and "a job or two I can hang on them" brings back the notions of evidence and law that the Op stressed in his first interview with Elihu Willsson.

Strangely, when the two other Continental operatives, Dick Foley and Mickey Linehan, arrive in the middle of *The Red Harvest* to help him, the Op makes no mention of searching for evidence or indictable crimes. Instead he explains his actions in Personville as being entirely situational and implicitly illegal: "It's right enough for the Agency to have rules and regulations, but when you're out on a job you've got to do it the best way you can" (78). Here the Op returns to using commercial language to describe what he is doing in Personville, but from that point on the notion of legality goes out the window.

As opposed to being a search for evidence to be used in the cleansing of the town or fun and games or pragmatism, in one of the most powerful passages in the novel the Op speaks of his role in Personville with the consciousness of having abandoned legitimate, legal, and humane tactics and having been poisoned. The Op acknowledges that he could have had Elihu's support and could have solved Personville's problems legally, but seeing the gangsters kill one another off is "more satisfying." And that satisfaction has to do with a growing attraction to violence, violence that has taken over his consciousness so that he has come to view common household items— a bit of wire, a cigarette lighter, an ice pick — as potential murder weapons. The passage ends with the Op's acknowledgment that he has become "blood simple" and the cause for this is "this damned town.... It's poisoned me" (104).

This passage is the culmination of the "poisonville" theme of the novel — the corrosive effects of a corrupt environment upon all who participate in it. The Op's purpose turns from a legitimate enterprise based on law and objectivity into a violent, cruel, personal vendetta. During the course of the novel the Op does not simply stir things up so that evil destroys itself, he consciously and sometimes gleefully sets out to ruin people — principally Whisper and Noonan. In doing this, the hero, by losing his better self, has the potential to become a villain. What saves him is the Op's awareness of and self-disgust for what he sees happening to himself. To make this point, Hammett inserts the central recognition of the Op's descent into personal chaos in the middle of his acknowledgement that he has been poisoned by "poisonville":

> I ... played with them like you'd play trout; and got just as much
> fun out of it. I looked at Noonan and knew he hadn't a chance in

a thousand of living another day because of what I had done to him, and I laughed, and felt warm and happy inside. That's not me [104].

After this speech, suspected of Dinah Brand's murder, the Op continues to be a witness to the lawlessness and violence in the town, but he is no longer in a position to manipulate people or events. And in the end there is no atonement: the Op just leaves.

INNER LIFE

One of the things that the novel form of *The Red Harvest* enabled Hammett to do was to provide glimpses into the Op's inner life. It is the whole point of the "poisonville" theme. Linked with the tension in the novel between impersonal, legal acts and personal, extralegal acts, moreover, Hammett developed other facets of the Op's inner life. Indeed, the increasing isolation of the Op in the novel — his alienation from the Continental Agency and its operatives along with the absence of the kinds of policemen he had worked with in all of the earlier cases— brings with it a new emphasis on frustration and exhaustion. Hammett also includes demonstrations of the Op's sensitivity toward others early in the novel as a contrast to his cynical manipulation of Whisper and Noonan and the "blood simple" side of the Op that comes out in the last half of the book. One such occasion is the Op's apology to Albury after his arrest for the murder of Donald Willsson. The Op tells readers that "on the way down to the City Hall with the boy and the gun I apologized for the village cut-up stuff I had put in the early part of the shake-down" (41). The Op acknowledges the necessity for cruelty in the execution of his job but also shows sympathy and compassionate understanding for a man undone by human frailty. Something similar occurs in the Op's treatment of Dan Rolff where the Op explains that he attacked Rolff in order to give back a degree of self-respect to a hopeless romantic and chronically ill man trapped in a bizarre relationship in a corrupt and cynical world.

Hammett also contrives to bring the Op into contact with mortality in several places in *The Red Harvest*. As opposed to the multitude of casual or offstage murders, Hammett includes two affecting, detailed encounters with death. The first is the scene with the dying Myrtle Jennison in the hospital, an incident in which Hammett stresses gruesome details. It's bad enough that disease has ravaged Myrtle Jennison's body, making it swollen and loathsome, but worse than that is her hysteria, which goes from "sniggering" when she throws the bedclothes off to show the Op her disease-ravaged body to despair when she tells the Op, as he leaves, that "it's hell to die ugly as this" (62). While Hammett withholds any response from the Op to this grotesque spectacle, he does provide a brief comment from the Op on Reno's death. While, as seen above, the Op's narration expresses admiration for the dying man's stoicism, later, on the last page of the novel, he notes with understatement that "sitting there listening to and watching him talk himself to death wasn't pleasant" (142).

While understatement characterizes the Op's responses to mortality, perhaps the most singular look into the Op's inner life in *The Red Harvest* comes in the two laudanum-induced dreams Hammett invents for him in chapter 21. The first of them begins with a tantalizing autobiographical fragment: "I dreamed I was sitting on a bench, in Baltimore, facing the tumbling fountain in Harlem Park" (107). Baltimore's Harlem Park, bounded on the south by Edmondson Avenue (also mentioned in the dream), is located at the beginning of Stricker Street, the location of Hammett's boyhood home. The first dream also brings with it the temptation to see the catalogue of cities and streets (Gay Street and Mount Royal Avenue in Baltimore; Colfax Avenue in Denver; Aetna Road and St. Clair Avenue in Cleveland) as evidence of Hammett's peripatetic life as a Pinkerton operative. In the dream itself a veiled woman "[the Op] knew well" but had "suddenly forgotten" appears, tells him something he cannot hear, abandons him to run after fire engines, and, after an exhausting search across the country, meets him in the Rocky Mount, North Carolina, train station and begins kissing him. In the second dream, the dreamer, intent on killing "a man I hated," undertakes a lengthy and exhausting pursuit of the enemy, "a small brown man who wore an immense sombrero," through the streets of a strange city (108). With a knife in his hand, the dreamer even chases him by running on the heads and shoulders of a crowd of people. The dream ends when the dreamer follows his enemy to the top of a tall building where the man jumps off the edge. Grabbing him by his head, the sombrero comes off and the dreamer finds that he is grasping a "smooth hard round head no larger than an egg" (108). At the end of the dream the dreamer and his opponent fall off the building together.

Marling (54) suggests that on one level the two dreams represent the Op's "coked up" version of the events leading up to Dinah Brand's murder with the brown man's egg head in the second dream representing the handle of the ice pick in Dinah Brand's chest. Maybe or maybe not. Not much in the first dream seems to have any connection with the immediate events surrounding Dinah Brand's murder and the only connection with reality in the second dream rests on the unsupportable assumption that all ice picks have round handles. If it's not events that the dreams recount, perhaps it's people. It is difficult, however, to consistently and definitively attach people in *The Red Harvest* to people in the Op's dream. A case can be made, for instance, for Elihu Willsson as the sombrero man the Op cannot catch and who involves him in mutual destruction: Hammett, after all, has the Op describe Elihu's head as "small and almost perfectly round." In the case of a veiled woman, the only viable female in the novel is Dinah Brand. If the veiled dream woman is Dinah Brand, then the Op has completely transformed her from an excessively forthcoming and concrete being into a mystery woman whose secrets are withheld. It's not easy to make these cases, but perhaps that was the reason that Hammett inserted the Op's passage about his poisoned imagination into the scene before the dreams. Both of the Op's dreams are basically about frustration; in the first it comes from the dreamer's inability to learn the identity of the veiled woman and, especially, what she has to say to him; in the second it comes from the dreamer's inability to capture and kill an enemy who transforms when he finds him. Both dreams center on attenuated pursuit ("I walked almost as far as in the first dream, but it was always in the same strange city" [108]), and both dreams end in failure. The unknown identities of the second parties are also something the dreams have in common. Even though readers can suggest identities for them from among the characters in the novel, in the first the veiled woman is basically someone the dreamer should know but cannot remember, and in the second the unnamed and unspecified antagonist is disguised and, in the end, transforms himself. Thus, while the two dreams may contain representations of people in the novel, the most apparent fact that they reveal is the frustration and exhaustion of the searcher. And this corresponds to one of the major motifs linked to the Op — his weariness and isolation.

SOME CONCLUSIONS

There are a lot of things in *The Red Harvest* that demonstrate Hammett's inexperience as a novelist. For one thing, he introduces too many characters and then doesn't know what to do with them. The characters of Lew Yard and Pete the Finn stand witness to this. This extends to the whole purpose of the Op's job in Personville. The scenes of the labor unrest and the evil of the copper magnates introduced in the beginning of the novel disappear almost immediately. Likewise during most of the novel Hammett pays so much attention to police corruption and Chief Noonan that it seems as if he doesn't know what to do with the other three bad men identified as the centers of corruption in the town. Indeed, Hammett never acknowledges that the real corruption of the town doesn't come from capitalists or bootleggers or gamblers or even from crooked politicians alone but from the lack of value placed upon human life. The novel does almost nothing with setting. While it starts off with a snapshot of the town, setting matters very little afterward.

The Red Harvest has two principal strengths: the character of the Continental Op and its frenetic pacing. In it Hammett was able to provide a fuller portrait of the hero he invented in 1923 and to adjust that character to accommodate changes in his own and other writers' detective fiction. The fuller portrait of the Op, moreover, made the Op a somewhat different character from the one portrayed in the 24 short stories. There are paradoxes. The new Op is both more forthright and more manipulative than in the early works: he often says what's on his mind but he also uses people for what are essentially his own ends. The new Op is both an agent of justice and order and a renegade vigilante pursuing private justice. He begins as one who can control events and ends in some ways as the victim of those events. In the pursuit of justice the Op becomes tainted by the epidemic of violence that is so tied to the environment in which he must do his job. He realizes that his character has been warped and, in the end, can do no more about this than leave before peace and order have been restored. Most notably, unlike the early stories, the Op of The Red Harvest is a lone hero increasingly isolated from everyone, even from well-intentioned people. In all of this the Op is a far more complex and interesting character than he was in the short stories.

The Dain Curse

Like The Red Harvest, The Dain Curse appeared first as a four-part serial in Black Mask: "Black Lives" (November 1928), "The Hollow Temple" (December 1928), "Black Honeymoon" (January 1929), and "Black Riddle" (February 1929). In The Red Harvest, it doesn't make a whole lot of difference who did what to whom. Everyone in the novel, even the Op, is guilty of something. In The Dain Curse, though, it does make a difference because it is a very different kind of fiction than anything Hammett had tried before. Any number of things caused this change — the advent and popularity of "proper" detective fiction on the East Coast and from Britain, Hammett's role as a critic for The Saturday Review of Literature, his newfound popularity and semiprosperity, and his reevaluation of the character and themes that had sustained him since the publication of "Arson Plus" in 1923.

"MR. CONTINENTAL"

While *The Red Harvest* develops the Op as the lone wolf, a vigilante detective fueled by a sense of mission as well as by his own vindictiveness, in *The Dain Curse* Hammett brought him back into the fold of the agency. Mickey Linehan, in fact, calls him "Mr. Continental" (256). Indeed, in *The Dain Curse*, Hammett introduced more named Continental employees than in his earlier fictions. Continuing his buildup from *The Red Harvest*, Mickey Linehan of the cast of Continental ops appears most often and has the most dialogue in *The Dain Curse*. The majority of Linehan's dialogue, however, is characterized by "sour cracks" exchanged with or directed toward the Op (e.g., "I ought to tell her what happened to that poor girl up in Personville that got so she thought she could trust you" [263]) and the Op's narrative usually makes snide remarks about Linehan's appearance ("Mickey Linehan was leaning his lop-sided bulk against a stone wall" [168]). In addition to this less than complimentary presentation of Linehan, Hammett also describes one of his new ops, MacMan, as unimaginative and stolid, but utterly dependable.

Most of the other agency detectives receive even less attention than Linehan and MacMan. In addition to Linehan, Hammett also brought back Dick Foley from the earlier stories but gave him no dialogue or significant action aside from his following suspects offstage and writing reports at the office. Even more briefly he mentions operatives Al Mason ("slim, dark, sleek" [163]), and (no first name given) operative Drake. Apparently forgetting that he had named the agency's night man Fiske in the earlier Op stories, Hammett notes in *The Dain Curse* that the Op talks on the telephone to Field, "the agency night-man" (243). In addition to these characters, the Op makes brief mentions of the Old Man several times during the course of the novel. As opposed to the remote and demanding role he had played in *The Red Harvest*, here the Old Man functions solely as administrator, assigning jobs and worrying about the Agency's bottom line: "The Old Man said, 'I certainly hope so,' rather coldly, not enthusiastic over having five operatives at work on a job that the supposed client might not want to pay for" (271). Just as there is an expanded cast of Continental ops in *The Dain Curse*, the agency's offices and routines receive fuller treatment in the novel than in the earlier Op fiction. Readers learn that there is a reception room and learn about the operatives' room where the ops hang out "swapping lies." Here, as in the short stories of the late 1920s, the Op has his own office and we learn once more that the agency is not located on the ground floor of its building because people use the building's elevator. Hammett also glances at the fact that the Continental is a national company — inserting a decoded telegram from the New York office — and that it is busy with a wide variety of cases. Thus, between the major installments of the novel, the Op goes "up to the mountains to snoop around for a gold-mine owner who thought his employees were gypping him"(187) and bargains with the ex-wife of a criminal for a photograph of her ex-husband.

The personnel and purpose of the Continental Detective Agency may be mentioned a bit more frequently in *The Dain Curse* than in any of the earlier Op fictions; nonetheless, even though the names are the same, things aren't the same. Most of this has to do with the Op. He functions more like a boss in *The Dain Curse* than ever before. Although technically he has to go through the Old Man for additional resources, the Op of this novel seems far more in charge of the agency's affairs than before. That there is an operatives' room at headquarters and he has his own office gives one sign of this. Another sign is that the Op consistently treats the other Continental employees as subordinates, ordering them around, and, in fact, usually condescending to them. None of the other ops seems worth much in the narrator's view: they may serve the right cause, but Linehan is a wiseguy slob and MacMan is mechanical. The Old Man, while the same character as in the early works, has a minimal role. Also, while Hammett returned to dropping an occasional bit of practical advice to readers about how detectives do their jobs, there is far, far less of it than in the earlier works. So, in spite of reviving the agency after having put it on the shelf for *The Red Harvest*, the narrator's (and the readers') attitude is different in *The Dain Curse*. Much of this comes from the fact that Hammett chose a new pattern for the plot of *The Dain Curse* and that new pattern demanded a new confidante.

THE COPS' SWAN SONG

In terms of the way Hammett treated the police, *The Red Harvest* was a pure anomaly: in all of the early works Hammett treats the police with respect and, in fact, in many of the early short stories police officers act as the Op's unofficial partners. It looks like the same thing is going to happen in *The Dain Curse*. In the opening parts of the novel Hammett reintroduces the San Francisco Police Department along with the same personnel he had used in the Op stories preceding *The Red Harvest*. There's Lieutenant Duff, Sergeant O'Gar, Detective Pat Reddy, and Phels, the department fingerprint expert, who goes all the way back to "Sticky Fingers," the second Op story. Hammett even invented a new police expert for *The Dain Curse* in McCracken, "a San Francisco police department bomb-expert" (255). At first the Sergeant O'Gar of *The Dain Curse* seems to match the character Hammett returned to so often in his short stories. The Op describes him as "a burly, stolid man of fifty, who wore wide-brimmed black hats of the movie-sheriff sort. There was a lot of sense in his hard bullet-head, and he was comfortable to work with (153).

This is essentially the same description Hammett used in the short stories with one significant exception: now O'Gar is "stolid." In his first appearance in *The Dain Curse*, however, O'Gar continues to share the same wisecracking relationship with the Op that he had in the pre–*Red Harvest* pieces. Thus, when the Op enters the first murder scene, Hammett puts in this interchange over the victim's body:

> "It's a man," O'Gar said as I put the blankets over him again. "He's dead."
> "What else did somebody tell you?" [153].

But while some things remain the same about O'Gar, in *The Dain Curse* he is a diminished character. First, there is the addition of "stolid" to the description of O'Gar as having "sense" and being an amiable coworker. O'Gar, however, isn't really a coworker in the novel but one who is much more subordinate and subservient to the Op than he had been in the short stories. At the scene of the first murder cited above the police seem to await the Op's arrival and opinions. That is even more the case at the scene of Edgar Leggett's murder. There, even though the cops are on the scene with O'Gar in charge, the Op takes over the whole business, from suggesting that Leggett's letter be read aloud to diagnosing the cause of Leggett's death as murder (in spite of the presence of a physician and two seasoned police detectives) to pinning the murder on Leggett's wife.

If O'Gar diminishes in *The Dain Curse*, Pat Reddy shrinks even more so. A police character who plays a significant role and with whom the Op develops a paternal relationship in "The Scorched Face," here Hammett reduces Reddy to little more than a rookie detective ("a big, jovial young-ster, with almost brains enough to make up for his lack of experience" [154]), and makes him function in the same kind of passive role as O'Gar fills. Finally, if the role of the police is marginal at best in the first two murders in the book, they play no role whatsoever in the windup of the blood-bath at the Temple. Here, Hammett switches immediately from the Op's killing of Joseph to his chewing over the events at dinner with Fitzstephan. About the police in San Francisco, then, they're not as much in charge as they had been in the early Op stories and, ultimately, they don't make any difference to what goes on in *The Dain Curse*.

That the San Francisco cops make no difference to the book is inci-dental — they simply didn't fit in with the kind of novel Hammett was writing but it was comfortable to include them as furniture in the first half of the book. This is not the case in the second half. Hammett purposely intended to make inept law enforcement a subsidiary feature of Gabrielle Leggett's adventures in Quesada. The action moves out of San Francisco into the boonies—"a one-hotel town pasted on the rocky side of a young mountain that sloped into the Pacific Ocean some eighty miles from San Francisco" (217). In his earlier fiction Hammett had generally treated coun-try cops kindly. But the whole machinery of the law in Quesada struggles to reach incompetence. The best of them is deputy sheriff Ben Rolly, des-tined to become like his father — "an amiable, aimless-looking man in shabby clothes" (221). Along with Rolly there's Sheriff Feeney, "fat, florid, and with a lot of brown moustache" (230), Marshal Dick Cotton, "a pompous, unintelligent man in his late forties" (230), and District Attor-ney Vernon, "sharp-featured, aggressive, and hungry for fame" (230). As the novel draws to a close, Marshal Cotton is arrested for killing his wife, Vernon constantly preens for the assembly of newspaper reporters, and throughout they are all clueless and manipulated. Other than con-fusing crime scenes and generally muddying the investigative waters, they play no role in discovering who blew up Fitzstephan or who killed Eric Collinson.

THE REAL WORLD

All of Hammett's Op pieces before *The Dain Curse* center simply on crime and detection. In the short stories there is room for little else and in *The Red Harvest* he created a world preoccupied with crime and crim-inals. Crime and detection, of course, are no less central to *The Dain Curse* than they had been to the earlier works, but instead of concentrating solely on garden-variety domestic crimes or generic gangland criminals, in his second novel Hammett added issues of contemporary interest — spiritu-alism, drug addiction, and criminology — to serve as background and to supply interest for readers, on top of that provided by the detective plot.

Spiritualism was an American preoccupation in the 1920s. It was part of the religious ferment that followed World War I. It was also in the news and had a connection with detective fiction in the person of Arthur Conan Doyle. An avid believer in the spirit world, Doyle published seven books on spiritualism between 1920 and 1929 (*A Public Debate on the Truth of Spiritualism* [1920], *Spiritualism and Rationalism* [1920], *Fairies Photo-graphed* [1921], *The Wanderings of a Spiritualist* [1921], *Psychic Experiences*

[1925], *The History of Spiritualism* [1926], and *What Does Spiritualism Actually Teach and Stand For* [1929]). And Conan Doyle also took to the lecture circuit, speaking in behalf of spiritualism in cities around the world—1923, in fact, saw him on platforms in California. All of this, in itself, was moderately noteworthy, but when Harry Houdini got into the act, spiritualism became even bigger news. A friend of the inventor of the modern detective story, Houdini was emphatically not convinced by Doyle's arguments and demonstrations and saw spiritualists as charlatans and hoaxers. In 1923 Houdini and Doyle traded arguments in letters printed in *The New York Times* and the next year Houdini published two exposés of spiritualists' legerdemain—*A Magician Among the Spirits* (1924), and *Houdini Exposes the Tricks Used by Boston Medium "Margery"* (1924). In 1925 Houdini made debunking spiritualists the basis of his popular show at the New York Hippodrome.

Hammett introduces the topic of spiritualism early in *The Dain Curse* and links it with the Op and Fitzstephan in the same year (1925) and the same place that the Doyle-Houdini letters appeared. Thus, in chapter 3 the Op gives this background:

> I had met him five years before, in New York, where I was digging dirt on a chain of fake mediums.... Fitzstephan was plowing the same field for literary material. We became acquaintances and pooled forces. I got more out of the combination than he did, since he knew the spook racket inside and out [154–5].

While in the first part of the novel (the "Black Lives" installment), Hammett uses bits of material about diamonds and the jewelry business he had picked up while working for Albert Samuels (to whom the book is dedicated), the second installment, "The Hollow Temple," very much relies on spiritualism. Chapters 9 through 11 take place at the Temple of the Holy Grail where the Op experiences some of the chemistry and physics used by fake mediums, and in chapter 12 ("The Unholy Grail") he gives Fitzstephan the lowdown on how cleverly the Temple was rigged to make believers out of its victims—"I'm not the easiest guy in the world to dazzle, I hope, but he had me going" (211). He also illustrates the fervor of believers by telling Fitzstephan about showing one of the Haldorn's faithful, Mrs. Rodman, all of the rigged-up apparatus at the Temple of the Holy Grail and her counterargument that even the images at a Christian cathedral are made of earthly material. Just as Hammett goes beyond the needs of the detective plot here to give a snapshot of the phenomenon of spiritualism, he also provides readers with its local habitations and names. Twice in *The Dain Curse* he notes the connection

between the contemporary interest in spiritualism and California —first
when Eric Collinson tells the Op that the Temple is "another cult.... You
know how they come and go in California" (167), and again when the Op
unravels the Haldorns' plan to set up their spiritualism scam: "They
brought their cult to California because everybody does, and picked San
Francisco because it held less competition than Los Angeles" (209–10).
After setting the place, Hammett names names. Early in the novel
Fitzstephan rattles off the names of spiritualists when he talks about Edgar
Leggett's companions: Marquard, Denbar Curt, and the Haldorns.
Fitzstephan also mentions the standard history of the Rosicrucians, Arthur
Waite's *The Brotherhood of the Rosy Cross* (1924). A bit later in the narra-
tive Eric Collinson alludes to the "Holy Roller" and "House of David"
when speaking of the Temple of the Holy Grail. And in his explanation of
the bogus spiritualists' planning, the Op recites names from the newspapers: "Thinking in that direction meant, pretty soon, thinking about
Aimee, Buchman, Jeddu what's his name, and the other headliners" (208).
Here, Hammett drops the names of some of the leading figures in the fringe
religious movements of the time. Collinson's two references bring in the
Holy Rollers, a group that spoke in tongues and included nudity as an
expression of the Holy Spirit, and the House of David (the Israelite House
of David, Church of New Eve, Body of Christ), a Midwestern communal
sect whose jazz band (the Jesus Boys) and hirsute baseball team toured the
country before and during the Depression and whose leader, Benjamin
Purnell, proclaimed himself Jesus' brother and was arrested on morals
charges in 1926. The Op brings in three of the biggest names of evange-
lism of the period: Aimee is Aimee Semple McPherson whose Angelus
Temple in Los Angeles accommodated 5,000 worshippers and whose Four
Square Gospel radio station (KFSG) reached out across the western states;
Buchman is evangelist Frank Buchman who launched a movement called
Moral Rearmament; and Jeddu is Jeddu Krishnamurti who had been pro-
claimed the new Messiah by Annie Besant, the head of the Theosophical
Society.

Hammett uses spiritualism as the basis for the plot in the second
quarter of the book and connects what's going on in *The Dain Curse* to
what was going on in the real world. That's not quite the case with one of
the novel's other contemporary connections: drug addiction. While the
Op alludes to Gabrielle's drug addiction a number of times in passing during the first half of the novel, it serves as just another character trait
superficially linked with her daring and risky lifestyle and with her "degenerate" appearance (her pointed ears and her sharp teeth). But more on that
later. It's not until the last quarter of the novel (the "Black Riddle" section)

that drug addiction assumes real importance. Significantly, however, it has little relevance to the detective plot.

Drug addiction gets its first serious consideration in chapter 19 when the Op proposes to stay with Gabrielle at Quesada and show her that "your curse is a bunch of hooey" (261). She brings up her need for drugs and the Op comments on public misconceptions about addiction:

> "Do you like using the stuff?"
> "I'm afraid it's too late for my liking or not liking it to matter."
> "You've been reading the Hearst papers," I said [261].

The next three chapters show the Op's management of Gabrielle's rehabilitation. From Vic Dallas's drug store in San Francisco he, illegally, procures morphine and a concoction of calomel-ipecac-strophene-strychnine as the pharmaceutical side of the cure. And he stays with Gabrielle as she fights through withdrawal. Hammett describes the effects on both the Op who spends this time gritting his teeth together and on Gabrielle whose every nerve and every sense throbs from the physical and psychological agony of withdrawal. Finally, coincident with the final revelations about the crimes in the novel, Gabrielle is cured.

Technically, none of this is necessary to the detective plot. Before Gabrielle's detox begins, the Op knows the answer to the overarching crime problem that holds *The Dain Curse* (albeit tenuously) together — indeed he even tells Aaronia Haldorn that he knows the answers in the middle of chapter 21. The drug business is there because it develops both Gabrielle's and the Op's characters and, of course, because drug addiction was a hot topic at the time.

Congress passed the first real anti-narcotics laws in the first quarter of the twentieth century. The Harrison Narcotics Act of 1914 made cocaine and heroin controlled substances, obtainable only by prescription; in 1922 the Narcotic Import and Export Act attempted to further control and limit the use of opium; and in 1924 the Heroin Act outlawed the possession and use of heroin. More important for the novel than these governmental actions were the anti-drug efforts of William Randolph Hearst's newspapers. With a history of stirring up hysteria about drugs going back to stories about Chinese killing and raping under the influence of opium, in the 1920s the Hearst papers took on drugs as a cause célèbre. Headed by writer Winifred Black (writing as Annie Laurie) the Hearst papers came back to drugs again and again.

The Op's contemptuous reference to the disinformation of the Hearst papers and his cure of Gabrielle's habit accomplish several things. They connect readers with a world outside of fiction and make a comment on issues that, strictly speaking, have no connection with the detective plot. On top of that, Gabrielle's cure strengthens the themes of self-reliance and of willpower that assume large importance in the last quarter of the novel.

The drug theme in *The Dain Curse* is linked with the theme of willpower and so is the material on physiognomy mentioned throughout the book. Hammett reexamined Lombroso's notions of criminal physicality as one of the themes of *The Dain Curse*. The first instance is when Hammett repeatedly presents Alice Dain Leggett as thoroughly pleasant looking and comfortably domestic ("She was a woman about my age, forty, with darkish blond hair, a pleasant plump face, and dimpled pink cheeks" [145]) and then reveals her history as a demented, cold-blooded killer. Then he does the reverse with Gabrielle. Throughout the early parts of the novel Hammett mentions in passing certain physical signs in Gabrielle's appearance that seem weird. Then, in a chapter entitled "The Degenerate," he brings Lombroso's theory out into the open. Hysterically, Gabrielle catalogues her facial features— her lobeless ears, small forehead, sharp teeth, small face — and, comparing herself to an animal, she tells the Op that she has "the physical marks of degeneracy" (257). The Op counters Gabrielle's apparent "degeneracy" with Alice Leggett's appearance that he had seeded earlier in the novel: "Wasn't she as normal, as wholesome-looking as any woman you're likely to find" (258). And he argues that Gabrielle's appearance has nothing to do with any supposed inherited criminal tendencies: "Physically, you take after your father, and if you've got any physical marks of degeneracy — whatever that means— you got them from him" (259). Indeed, in his dialogue with Gabrielle, the Op argues on behalf of willpower as the determining factor in human behavior versus biological determinism and environmental influences.

All of this material about spiritualism, drug addiction, and criminal nature suggests several significant things about *The Dain Curse*. First of all, it means that Hammett approached his second novel about the Continental Op in a very different way from the way he had approached his short stories and *The Red Harvest*. *The Dain Curse* is no longer simply a story about a detective catching criminals. Here, Hammett faced one of the basic problems of detective fiction — how to make what is essentially short fiction into a novel — and his answer to this conundrum was not simply to add more action as it had been in *The Red Harvest*. Like other writers of the 1920s, what he did was to add supplementary material and link it as background to the bare bones of the story of unraveling who did what to whom. This added material ramifies in several ways. First it makes the hero more than simply a manhunter but someone with broader experience and knowledge, someone, in short, who is just as much an intellectual as a thief taker. In *The Dain Curse*, therefore, the Op possesses wide (but notably not esoteric) knowledge and thinks about thinking both in his conversations with Fitzstephan and those with Gabrielle. Just as importantly, this new approach posits different kinds of readers from those assumed by the *Black Mask* stories. *The Dain Curse* aims at readers who will understand the allusions to spiritualists and religious fakirs, who have the same contempt for the Hearst newspapers as that voiced by the Op, and who possess skepticism like the Op's about whether there is a biology of criminals. Not only that, *The Dain Curse* expects readers to want a much more talky book than the action-packed *Red Harvest*.

IT'S ALL ABOUT SEX

Before *The Dain Curse* almost everything in Hammett's detective stories is about illicit gain. With the exception of "Night Shots," simply wanting money stands behind the crimes in all the short stories and *The Red Harvest*. Even in "Crooked Souls" where Hammett could have made much more out of a warped parent-child relationship, he didn't.

Much of what occurs in *The Dain Curse* happens because of aggressively sexual men. The prehistory of the novel begins with Edgar Leggett's longings for his sister-in-law and not his wife. But this is a mild case compared to what happens in the rest of the novel. In the second part of the book Hammett revs up the male libido theme with Joseph Haldorn. One aspect of Joseph's delusions of godhead is his rampant sexuality that culminates in the scene where he is about to sacrifice his wife on the altar at the Temple of the Holy Grail in order to possess the drugged-up, virginal Gabrielle. Indeed, much of what goes on in the scenes at the Temple stems from Joseph's manipulation of people and events so that he can control Gabrielle's mind and body.

After the Temple episode Hammett included what amounts to a digression with the details about Marshal Dick Cotton being driven to murder by suspicions about his wife's infidelity. The last portion of *The Dain Curse*, however, makes piggish male behavior its main focus. The Op's conversation with Gabrielle in chapter 19 centers on aggressive male sexual behavior and the questions "Why do men —? Why have all the men I've met —?" (260). Here Gabrielle ticks off a list of men who have made lewd advances to her. It includes lawyer Madison Andrews ("but you can't blame the curse with him — it's habit. Was he very bad?" [260]) and she reveals for the first time that Owen Fitzstephan has made untoward advances to her. Indeed, hyperaggressive male sexuality stands behind almost all of the crimes in the book, as revealed in the Op's final confrontation with the book's master villain: "She'd had a bad time with Andrews, and even with Eric, but she didn't mind talking about them. But when I tried to learn the details of your wooing she shuddered and shut up" (283). Fittingly, perhaps, in each case libido-driven male behavior ends in disaster: Leggett is murdered; Joseph is shot down by the Op; Andrews runs off, about to be exposed as an embezzler; and Fitzstephan ends up as a mutilated freak.

Women (Mostly) Are Predators

If *The Dain Curse* makes a point of portraying men as pigs, it's not much kinder in describing the role women play in relationships. Of course the first and best example of this is in Hammett's portrait of Alice Dain. In her confession Alice describes the beginning of the relationship between the Dain sisters and Maurice (Edgar Leggett) and reveals both the demented rivalry between the sisters and Leggett's main attraction for them as a way out of poverty. Consequently Lily "trapped him — that is crude but exact — into matrimony" (181). The narrative goes on to characterize Alice quite literally as a predator: "This was a blonde woman whose body was rounded, not with the plumpness of contented, well-cared-for early middle age, but with the cushioned, soft-sheathed muscles of the hunting cats, whether in jungle or alley" (180). But Alice Dain isn't the only woman with these characteristics in the novel. There's Aaronia Haldorn and at their first meeting she almost scares even the Op. He makes much of the beauty of her face, especially her eyes, but he also concludes that "It was as if her face was not a face, but a mask that she had worn until it had become a face" (169).

Later in the novel the Op makes it clear that she was the real brains behind the Temple of the Holy Grail scam: "They — or she: Joseph was a light-weight — rigged up a cult" (209). In the last parts of *The Dain Curse* Aaronia has moved on seemingly effortlessly from Joseph and has teamed up with Madison Andrews, and Hammett also suggests that throughout everything in the book she was hooked up with Fitzstephan. Indeed, she is one of the few people in the novel who physically threatens the Op, as she does near the close of the action. Along with Alice Dain and Aaronia Haldorn, Hammett almost casually adds that Fink, the mechanic who engineered the Haldorn's spook-effects, is deserted by his wife after the debacle at the Temple. So, just as in the male department, in the female department of *The Dain Curse* there doesn't seem to be a lot to choose from. But there is.

There Are (a Few) Swell Guys

Chivalry underlies the whole first movement of the novel. It's what the whole romantic story of Edgar Leggett (Maurice Mayenne) is all about: Leggett confesses to a crime he did not commit in order to protect his daughter and as a result endures years of suffering and privation on Devil's Island. And Eric Collinson belongs to the same category. Fitzstephan calls him "the Chevalier Bayard," alluding to Pierre du Terrail Seigneur de Bayard (1473–1524), a legendary exemplar of courtesy and chivalry. From his fumbling fib at the start of the novel about what time he brought Gabrielle home (midnight versus 3:00 A.M.), all of Collinson's bumbling actions spring from his devotion to Gabrielle's reputation, safety, and integrity. He, however, is totally ineffectual and, in fact, serves as an impediment to what the Op tries to do. Oddly enough, though, Hammett gave him his own name — the pseudonym he used in his first pulp publications (Peter Collinson). He also has him killed as a direct result of his absolute devotion to Gabrielle. In all, Eric Collinson is reminiscent of the characters in the romance novel that the Op skims in his early Op story "Death on Pine Street": "I found a book and spent the next half-hour reading about a sweet young she-chump and a big strong he-chump and all their troubles" (200).

With the Op it's anyone's guess whether he's in the same category as Leggett and Collinson. While throughout the novel the Op protests that he is just a hired hand and has no emotional attachment with any of the principals, near the end Hammett includes a suggestion that the Op's relationship with Gabrielle is more than that of detective and client. Mickey Linehan wisecracks that the Op's relationship with Gabrielle is like the one the Op had with Dinah Brand in *The Red Harvest*. But there are suggestions in *The Dain Curse* that the relationship here is both more intense and more emotional. Thus, when Gabrielle emerges from detox she asks the Op why he stayed with her, why he cured her of her addiction, and he replies,

> "I'm damned if I'll make a chump of myself by telling you why I did it, why it was neither revolting nor disgusting, why I would do it again and be glad of the chance" [282].

Here there is the pretty definite suggestion that the Op has developed an emotional attachment with Gabrielle and that, chivalrously, he is denying himself the gratification of admitting his feelings and of attempting to form a romantic relationship with her. Several pages later it even seems as if Gabrielle pulls herself up short when she picks up on the Op's feelings for her after she describes him as someone good to have around, but who is nonetheless immune from warmth and other kinds of "human foolishness" like love. The Op, however, gives Gabrielle an unexpected answer to which, in the final words in the chapter, she is taken aback.

> "I'm not sure I wouldn't trade places with Fitzstephan now — if that big-eyed woman with the voice was part of the bargain."
> "Oh dear" [285–86].

The "big-eyed woman" is not Gabrielle but Aaronia Haldorn, about whom the Op had recently commented to Fitzstephan that "I like her: she's shifty" (284). The Op's response to her mentioning love clearly confuses Gabrielle, but, more importantly, it's meant to be confusing to the reader because it presents questions without answers. Is the Op, for instance, dropping Aaronia's name as a self-denying way of distracting Gabrielle from the truth of his own feelings for her, or is he really attracted to the exotic and dangerous Aaronia instead of the naïve and virginal Gabrielle? Who knows? But that's all right. Hammett intended this to be confusing. It's what he used to do in his sex stories for *The Smart Set* and for the pulps and in no small measure *The Dain Curse* is an updated version of those stories.

Before *The Dain Curse* Hammett had assiduously avoided the topic of sex in his detective stories. Passion almost never serves as the motive for the crimes in them and, as seen above, Hammett made emotional connections and sex into things that could only serve as detractions and impediments to keep a detective from doing his job. Clearly this isn't the case with *The Dain Curse*. The novel not only bases much of what happens on motives of passion but also includes a section near the end in which Hammett presents a short course on female sexuality to Gabrielle. Then, too, the novel presents the hero, albeit briefly, as an emotional, sexual being. These things may be different from what Hammett had done in his detective stories, but they are decidedly not different from what he had done in the "sex stories" he had written in the 1920s. In "In Defence [sic] of the Sex Story" Hammett proclaimed that

> sex has never made a poor story good, or a good one poor; but if Mr. Bedford-Jones will make a list of the stories that are still alive after several centuries, he'll find that many of the heartiest survivors have to do with the relations between the sexes, and treat those relations with little of the proper Victorian delicacy [7].

The "Victorian delicacy" motif formed one of Hammett's motives in his sex stories: stories like "The Dimple" and "Esther Entertains" are about adultery and promiscuity and in them he deals with subjects that came as close as one could to the edge of publishing propriety. In some of the sex stories, however, it's hard to tell whether Hammett intended to shock and titillate or to make serious points. This isn't the case with *The Dain Curse*: in the presentation of the prehistory of the Dain/Leggett relationship and in the discussion of Gabrielle's sexuality in chapter 19, Hammett intended the novel to be a serious and meaningful discussion of sexuality — no matter how awkward and naïve some of this seems today. Another element that carried over from the sex stories is that *The Dain Curse* is all about rotten relationships, and that men and women contribute equally to poisoning those relationships. In the sex stories Hammett goes back and forth from centering on stupid and venal men to centering on stupid and venal women. In the battle of the sexes it's hard to pick a favorite. Things come out in the novel in the same way. Line up Alice Dain and Aaronia Haldorn against Joseph Haldorn and Owen Fitzstephan and there's blame to be attached all around. These things, along with Hammett's presentation of the Op's ambivalent emotional commitments in the novel, connect *The Dain Curse* most firmly with Hammett's technique not just in his sex stories but in all of his early fiction. Thus, just as one doesn't know whom to blame most in "The Parthian Shot" or whether Hagedorn in "The Road Home" will continue the chase out of a sense of duty or because of a hope of gain, in *The Dain Curse* Hammett leaves the question open about whom the Op is most attracted to: Gabrielle or Aaronia.

THE NEW DETECTIVE STORY

If Hammett's addition of the Op's relationship with women (whatever it is) is something new in *The Dain Curse*, there are other significant changes in the Op as well. For one thing, as noted above, he is much more in charge than he had been in the earlier stories, more in charge of the doings of the Continental Agency and more in charge even of the police. His familiar relationship with Dick Foley disappeared with *The Red Harvest* and in *The Dain Curse* his relationship with the other Continental ops becomes even more strained than it had been in the first novel. The Op no longer seeks the professional or personal company of ops or cops but instead seeks out Owen Fitzstephan, a character from a decidedly different class from those with whom the hero used to congregate. Fitzstephan is not only from a different social class — notably he lives in a building on Nob Hill where visitors need to be announced and his diction is peppered with the same kind of college-boy slang Hammett manufactured for Jack Counihan in "The Big Knock-Over" — but, to boot, he is a writer and an intellectual. At least partly because he chose a plot based on the device of the assistant detective as the guilty party, Hammett had to change the social standing and relationships of his hero. He also, as a consequence of this, had to change the way the Op speaks. Thus, although the Op uses a smattering of gangster slang in his conversations with Fitzstephan, his diction in *The Dain Curse* is far more that of standard American English than in any of Hammett's previous Op fiction.

Another change in the Op of *The Dain Curse* is that there is a lot more emphasis in his character upon thinking versus a focus on practical matters. When Hammett first introduced the Continental Op some of his uniqueness for his audience lay in his explanations of what detectives do: how they shadow suspects, how they trace luggage, other "real world" aspects of the detective business. In the novels this mostly disappears. In the hurly-burly of action in *The Red Harvest* there's little time for digressions on detective technique and there's little inclination for the Op to talk shop. With the focus on technique gone, Hammett shifts to emphasizing the Op's actions and his almost preternatural intelligence. Thus, before readers know the facts, the Op announces that he knows the solutions to the murders of Donald Willsson and Tim Noonan in *The Red Harvest*, and the same thing occurs in *The Dain Curse* when the Op brings up Alice Dain's guilt before presenting the logic behind the accusation, and, more pointedly, near the end of the novel when he tells Aaronia Haldorn that he knows all of the answers before confronting the killer and revealing the answers to readers in the next chapter. One of the differences between the two novels, however, is that *The Red Harvest* makes up for the loss of attention to practical detective technique by substituting lots of action whereas *The Dain Curse* fills that absence with talk. And a portion of the Op's talk centers on the nature of thinking and motivation.

Some of the material about thinking concerns basic issues about motivation and what makes people what they are. In the Op's conversations with Gabrielle near the end of the novel he mentions the difficulty of understanding oneself and one's world: "Thinking's a dizzy business, a matter of catching as many of those foggy glimpses as you can and fitting them together the best you can" (258). Although examining and debating psychological theories isn't part of the Op's job, nonetheless the topic of motivation comes up relatively early in the narrative when the Op introduces it in connection with Fitzstephan and his literary pursuits. During the opening parts of the novel Fitzstephan is writing an article for the *Psychological Review* that denies the existence of the unconscious mind and labels psychoanalysts and behaviorists as "faddists." Twenty-five pages later, though, Fitzstephan seems to reverse himself. In discussing Alice

Dain's character and motivation the Op argues a practical approach ("You won't find the key to her in any complicated derangements. She was simple as an animal, with an animal's simple ignorance of right and wrong, dislike for being thwarted, and spitefulness when trapped" [185]) and Fitzstephan objects to such a prosaic view of character and motivation by saying, "It's fellows like you that take all the color out of life" (185). In a semifacetious manner he then goes on to drift in metaphysics by suggesting the possible reality of a stain in the blood and the existence of the Dain curse — things that the Op does not accept. At the end of *The Dain Curse* the Op truncates the whole debate by concluding that while the criminal's acts can't be accounted for by rational analysis he is unwilling or unable to explain the villain's motivation and simply labels him as "goofy." While Hammett no doubt intended this argument about intellect and motivation to possess some interest in itself as an intellectual matter — his review of Mary Austin's *Everyman's Genius* in 1925 demonstrates that he had read and thought a bit about how the mind works— he also intended it to serve as a part of the cat-and-mouse structure of the novel. Indeed, much of what Fitzstephan says on the subject is deliberately intended to confuse and misdirect the Op's thinking about the series of crimes in the novel.

If the Op ultimately does not fall for any of the intellectual ruses and misdirection placed in his path, he does talk throughout the novel about how thinking applies to what detectives do. First comes the universal skepticism embodied in the Old Man in the earlier stories. Thus, in recounting events in the Temple of the Holy Grail, Fitzstephan complains about the Op's skeptical way of thinking: "Later, after you've finished your story, you can attach your ifs and buts to it, distorting and twisting it, making it as cloudy and confusing and generally hopeless as you like. But first please finish it" (214). After skepticism for the detective come facts and the patient examination of those facts. A number of times during the course of the narrative the Op emphasizes the prime importance of collecting facts and analyzing them. He repeats the notion that "you don't catch murderers by amusing yourself with interesting thoughts. You've got to sit down to all the facts you can get and turn them over and over till they click" (248).

If the Op and Fitzstephan go back and forth about aspects of how the mind works, they also talk about detective stories and the way that they work. This begins when the whole Leggett affair comes up early in the novel and the Op brings in and ridicules the master criminal story:

> "What do you think he is? King of the bootleggers? Chief of an international crime syndicate? A white-slave magnate? Head of a dope ring? Or the Queen of the counterfeiters in disguise? [157].

Later the Op mentions his dislike for highbrow puzzle stories: "But spring the puzzle. Don't be literary with me, building up to climaxes and the like. I'm too crude for that — it'd only give me a belly-ache" (232). Just as the Op does in this passage, Fitzstephan also complains a couple of times about stories that don't directly get to the point. First there is the passage cited earlier ("But first please finish it"), and then, 35 pages later he says that he likes mindless adventure detective stories like those of the Nick Carter school because they don't include knotty problems that need to be assessed and reassessed. All of this talk about how narratives work in detective stories establishes the same kind of misdirection Hammett included in the debate between the Op and Fitzstephan about motivation. Thus, the Op ridicules master criminal stories and the novel turns out to be a story about a villain who sees himself as a master criminal. All of the impatience the Op and Fitzstephan express with regard to puzzles and the convolutions of puzzle stories turn out to be ironic comments on the plot of *The Dain Curse*, which depends on "distorting and twisting...[and] making it ...cloudy and confusing and generally hopeless." In addition to its function in the novel, all of the talk about detective stories in *The Dain Curse* is another sign of Hammett's moving toward the patterns of East Coast "Golden Age" fiction in which playfully self-conscious references to detective stories serve as one hallmark of the genre.

SOME CONCLUSIONS

Running to 103 pages in its original form in *Black Mask*, *The Dain Curse* is slightly longer than *The Red Harvest*. Even with those extra five pages, however, it's still too short and, on top of that, it's much more disjointed than the first novel. Throughout the book Hammett packs in more subsidiary characters and crimes than he has the time or space to properly cover. Perhaps as a carryover from *The Red Harvest*, he felt the need to include as many crimes in *The Dain Curse* as he possibly could; as a consequence, some of them receive short shrift, like the Upton-Rupert business in the first episode, and some, like the Cotton-Widden conflict in the third part, are just plain muddy and confused. Frankly, a lot of the novel's muddiness exists because it is not long enough. Not only that, some of the material in the novel seems self-indulgent and unnecessary. A case in point is Hammett's creation of a romantic and exotic prehistory for Edgar Leggett wherein his sojourn at Devil's Island and travels in Central America have little bearing on essentials of the Dain-Leggett curse.

The action in *The Dain Curse*, too, differs significantly from that of *The Red Harvest* where the solutions to the inserted crime puzzles serve only as rest stops in the plot of cleaning up the city. Because Hammett did not want to reveal the frame story until the very end of the book, the episodes in *The Dain Curse* seem separate and their solutions seem final solutions instead as parts of an ongoing plot. Even the geography conspires against the coherence of the plot when, between the first two episodes, the Op leaves town and after the business at the Temple of the Holy Grail the novel shifts to an entirely new setting with an entirely new cast of characters.

It is clear after reading not too many pages that Hammett is trying to do something different in *The Dain Curse* than he had done with *The Red Harvest* or the Op short stories. Whereas throughout the 1920s Hammett had compartmentalized his fiction, keeping sex stories separate from adventure stories and adventure stories separate from criminal stories and criminal stories distinct from detective stories, in *The Dain Curse* for the first time he combined elements of the sex story with those of the detective story and, in general, gave more attention to psychology and analysis. But even though in many ways *The Dain Curse* was for Hammett an experiment, some of its weaknesses come from the fact that it wasn't experimental enough. Perhaps to ensure its success, Hammett didn't want to or couldn't give up some of those things that led to his popularity as a *Black Mask* writer — the Continental Agency, the San Francisco police, the nonstop action, and especially the hero who had been with him since 1923. That Hammett realized this seems apparent: only months after completing *The Dain Curse* he began to write about a different hero, Sam Spade, and a novel that was to be different from both *The Red Harvest* and *The Dain Curse*. On the way to *The Maltese Falcon*, however, Hammett had to teach himself more about how to write detective novels.

In its storytelling, *The Dain Curse* differs significantly from anything that Hammett had attempted. One of the reasons for this—perhaps the main reason for this—was that by the time he began writing his second novel Hammett had been pretty thoroughly exposed to the new eastern, highbrow detective fiction. Reviewing for *The Saturday Review of Literature* he had written about a number of the new detective writers who appeared at the end of the 1920s, including S. S. Van Dine (*The Benson Murder Case* in *SRL* in January 1927) and Dorothy Sayers (*The Unpleasantness at the Bellona Club* in *SRL* in October 1928). The new "Golden Age" fiction made the short story about what a detective does into a short novel by playing games with the readers— deliberately trying to confuse them, leading them down false alleys, and finding increasingly devious ways to obscure facts that become meaningful only at the end of the story. Hammett made *The Dain Curse* this kind of book and his use of the assistant detective as villain along with all of the other puzzle apparatus in the novel mirrors what was happening in Britain with Agatha Christie, Sayers, et al and on the East Coast with S.S. Van Dine and Ellery Queen. It was a kind of fiction that leaves behind underworld characters and cops, it talks more and describes action less, and it was meant to appeal to a different kind of audience.

One of the defining features of the new "Golden Age" fiction resided in its playfulness. While what has become the classic detective novel deals with perverse acts committed by devious and warped people, it is also a game, a contest between the writer who wants to outwit the reader and the reader who wants to solve the puzzle before the writer wins by revealing it. In his *Saturday Review* pieces Hammett's biggest complaint (after the accuracy of details) about writers was the predictability of their plots. Readers, he maintains, aren't supposed to see what's coming and surprise is what they want from their detective stories. This, of course, is the way Hammett intended *The Dain Curse* to work. Indeed, one of the novel's defects from a classical detective novel point of view is that it works too well — the surprise at the end of the novel is too much of a surprise. Hammett does drop in an occasional oblique hint — like the early mention of Fitzstephan's connection with spiritualism ("he knew the spook racket inside") — and, in retrospect, it's a small sign consistent with his guilt. His problem, however, was that Hammett couldn't seed much in the way of real hints about the motive that holds the whole novel together (Fitzstephan's lust for Gabrielle) because doing so would have been taboo.

Playfulness in *The Dain Curse* extends beyond what Hammett tried to do with the main plot of the novel. He also used the novel to amuse himself and, to some extent, to parody himself. In an interview with Albert Samuels, William Nolan learned that Hammett inserted the names of a number of his fellow employees at Samuels' Jewelry into *The Dain Curse*: "Leggett was our switchboard operator.... David Riese, who also worked for us, became a doctor in the novel — and a minor character was named after our Mrs. Priestly, who was in silverware" (*Casebook* 51). Nolan also points out that Hammett may have modeled the villain of the piece upon himself:

> His portrait of Fitzstephan might well have served as a self description: "...a long, lean, sorrel-haired man of thirty-two with sleepy gray eyes, a wide, humorous mouth, and carelessly worn clothes; a man who pretended to be lazier than he was, would rather talk than do anything else and had a lot of what seemed to be accurate information and original ideas on any subject that happened to come up, as long as it was a little out of the ordinary." ([Nolan's ellipsis] *Casebook* 54).

One can add to this presumptive self-portrait that at the root of all of the evil in *The Dain Curse* lies Fitzstephan's appetite for Gabrielle and her off stage rejection of him. Sexual appetite, it seems, also was one of the ways that Hammett defined himself during this period. Layman mentions the "new sexual freedom Hammett was exercising" in 1927 (85) and connects it with the aggressive male sexuality that characterizes Hammett's poems ("Yes," "Goodbye to a Lady," and "Curse in the Old Manner") published shortly before he took up writing novels. With this in mind, the presentation of the dark side of sexual ardor in the character of Fitzstephan along with the Op's chaste and ultimately Victorian treatment of Gabrielle's problems with men and sex replicates the same ironic playfulness that characterizes all of Hammett's early prose as well as presenting an ironic comment about himself.

4

The Last Op Stories

Near the end of 1927, Hammett's novels rather than short fiction came to occupy most of his attention. Beginning with *The Maltese Falcon* (published serially beginning in September 1929), he developed new heroes— Sam Spade, Ned Beaumont, Nick Charles— upon whom he would build his last three novels. But he did not give up the Op entirely until he had all but given up writing detective stories. Between *The Red Harvest* and *The Glass Key* Hammett wrote his last four Continental Op short stories. The first of these, "This King Business," appeared in *Mystery Stories* (January 1928) between the third and forth installments of *The Red Harvest*; "Fly Paper" came out in *Black Mask* (August 1929) after the last installment of *The Dain Curse*; *Black Mask* printed "The Farewell Murder" the month after the last installment of *The Maltese Falcon* (February 1930); and "Death and Company" appeared in *Black Mask* (November 1930) after Hammett had finished *The Glass Key*. "Death and Company" was Hammett's last appearance in *Black Mask,* and the ten short stories he wrote after it were intended for "slick" magazines: *Harper's Bazaar, American Magazine, Liberty,* and *Collier's*. None of these ten was about the Continental Op.

"This King Business"

The length of what *Black Mask* called a "novelette," "This King Business" recounts the Op's travels to Muravia on behalf of the family of Lionel

Grantham in order to quiet their fears about the somewhat unsettled young man messing about in the Balkans with $3 million at his immediate disposal. The Op finds that the young man has been drawn by a couple of shady government officials into a plot to unseat Muravia's current more or less republican government, a plot that he believes will include making him king so that the country can reap the benefits of having an American on its throne. After consorting with the plotters, the Op manages to save Grantham from disaster by helping to make him king, by having him abdicate the same day, and by then turning the country's government over to the minister of police rather than the sinister Icelandic soldier of fortune who is in charge of the country's army

At first glance, "This King Business" seems to come right out of Anthony Hope's *Prisoner of Zenda* (1894) with its imaginary country, Byzantine political plots, and fantasies about kingship. Be this as it may, Hammett had more immediate sources for the plot of the story. For one thing, "This King Business," like *The Dain Curse*, demonstrates Hammett's increasing use of current (or semicurrent) events in his fiction. The Op alludes to two of the real dynastic shenanigans that went on during the period after World War I: the 1925 revolt in Iran that led to the ascent of the Pahlavi dynasty, and the imbroglios in Albania that made Ahmed Zogu first prime minister and then, in 1928, King Zog I. The first of these incidents Hammett connects with Colonel Einarson as an outsider ambitious to gain power (Einarson carries a picture of the Shah of Persia) and the Albanian dynastic situation he uses both as background for several of the coups d'etat in the story and as a precedent to Lionel Grantham's royal fantasies.

Hammett took these bits of contemporary political history and used them for a re-telling of the underlying story of the novel he was writing at the time: that is, he made "This King Business" into the optimistic version of *The Red Harvest*. The purpose of both "This King Business" and *The Red Harvest* is the same, but what happens in the stories is radically different. Fundamentally, both *The Red Harvest* and "This King Business" are about saving communities. Indeed, in *The Red Harvest*, whether he likes it or not, the Op is in the king business by restoring the monarchy of Elihu Willsson, "the czar of Personville." In the novel, from the practical point of view the Op succeeds, but in the larger sense he fails. He sets the bad guys against one another, restores order in the town, and gives it back to Willsson. But, after all of the mayhem and grief connected with the process of cleansing the town of its corruption, at the end of the novel the Op knows that none of it will have a lasting effect: "You'll have your city back, all nice and clean and ready to go to the dogs again" (134). The Op, then, knows that he has failed to cleanse Personville. "This King Business" may be fantasy, but in it Hammett makes the Op thoroughly succeed in the king business. He not only helps to oust an incompetent government and temporarily makes a naïve but honorable young man king, but then he also unmakes that kingship and opens the way for the country to have a legitimate, efficient, and probably laissez faire government. Just as what happens in "This King Business" echoes what happens in *The Red Harvest*, the character patterns present certain similarities. Both the novel and the "novelette" bring the Op into contact with a flirtatious woman companion whose principal trait is practicality, and they both feature a fat chief of police. "This King Business," however, the woman companion is not like the slatternly Dinah Brand in *The Red Harvest* but is pretty, well groomed, and idealistic. And the fat chief of police is not like the pathetic Chief Noonan but represents the future salvation of the community. But in "This King Business" Hammett also plays with one of his older character stereotypes.

The framework Hammett uses in "This King Business" is that of the adventure story. Back in his apprentice days the one form of popular fiction that Hammett tried but seemingly found less than convivial was the action/adventure story — he only wrote a few of them ("The Road Home," "Laughing Masks," "Nightmare Town," and "Ber-Bulu"). With "This King Business" he took up the form again. First there is the setting: after "Ber-Bulu," it's Hammett's only story set outside the United States, and, like that early piece set in the Philippines, "This King Business" depends in some small measure on its exotic locale. More importantly, characters in adventure stories differ from characters in detective stories. Thus, in "This King Business," the lead character risks his life not situationally as the Op does in the detective stories but consciously for a high purpose: the fate of a nation. And Hammett connects this novel idealism with the figure of the soldier of fortune, a character type that links "This King Business" with several of Hammett's early adventure stories. In several of the early stories Hammett portrayed rootless young men drifting about and looking for adventure. In "Laughing Masks," for instance, he portrays the hero, Phil Truax, as representative of this class of characters:

> Since his discharge from the army he had been drifting, finding himself at odds with the world, gambling, doing chores for political clubs—never doing anything very vicious, perhaps, but steadily being more and more enmeshed in the underworld [105].

This is the same persona that the Op invents for himself when he talks to the conspirators in "This King Business": he tells them that after service in the war he has drifted about Europe "doing odd jobs," some of which have not been "ladylike" (674). This is the stuff of the adventure hero. So is the linkage with danger and sadism: in "This King Business" Colonel Einarson's combination of competence and cruelty echoes that of Boris Kapaloff in "Laughing Masks." Finally, as in his adventure stories, "This King Business" contains an idealistic and unsullied romance between Lionel Grantham and Valeska Radnjak. Significantly, Hammett even took the name of the most intriguing woman in "This King Business," Romaine Frankl, from Romaine Kapaloff, the damsel in distress in "Laughing Masks."

Romaine Frankl, however, is no damsel in distress, and "This King Business" is not quite an adventure story. It's an adventure story turned on its head. For one thing, early in his career Hammett came to see the character of the soldier of fortune as a disreputable type, unfit for the hero's role: thus, in "The Ruffian's Wife" the international soldier of fortune gets labeled as a "sneak thief." Consequently, in "This King Business," the Op is not what he pretends to be (a soldier of fortune), but a detective hired to do a job that has to do with domestic issues—saving a family's money and reputation. The soldiers of fortune in the story are Lionel Grantham, the naïve boy, and Colonel Einarson. One is a bit of a nincompoop and the other is a bit of a villain. Hammett not only endowed Einarson with villainous qualities (cruelty, arrogance, etc.) along with his idolization of the throne-grabbing Shah of Persia but he also added an element of absurdity to the character: he's from Iceland, and, after the Middle Ages, whoever heard of Icelandic soldiers of fortune?

The final view of soldiers of fortune in "This King Business" comes at the end of the story from Vasilije Djudakovich, Muravia's minister of police, who sees Grantham and the Op not as saviors but as "a pair of adventurers who are making a profit out of his country's troubles" (703). In addition to this reversal of the stereotype of the soldier of fortune, there's the woman. Romaine Frankl is no adventure-story damsel in distress or even a sloe-eyed temptress. She's a spunky, intelligent, calculating, coquettish, practical, affectionate, sophisticated, diminutive dynamo.

Romaine Frankl is Dinah Brand from *The Red Harvest,* cleaned up. Throughout "This King Business" Frankl is the Op's confidante. At each juncture in the action he goes to her house seeking advice and sharing information with her. As in *The Red Harvest* during these conferences, there is some boozing and light flirtation. Like Dinah Brand, Romaine Frankl is determined and single-minded. Just as Dinah Brand is open about using her sexuality for practical, nonromantic ends, so is Frankl: "I've capitalized that beauty and charm in half the countries in the world" (692).

In "This King Business," however, the single-mindedness ultimately connects with the woman's dedication to her country and commitment to her lover, Vasilije Djudakovich, rather than to Dinah Brand's avarice. In addition to this, unlike the sentimental impracticality evident in the romance of Lionel Grantham and Valeska Radnjak, the object of Grantham's starry-eyed devotion, Hammett makes Frankl a wholly practical woman. This practicality extends from small things (like her tearing a button off of the Op's union suit so that she can be seen sewing it on in order to further the image she wishes to create for others) to some very large things. And the largest of these is her relationship with the Op. Thus, although she flirts with the Op she is dedicated to Vasilije Djudakovich, the fat minister of police and the country's ultimate savior. Her final words in the story to the Op, however, are, "When Vasilije dies— and he can't live long, the way he eats— I'm coming to San Francisco" (709).

If Romaine Frankl is an echo of *The Red Harvest*, Lionel Grantham is a study for Eric Collinson in *The Dain Curse*. Like Collinson, Lionel Grantham is a completely idealistic and romantic young man. Hammett insists on that latter point by attaching the word "boy" to every mention of him in "This King Business." He is young, idealistic and very rich — a potentially disastrous combination. His idealism leads him to believe that he can make a difference to Muravia: "The money that I have would go a long way in this small, impoverished country" (670). His idealism also makes him loathe violence and cruelty. In his first meeting with Grantham, the Op comments on the boy's repulsion when witnessing Colonel Einarson's protracted flogging of the soldier who attempted to assassinate them. On top of this the Op shows Grantham in the throes of a completely and wholly romantic relationship with Valeska Radnjak, the Balkan beauty. She is totally goofy about him and he is just as goofy about her. It's something that both amuses the Op and also makes him feel protective and paternal when he acknowledges that the love between the two has nothing to do with wealth or power. What the Op does realize, however, is that Grantham is being used and exploited by Einarson, and that both his money and his life are at risk once the coup to make him king succeeds. In "This King Business" it's the Op's job to get the young man out of the trouble that his naïveté and sentimentality have gotten him into. And, of course, he does this. Unlike Eric Collinson, whom the Op treats as a dope throughout most of *The Dain Curse*, during the course of the action in "This King Business" the Op briefly recognizes that Grantham is more than a bumbling nincompoop. This happens during a crucial moment of the coup when Grantham demonstrates a combination of sentiment and courage by offering his life for the cause in which he believes. And the Op states that "but it's God's own truth that even I — a middle-aged detective who had forgotten what it was like to believe in fairies—felt suddenly warm inside my wet clothes" (696). That feeling, of course, doesn't last long because the Op still has to deal with the very practical matter of saving Lionel from a world in which idealism and principles almost inevitably lead to folly and then to disaster.

One of the ways to avoid folly and disaster in "This King Business" is to be lazy and fat. In some ways Vasilije Djudakovich, the minister of Muravia's police, is the most interesting character in the story. While he doesn't appear often, Hammett seems clearly fascinated with him. For one thing it gave him a chance to describe a fat man, and Hammett enjoyed describing fat guys: "Maybe he wouldn't weigh more than five hundred pounds, but, looking at him, it was hard to think except in terms of tons" (664). The thing about Djudakovich is that he's not just fat, he's also lazy. Hammett liked laziness. In the first run of Op stories it was one of the characterizing features of some of Hammett's favorite characters: Deputy McClump in the first story, "Arson Plus," is notably lazy, and the Op describes Pat Reddy in "The Scorched Face" as "a big blond Irishman who went in for the spectacular in his lazy way" (365). And in "This King Business" Hammett made laziness not simply into a curiously likable character trait but also into a principle of government. At the end of the story when the Op talks about Djudakovich being an ideal leader for Muravia, he says, "I'm told he was a good Minister of Police because inefficiency would spoil his comfort. Maybe he'd be a good king for the same reason" (701).

The Op appreciates efficiency. It's one of the things he admires about Djudakovich, and it's even one of the things he admires about the sinister Colonel Einarson, but from the other end of the spectrum of work. When the Op watches Einarson flog the soldier into a bloody pulp, even though he sees it as repulsive, he also respects him for doing a job in a careful and disciplined manner like a carpenter or a stoker: "Here was a job to be done in a workmanlike manner, without haste or excitement or wasted effort, without either enthusiasm or repulsion. It was nasty, but it taught me to respect this Colonel Einarson" (672). While not brutal, in "This King Business" the Op also has a job to do, and he does it in a workmanlike manner. And that means unsentimental practicality. As is always the case, this comes out when the Op is involved in violence. Instead of gentlemanly fisticuffs in the opening movement of the story, the Op feigns surrender and then kicks the soldier-assassin in the belly and pulls his hair as the most effective way of getting the job done. The same kind of practicality comes out in the Op's strategy for extracting Lionel Grantham from the mess in Muravia. Rather than simply leaving the country with Grantham's original assets, the Op bargains with Djudakovich not just for the return of Grantham's $3 million but for several million more and is bemused (but not surprised) when Grantham returns the extra cash to Muravia.

While this fusion of hardheaded or hard-boiled characteristics with disguised sentimentality (seen here most clearly in the Op's ultimately paternal attitude toward the "boy" Lionel Grantham) reflects some of the same character points that Hammett made in all of the Op stories, in "This King Business" there are some new things about the Op. For one, this story accelerates the trend in the later Op stories of making the hero more of a boss than an operative, and, even more than in *The Red Harvest*, it distances him from the agency. For another thing, there is the revisionist biography put forth in the story. In the earlier Op pieces Hammett showed the Op as the common man. He seems to have no interests beyond being a detective: his associates are cops, ops, or crooks; his style of living is rarely mentioned, but when it is it is that of either a minimalist or a common man; his finances seem modest; and he seems little inclined toward sophisticated society or high culture. There is also the obvious point that he speaks as the common man speaks. Although the age that Hammett invented for him was right for it, nowhere in the stories of the pre–*Red Harvest* period is there any mention of the Op having served in World War I or of having traveled anywhere outside the United States. In "This King Business" suddenly Hammett invented new bits of the past for the Op — that he held a captain's commission in military intelligence during the war and that he speaks a couple of European languages. While they have no real impact on the Op's character (at the end of "This King Business," for instance, he still grouses about his expense account), these newly minted biographical facts connect the Op more with Hammett's aims for intellectualizing his character in his next novel, *The Dain Curse*, than with the Op that he had written about in the 24 previous stories. What does seem different about the Op in "This King Business" is his relationships with women. As seen before, Hammett deliberately kept sex out of the Op stories. In the short stories the issue of sexuality comes only in the temptations offered to the Op by evil women. *The Red Harvest* and the Op's relationship with Dinah Brand changed things, but in that novel the Op clearly and consistently has the upper hand in the relationship. That's not the case in "This King Business." While Hammett gives no insight into the Op's real feelings for Romaine Frankl, in their relationship she is the aggressor and is the one in charge.

"This King Business" demonstrates a number of things — Hammett's development of old and new facets of the Op's character, the reciprocal relationship between this story and *The Red Harvest* and *The Dain Curse*, and Hammett's increasing use of current events and decreasing emphasis on the work of the professional detective. Perhaps the most significant aspect of the story, however, is that in it Hammett makes his first deliberate and forthright statement about human rights. Almost at the end of the story the Op suddenly uses Colonel Einarson's death as the occasion for a digression on lynching that begins with "I hate mobs, lynchings— they sicken me. No matter how wrong the man is, if a mob's against him, I'm for him" (708).

The story ends with the Op wishing he could turn a machine gun on this and any other lynch mob. The Op's outburst in response to the soldiers literally tearing apart the villainous Colonel Einarson is gratuitous and dramatically uncharacteristic both for the Op and for Hammett. This is not only different from the way in which the Op had always responded to death and violence in all the previous stories, but it also disrupts Hammett's teasing closure of the romantic relationship between the Op and Romaine Frankl at the end of the story. It was almost certainly another one of Hammett's inclusions of current events in his fiction — in this case the state-by-state campaign for anti-lynching laws led by Ida B. Wells-Barnett after the U.S. House of Representatives passed the Dyer Anti-Lynching bill only to have it rejected by the Senate in 1922. But it is also perhaps the first sign that Hammett recognized that social justice was more important than the action of a fictional detective, no matter how authentic he tried to make that detective.

"Fly Paper"

Hammett wrote "Fly Paper" after he had finished *The Dain Curse* and before the publication of *The Maltese Falcon*. It is another novella-length story that begins with the Op trying to track down one more wayward offspring, this time the daughter of a wealthy East Coast family. He first encounters an incompetent confidence scheme run by Holy Joe Wales and Peggy Carroll intended to dip into the deep Hambleton family pockets. In the process of exposing the scheme the Op discovers the body of the daughter, Sue Hambleton, dead as a result of arsenic poisoning. While questioning the confidence duo, the gigantic criminal, Babe McCloor, Sue Hambleton's lover, appears and shoots Wales and escapes. Then ensues a protracted hunt and chase through the streets of San Francisco on foot, by car, and by streetcar. This ends when McCloor, by coincidence, attempts to hijack the taxi occupied by the Op and another Continental operative. There is a fight, another chase, and finally the Op shoots McCloor in both kneecaps. While the capture of McCloor wraps up the second murder in the story, the Op still has no answer to how or why Sue Hambleton died. In a conference at the Continental offices the Old Man reveals the meaning of the enigmatic clue — a copy of *The Count of Monte Cristo* wrapped in fly paper — and, with the news that Babe McCloor was hanged for his crimes, the case is closed.

After his excursion into the adventure story with "This King Business," "Fly Paper" was a return to Hammett's familiar territory — the territory of the 24 stories about the Op that he had written before *The Red Harvest*. In "Fly Paper" Hammett returned to San Francisco, after experimenting with new elements in his hero's character in the two novels and "This King Business." Thus, as opposed to town cleaning or king making or unraveling the labyrinthine ways of a criminal genius, "Fly Paper" begins as a missing persons case, the kind of thing that was probably one of the staples of the private detective business and, in turn, the spring board for the plots in a number of the previous Op stories. Recall that a number of other Op stories ("The Girl with Silver Eyes," "The Golden Horseshoe," "The Scorched Face," and "This King Business") all start off with an affluent family hiring the Continental Detective Agency to find someone. Likewise, in "Fly Paper" Hammett returned to showing his hero acting in concert both with other detective agency operatives and with the police. While Hammett had written some of his old favorites like Dick Foley and Mickey Linehan out of the series, in "Fly Paper" he reintroduces MacMan (whom he invented for *The Dain Curse*) and he brought back the Old Man and gave him a far more significant role in the story than the one he played in all of the previous stories. Like the early Op stories, almost incidentally "Fly Paper" drops in small details about the operations of the Continental Agency — its nationwide operations (the case begins with the New York branch of the Continental) and its attention to detail (the Op goes out carrying photos of both Sue Hambleton and Babe McCloor). If the agency once again plays a role in what the Op does in "Fly Paper," so do the police. There are cameo appearances of Lieutenant Duff, a somewhat larger one for Sergeant O'Gar, and at the railroad yard the crowd of those searching for McCloor includes a new cop, Harry Pebble, as well as a railroad policeman whose jaw has been broken by the fugitive. This was familiar territory. And operating in that territory also makes the Op shed the sophisticated accoutrements Hammett had invented in *The Dain Curse* and "This King Business." Thus, the Old Man, not the Op, solves the intellectual puzzle in the piece and, since much of the story involves hanging around with cops and criminals, the language in "Fly Paper" returns to revel in the language of the streets. Finally, like the best of the early Op stories, "Fly Paper" is about the streets of San Francisco. During the Op's first chase of Babe McCloor in the story, for example, in less than a page Hammett names twelve San Francisco streets (Market, Hyde, Taylor, Sixth, Mission, Ninth, Harrison, Third, Bryant, Eighth, Brannan, and Townsend) in order to add a jolt of realism to what is going on and to what the Op does. All of this recalls the Op stories of the 1920s.

Another element in "Fly Paper" that is reminiscent of early Op stories is the attention that Hammett pays to the details of detection. This, of course, was one of his principal aims in the first Op stories and also something that waned as the longer stories of the late twenties or that pretty much disappeared in *The Red Harvest*, *The Dain Curse*, and "This King Business." In their own particular ways, each of these works of fiction departs from the reality of crime, criminals, and detective and police work that Hammett knew as a Pinkerton and upon which he depended in his early Op stories. In the thirties Hammett, however, came back to thinking about the ways that real detectives work and this became one of the things that he harped about in his reviews in *The Saturday Review of Literature* and *The New York Evening Post*: there was no surer sign of incompetence among detective stories, Hammett kept on saying, than inaccurate descriptions of detective or police routine. This may have been one of the reasons that, after abandoning them in *The Red Harvest*, "This King Business," and *The Dain Curse*, he brought back the Continental and its operatives as well as San Francisco police personnel in "Fly Paper"—because real private detectives worked that way. Hammett had become confident enough not to tell his readers about the real world of crime and detectives but to show it to them. This appears, for example, in the way Hammett handled techniques for interviewing suspects. In "The Tenth Clew," written in 1924, Hammett approached the subject with the Op teaching readers about how and why it's done:

> One of the things that every detective knows is that it's often easy to get information — even a confession — out of a feeble nature simply by putting your face close to his and talking in a loud tone [72–73].

With five years of writing about the Op under his belt, in "Fly Paper" Hammett approached the same situation — getting information from the incompetent con man Holy Joe Wales— in this way:

> I went over and stood in front of him. I took his chin between my left thumb and fingers, raising his head and bending my own down until our noses were almost touching.

"Where you stumbled, Joe, was in sending the telegram right after the murder" [724].

It's the same thing, only in "Fly Paper" Hammett shows detective technique instead of talking about it. Another example is what he does with gunshot wounds in "Fly Paper." In one of the pieces in *The New York Evening Post* Hammett wrote around the same time as "Fly Paper" he tried to set readers straight about what happens when someone is shot with a large caliber weapon:

> When a bullet from a Colt .45, or any firearm of approximately the same size and power, hits you, even if not in a fatal spot, it usually knocks you over [910].

So, in "Fly Paper" he shows this in action when Babe shoots Holy Joe: "The bullets knocked Wales down on the sofa, back against the wall" (727). This is not only Hammett providing accurate detail about the world of crime and criminals, but it is also Hammett showing readers, once more, how to write a proper detective story.

Just as Hammett returned to writing about how real detectives do their jobs, he also returned to the kinds of criminals he wrote about in the earlier Op stories. For one thing, in "Fly Paper" they're stupid. He depicts Holy Joe as a bungler, Peggy Carroll as a harridan, and Babe McCloor as a muscle-bound berzerker. While Sue Hambleton never enters the story alive, the narration depicts her as a brainless, spoiled, thrill-seeking rich girl. They are all dumb and their stupidity is as much responsible for their undoing as the Op's actions. Just as he had done with some of the earlier gangster characters, however, Hammett expresses some admiration for the strong and stoic bad guy, in this case Babe McCloor. Patterned on Red O'Leary from "The Big Knock-Over," McCloor is an awesome physical specimen ("two hundred and fifty pounds of hard Scotch-Irish-Indian bone and muscle" [712]) and an irresistible force. Hammett bracketed "Fly Paper" with exhibitions of McCloor's strength in action, first when he destroys Vassos' speakeasy at the beginning and then with the fight that pits the Babe against the Op and MacMan at the end of the story. Just as important as McCloor's physical strength, "Fly Paper" also shows off his stoicism. Most pointedly this comes out in the hospital scene with McCloor recuperating from two shattered kneecaps: "He lay on his back in bed with a couple of pillows slanting his head up. The skin was pale and tight around his mouth and eyes, but there was nothing else to show he was in pain" (739). This is the same kind of thing that the Op witnessed with Whisper and Reno in *The Red Harvest.*

Along with his return to portraying both the simpleminded aspect of criminals as well as using one of them to convey admiration for those who accept pain without flinching or whining, in "Fly Paper" Hammett's fascination with gangster slang returns with a vengeance. Once again, this is something absent in *The Dain Curse* and "This King Business." In "Fly Paper" gangster slang is an integral part of the characters of Peggy Carroll and, to a greater extent, Babe McCloor. In two pages of conversation with the Op, for instance, McCloor uses improper grammar (including Hammett's characteristic use of double negatives, "I didn't pay no attention to your mug") and more mundane bits of gangster patois ("beefing," "mug," "croaker"). But Hammett also gave him a mouthful of more colorful slang expressions: McCloor uses "devastated" for injured, "jungled up" for hidden, "boiler" for car, "hammer and saws" for law officers, "tooting up the wrong ringer" for "barking up the wrong tree," "barbering" for talking, and "heel and toe" for leaving. Hammett wrote for him his best passages of underworld slang and it became an integral part of McCloor's character. And, as in the earlier Op stories, this kind of language also creeps into the Op's dialogue — in his interview with McCloor, for instance, he asks him why he "gave her the goog," which the gangster immediately understands as referring to his giving Sue Hambleton a black eye.

All of the Op's character in "Fly Paper" comes from his occupation as a manhunter. The action in "Fly Paper" centers on, first, the Op's knowledge of how to deal with petty criminals, and then on the protracted chase of McCloor. Framing these is the puzzle of how Sue Hambleton was killed, but this is a part of the story that readers almost lose sight of when the action shifts to hunting and chasing McCloor. As always, the action of the story demonstrates how adept and dogged the Op is in the prosecution of his duties as a detective. Interestingly, in "Fly Paper" the Op's role as a detective makes him a more active hero than in most of the earlier pieces. There is not only his frenetic chase of McCloor around San Francisco, but "Fly Paper" also contains a protracted fight scene between the Op, MacMan and McCloor that suggests a different emphasis in his character. Significantly, unlike the earlier stories, in "Fly Paper" Hammett does not include any mention of the Op being short and fat and, in fact, the physical details of his fight with the "giant" McCloor suggest that the short and fat description of the Op was a means of characterizing his hero in the early stories when the Op needed something extra to distinguish him from other detective heroes in the marketplace than to the description of a hero involved in a violent world peopled with large, strong, passionate, determined, violent, strong men.

In the stories preceding "Fly Paper" and in *The Red Harvest*, the Op functions more as a boss than an employee, and the Continental Agency, while it does not disappear entirely, plays an increasingly negligible part in what goes on. In *The Red Harvest* the Op avoids, as much as he can, any official contact with the agency, and in "This King Business" even though the agency is mentioned briefly at the beginning and the end, the Op is not even on the same continent as his employer. Hammett renewed readers' acquaintance with the agency in *The Dain Curse*, but in it, as in the stories of the late 1920s, the Op seems more of a leader than an employee. In "Fly Paper" the presence of the agency does not loom large, but it has more importance than in the stories immediately preceding it. The agency and its personnel play a new role in "Fly Paper." There are, of course, perfunctory mentions of named operatives and the practical assistance provided by the agency's nationwide offices, but its new importance in "Fly Paper" revolves on the role played by the Old Man. Whereas in all of the earlier stories Hammett emphasizes the Old Man as an efficient, albeit cold-blooded, administrator, in "Fly Paper" he focuses on his brains. For one thing, he makes the Old Man, not the Op, the font of wisdom about criminal history. Thus, when the Op brings up that Sue Hambleton had been poisoned with arsenic the Old Man comes back with "Ah, arsenical fly paper.... The Maybrick-Seddons trick" (722), alluding to the 1899 trial of Florence Maybrick and the 1909 trial of Frederick and Eliza Seddon, both of which turned on arsenic being soaked out of flypaper and used as poison. It's not that the Op is an entire slouch in matters of criminal history — he does respond that he worked an arsenic poisoning case in Louisville in 1916 — it's just that the Old Man gets things and gets to things faster. Citing historical precedent, however, is only the rehearsal for what happens at the end of the story. There, when the Op is stumped about the death of Sue Hambleton and, as a last resort, is going to read through the book he found wrapped in flypaper in her apartment, the Old Man reveals that he has already read the book and found the pertinent passage about arsenic eating. The whole new relationship between the Op and the Old Man, in fact, starts in the first pages of "Fly Paper":

> The Old Man gave me the telegram and a check, saying: "You know the situation. You'll know how to handle it."
>   I pretended I agreed with him [713].

While Hammett gave the Op self-effacing lines in the early stories, this is the most pronounced example of humility in all of them. And, of course, like the Op's other disingenuous comments that reflect self-conscious humility, this one isn't quite true: readers realize that the Op will know how to handle things because he always does. What this line does, however, is to serve as an introduction to the double focus of "Fly Paper." The story is both a continuation of the kind of action gangster story that Hammett had written, like "The Gutting of Couffignal" and "The Big Knock-Over," and also a genius detective puzzle story like the kind that he had begun to write with *The Dain Curse*. Thus, the Op acts as hero for the middle parts of the story and the Old Man springs the surprise at the end.

Citing historical crimes like the Maybrick and Seddon cases and springing the literary surprise at the end of "Fly Paper" is one of the things that connects the story with a move on Hammett's part toward the kind of puzzle story he had been reviewing for *The Saturday Review of Literature*. Looking back at the first run of Op stories, very few of them are puzzle stories that slyly drop a clue to the solution into the text and then unveil it as a surprise at the end. By 1930, however, the new crop of East Coast detective story writers and British imports like Christie and all the rest made the puzzle story popular. Readers can see this influence on Hammett's using the assistant detective trick in the plotting of *The Dain Curse*. And its influence is there in "Fly Paper." Significantly, however, even though Hammett uses some of the techniques of the new breed of detective story writer, in "Fly Paper" he did not give up the essentials that made the Op stories popular in the first place. This is something that he tried to do in *The Dain Curse* and something that he accomplished more successfully in "Fly Paper."

"The Farewell Murder"

Published in *Black Mask* in 1930 after the last installment of *The Maltese Falcon*, "The Farewell Murder" takes the Op to the small town of Farewell, California. The Continental Agency has been hired to send an operative to Farewell by Theodore Kavalov, who believes that Captain Hugh Sherry and his servant Marcus intend to kill him for the disgrace Sherry suffered from his naïve involvement with Kavalov's barely legal war profiteering in Cairo at the end of World War I. On the night of the Op's arrival, he and Kavalov's son-in-law, Dolph Ringgo, investigate a nocturnal prank and the next day the Op visits Sherry. Sherry, very much the insouciant British gentleman, tells the Op that he has come to Farewell because in Morocco he was told by a voice coming from an orange tree that Kavalov was going to die. He also tells the Op that, having just had a dream in which he saw Kavalov with his throat cut, Farewell no longer holds any allure for him, and that he and his servant will leave town that day. The day after Sherry leaves servants find Kavalov in bed with his throat cut. Then follows a complex hunt for Sherry and Marcus that ends with their discovery in Spokane, Washington. Shipped back to Farewell, neither Sherry nor Marcus is forthcoming about their whereabouts at the time of the murder. In spite of evidence that the Englishman and his servant were elsewhere at the time of the murder, Farewell's nervous DA puts Sherry on trial for Kavalov's murder and he is easily acquitted. Then, because she fears for her husband's life with Sherry on the loose, Mrs. Ringgo asks the Op to return to Farewell. There he becomes a late arrival at a shoot-out involving Sherry, Marcus, and Ringgo and, with a trick reminiscent of Poe's making the dead speak in "Thou Art the Man," he pins the murder of Kavalov and all of Sherry's Halloween shenanigans on Ringgo.

With "The Farewell Murder" Hammett returned to playing with the Gothic elements that he had tried out early in his career in "Laughing Masks." But this time he knew more of what he was doing. In "The Farewell Murder" Hammett used a spookier atmosphere and added a different approach to plot and character than he had in his early work and made "The Farewell Murder" a more successful piece of fiction than his awkward and failed attempt at writing Gothic fiction in the early 1920s. From the very beginning of "The Farewell Murder" Hammett worked on atmosphere. The Op arrives in Farewell on a dark and stormy evening where he is met at the railroad station by an Igor-like servant who doesn't seem to speak English. As they speed through a dark tunnel of trees on the way to Kavalov's mansion, a black man apparently stabbed with a knife appears on the road, scaring the willies out of the driver, but when the Op goes back to investigate the apparition the black man has disappeared. The chauffeur runs off in terror, leaving the Op to drive the car to Kavalov's eerie mansion himself. Even though Hammett described the place with the Op's casual diction, Kavalov's mansion is significantly strange:

> Take a flock of squat cones of various sizes, round off the points
> bluntly, mash them together with the largest one somewhere near
> the center, the others grouped around it in not too strict accordance
> to their sizes, ... and you would have a model of the Kavalov house
> [749].

The house seems to come right out of an early 1930s Hollywood horror movie and, in fact, Farewell seems more like it's in Transylvania than in California.

At the beginning of the story Hammett cranks up not just the Gothic atmosphere, but he also carries over such spooky elements to events and the people. It starts off with the disappearing black man the Op encounters on the road and continues when the Op and Ringgo go out into the woods on the dark and stormy night and find the family dog skinned and roasting on a spit. Everyone the Op meets is frightened. Not only does the chauffeur run off into the night "with scared, whitish eyes" (747), but when the Op arrives at the big house the gate keeper stammers, the servants mutter about strange goings-on, and the Op notices that his host has a pistol in the pocket of his evening clothes. In the characters Hammett couples fear with foreignness. The driver who speaks little or no English is a precursor to the introduction of the war profiteer Kavalov, who hired the agency to protect him. While Hammett provides for him only a scanty history attached principally to his shady business dealings and his devil-take-the-hindmost capitalism, Kavalov's diction in the story is a bit off from standard American diction and his name connects him with Boris Kapaloff, the sinister Russian integral to the Gothic intentions of "Laughing Masks." But the foreignness among the characters in "The Farewell Murder" doesn't stop there. The Op notes that Kavalov's daughter's face "had Asia in it" (751), and in addition to the weird inhabitants of the big house there is also the central threat provided by the British colonial Sherry and his African servant, Marcus. They, however, are quite different from the Kapalov crowd. They may not be Americans but they are something more than alien and spooky. Sherry and Marcus may be threatening but they are also engaging, ironic, suave, and enigmatic. Hammett also combines these elements in Sherry's character with the exotic and inexplicable part of the Gothic tradition. Thus, Sherry's casual description of why he has turned up in Farewell is the following:

> I was in Udja, ... and one morning a voice came to me from an orange tree. It said "Go to Farewell, in California, in the States, and there you will see Theodore Kavalov die." I thought that was a capital idea. I thanked the voice, told Marcus to pack, and came here [761].

What Hammett seems to have done here is to take the combination of brutish foreigner and sportsman character that he portrayed ineptly in "Laughing Masks" and split it into two people in "The Farewell Murder." Kapalov became the stolid Slavic brute and Sherry became the suave sportsman who treats people and events as if they were part of a game in which irony and aloof good humor are the preferred character traits.

On top of the atmosphere and the characters, the plot of "The Farewell Murder" depends on the Gothic tradition and the linkage of that tradition with that of the detective story. Abrogation of the laws of biology and physics forms the basis of one important branch of Gothic fiction: in these stories the dead walk, humans transform into wolves and bats, spirits defy time and space, voices from trees and dreams reveal the truth, and slugs from a .45 have no effect on ectoplasm. Hammett played around with some of this a bit with the scenes at the Temple of the Holy Grail in *The Dain Curse.* In "The Farewell Murder" he made the paranormal the factor that establishes the plot. Therefore, all of the preternatural business associated with Sherry's appearance in Farewell and the voice from the orange tree brings the Op to Farewell and gets the action of the story started. After the murder, the plot of "The Farewell Murder" hinges on the issue of defying time and space. The conundrum the authorities face is how Marcus and Sherry could have been in two places hours apart at the same time? And then, because it is a detective story, the conclusion of "The Farewell Murder" reveals the mechanics behind the Gothic machinery.

Because it is a detective story, the answer to the crime problem in "The Farewell Murder," of course, is that Sherry and Marcus can't be in two places at once. The illusion that they can be in two places at once, as well as all of the spooky effects encountered by the Kapalov household, is not because of an alternate reality but the result of an elaborate ruse set up by the murderer. This is pretty much standard detective story fare. In "The Farewell Murder," however, Hammett makes the additional point about the Gothic in that the mumbo jumbo about the spirit world and miscellaneous Halloween antics really only frighten and fool stupid people. Consequently, most everybody in Farewell is pretty dense. In the Op's comments about him and in his dialogue Hammett makes sure that the readers know that Kavalov is stolid, pompous, inept, and ignorant. Mrs. Ringgo, his daughter, isn't much better: "Her face ... was pretty, passive, unintelligent" (751). Kavalov's servants from the chauffeur to the household staff to the farmhands are all "useless." And when the local authorities take up the investigation of Kavalov's murder they fall into the same category: the sheriff mumbles through his moustache, and the district attorney chews his fingernails down to nubs because he is prosecuting a case about which he is entirely clueless.

Unlike "Fly Paper," in which Hammett put the Op back on the streets and returned to demonstrating his understanding of and connection with naïve and beetle-browed underworld characters, in "The Farewell Murder" he carried over the increased social and personal sophistication he had developed for the Op in "This King Business" and *The Dain Curse.* For one thing, unlike the Op's minimalist lifestyle implied in the early stories where his companions seem to be only cops and ops, in "The Farewell Murder" Hammett presents a formal dinner —complete with an extensive menu that includes caviar and *crème de menthe* — at which the Op clearly knows which fork to use. Just as in "This King Business" where the Op has acquired the background of an officer's rank and the ability to converse in foreign languages, in "The Farewell Murder" he is entirely at home in the upper-crust manners and rituals at the Kavalov castle. In this story Hammett replaces the stupid criminal upon which a lot of his early fiction depends with stupid victims and clueless agents of the law. This all suggests a movement away from the communal action of the early stories toward portraying the Op as an exemplar of an elite of intelligence and attitude. Indeed, as the Op stories progress from 1923 to the time of "The Farewell Murder" they move from showing the detective uncovering the truth before the readers' eyes with the help of the agency and the police, to the unaided detective knowing the truth and then, as a surprise, revealing the answer and explaining the process of discovery to both open-mouthed witnesses as well as to the readers. The inevitable result of this change is increased emphasis on the detective's intelligence as well as his separateness from the rest of the characters. This corresponds with Hammett's increased emphasis on the Op as a boss, the decreased importance of the characters and facilities connected with the Continental Detective Agency and the police department, and the additions and corrections he made to the social aspects of the Op's character. It has to do, as well, with the company that he keeps. Just as in *The Dain Curse* the Op leaves behind O'Gar and his other professional associates and spends his time with and appreciates the company and conversation of the intellectual and socially prominent master criminal, in "The Farewell Murder" the Op feels more at ease with Sherry than he does with the stolid and brutish inhabitants of Kavalov's mansion or with Farewell's law enforcement personnel. Some of this has to do with brains, but a lot more of it has to do with attitude. Early after his arrival at the big house Kavalov's son-in-law warns the Op that Kavalov has no sense of humor; this is a stark contrast to his reception at Sherry's cottage where the Op finds humor and irony and a degree of the brand of laziness that Hammett made an essential part of many of his favorite characters.

During the story the Op, of course, is not taken in by any of the Gothic shenanigans. Detectives never get taken in by masquerades and funhouse effects—which is just what the Op tells Ringgo at the end of "The Farewell Murder." Opposed to the characters who are incapacitated by the eerie events, throughout the narrative the Op does real world, material detective things. He looks for clues, watches people, and uses the resources of the Continental Detective Agency to find out who is who and who has done what. In his first meeting with Sherry, the Op even tosses in the German term for horror when he tells him that he knows what and why strange things have been going on in Farewell:

"That's why you've been trying to hurry it up?" I asked.

"I beg your pardon?"

"*Schrecklichkeit*," I said, "Rocky skulls, dog barbecues, vanishing corpses" [761].

Characteristically, however, even though the Op tells the readers at the end of the story that he knew what was what "right along," it's not the Op's reading of character or possession of facts that lead to the villain's undoing in "The Farewell Murder." As in so many of his other Op stories, evil is pretty much self-destructive. Thus, after Kavalov's death and Sherry's acquittal, since the agency is no longer under contract to settle affairs in Farewell, the Op would have let the whole matter slide had not Mrs. Ringgo come to San Francisco and hired the agency to look after her husband's safety. On top of that, at the end of the story the conspirators fall upon one another, resulting in Sherry's death. In "The Farewell Murder," however, there is more to wrapping up the case than that. Ringgo is too tough to confess when faced with defeat. The Op, however, is a better magician than the bad guy. Throughout the story it was the villain's purpose to create the illusion of the supernatural for his own ends. At the conclusion of the story the Op turns the tables and creates his own stage effects in order to bring the murderer to justice. Just as in Poe's story "Thou Art the Man" the narrator creates the illusion of a corpse being reanimated in order to bring a murderer to justice. The Op uses Sherry's corpse to bring the crime home to Ringgo: he pretends to hear Sherry's dying identification of Ringgo as the mastermind behind all of the goings-on in Farewell.

Hammett did much better with Gothic technique in "The Farewell Murder" than he had earlier. In fact it was no doubt the Gothic elements in this story that prompted his agent to put together a deal the following year that led to *Creeps By Night* (1931), an anthology of weird tales (including Faulkner's "A Rose for Emily") for which Hammett wrote a perfunctory introduction. In spite of his successful return to the Gothic and his increasing use of tactics like those of main-line golden age detective story writers, writing about the Op was something that increasingly held little interest for Hammett.

None of the Internet search engines can find a town in California named Farewell. Maybe there was one in the 1930s; maybe there wasn't, but the year before Hammett published "The Farewell Murder" was one of leave taking for him. In the spring of 1929 he left his family and established a separate residence in San Francisco. In October he and Nell Martin left California and moved to New York (Layman 114). He also tried to say good-bye to the Op. First, he created a new hero for *The Maltese Falcon*, which began serial publication in September, and then in October he tried to do without a hero in the disastrous short story "The Diamond Wager," a joke-caper yarn set in Europe to which he did not even attach his name but published under the name of Samuel Dashiell. The good-bye, however, was a short one; Hammett had one more Op story to write.

"Death & Company"

"Death & Company" took up five pages in the November 1930 issue of *Black Mask*. It was Hammett's last story for the magazine. He then had an agent and published his rapidly diminishing output of short fiction in slick periodicals.

The story begins with a conference between the Old Man, the Op, and a client, Mr. Chappell, who has come to the agency with a note he received demanding ransom for the return of his kidnapped wife. The note is melodramatically signed "Death & Co." The Op advises that Chappell meet the ransom demands and arranges for the police to watch the site where Chappell is to leave $5,000 for the return of his wife Louise. The day after Chappell goes to the drop site, the police who have been staking out the location report that they saw no one appear to pick up the money. Then a second ransom note comes in the mail. Chappell once again goes off with a packet of $5,000 and reports that the first payment had been taken from the drop site. The next day a Death & Company note arrives saying that because Chappell involved the police, Mrs. Chappell has been killed. The Op and the cops find her body at an apartment they eventually learn belongs to Dick Moley, "a gambler, gunman, and grifter-in-general" (123). Chappell then says that he has received a telephone call from Death & Company threatening his life. Waiting outside Chappell's house the Op sees Moley enter and, before he can intervene, the gunman kills Chappell. The story closes with the Op telling Moley that he has bought himself an unnecessary trip to the gallows because the Op knew all along that Chappell had killed his adulterous wife and rigged the phony kidnapping scheme, and that he would have tied things up legally without the gangster's intervention.

"Death & Company" is hardly a masterpiece. From the aficionado's point of view, this very short story leaves out plenty of crucial details— like how Chappell sends himself special delivery letters when he seems to be constantly under observation. "Death & Company" does, however, contain a number of Hammett's characteristic touches as well as clear indications of how the Op had changed since his first introduction seven years earlier. One such element is sex. The character of the adulterous or promiscuous woman was a common ingredient in a number of Hammett's later Op stories. While in some of the stories from the mid–1920s Hammett had drawn women who hold out the prospect of sex in order to tempt the Op — most notably in "The Girl with Silver Eyes," "The Whosis Kid," and "The Gutting of Couffignal" — in stories at the end of the decade he increasingly began to introduce adulterous or promiscuous women. Thus, "The Main Death" centers on the Op covering up a wife's extramarital adventures, and everyone in Personville knows that Dinah Brand is for sale to the highest bidder. On top of this, one of Hammett's recurring character stereotypes was that of the spoiled rich girl out for kicks — this character type comes into one of his earliest Op stories, "Crooked Souls," and reappears in "The Scorched Face," "$106,000 Blood Money," and "Fly Paper." Just as in his "sex stories" his overall attitude toward promiscuous women in the Op stories was ambivalent and ambiguous. In "The Main Death" and *The Red Harvest* and even, perhaps, in "This King Business" he presents sexual adventuring as an understandable and acceptable facet of the women characters, while in other pieces the action of the story visits punishment upon promiscuity — stricken consciences in "The Scorched Face" and "$106,000 Blood Money," and death in "Fly Paper" and "Death & Company." Readers, however, never meet the women who are murdered as a consequence of promiscuity or adultery in the last two stories: they only appear as corpses. Interestingly, the way in which Hammett presented the corpses in "Fly Paper" and "Death & Company," stories in which women die as a result of irregular relationships, is significantly different. In the first story, even though the Op notes that Sue Hambleton died wearing "yellow pajamas trimmed with black lace," his description stresses the physical attributes of death: the whiteness of her face and feet and the bruises on her face. The Op's description of Louise Chappell's body in "Death & Company," however, emphasizes sex: even though she has been dead for several days, before he mentions the bruises on her body the Op's description fastens on the fact that she is wearing a man's bathrobe over "pinkish lingerie." In "Death & Company," mentioning Louise Chappell's underwear may have been purposefully risqué for the times but it was mainly a clue. At the end of the story readers learn that she has been playing house with the gangster Moley for some time and hanging around alive and then dead in dishabille provides proof of her adultery first for her husband and then for the Op. The main point of Louise Chappell in "Death & Company," then, is the same as that which Hammett used with the women in his other stories of the time. Readers know nothing of her nature or character or motives because, unlike his practice in his sex stories, in these detective stories Hammett chose to focus on responses to adultery or promiscuity as opposed to its causes.

"Death & Company," however, isn't about adultery: readers don't know about Louise Chappell's affair until the end of the story. It, of course, is about the Op's competence and intelligence as a detective, but the principal focus of the story rests on Hammett's depiction of Chappell and the implicit contrast with the gunman Moley. When he introduces Chappell the Op describes him as a middle-aged man who is "solidly built," but who has loose features and a dead fish's handshake. Overall, he impresses the Op as being "shaky and washed out by worry or grief or fear" (117). During the story Chappell sweats, shakes, and seems to come close to swooning when the letter announcing his wife's death arrives. By the end of the story he shows signs of a complete physical breakdown: "Chappell was in a bad way.... He was shivering as if with a chill and his eyes were almost idiotic in their fright" (123). He is so near collapse that near the end of the story the Op calls a physician for him. Readers, however, learn at the end of the story that Chappell's emotional and physical breakdown is a result of something other than grief for the death of his wife. Maybe it was caused by the shock of discovering his wife's infidelity or by his guilty conscience or by his fear of discovery. But none of this matters to the Op or to Hammett. The most important thing in the story is Chappell's behavior. No matter the cause, Chappell is a portrait of a man who can't take it. Hammett makes him a little man who has committed a crime of passion and then manufactured a grandiose fiction to cover it up. That fiction is both patently melodramatic in its implication that Chappell and his wife are victims of a vast, organized, sinister master criminal organization, and it is also transparent to the Op and to the police who witness his increasingly futile attempts to pull the whole thing off.

Moley, on the other hand, is somebody who can take it. Hammett patterned him partly on Red O'Leary from "The Big Knock-Over" and, even more closely, on the reincarnation of O'Leary in "Fly Paper" in the character of Babe McCloor. With O'Leary, McCloor, and Moley one of the most significant character traits lies in their capacity for action: when something bad happens to them, they react immediately. Thus, when McCloor discovers that Sue Hambleton is dead he picks up his .45, hunts down Holy Joe Wales, and shoots him. It's the same thing that Moley does in "Death & Company," only he uses a .44. Another feature of these hard characters is that they base their actions upon principle. In "Death & Company" Moley tells the Op that he loved Louise Chappell ("...only I wasn't playing. I meant it" [126]), and that Chappell deserved to die for his wife's murder ("I've got a hunch I came pretty near giving the rat what he deserved" [126]). More important than either of these traits, however, is that Moley and his progenitors accept the consequences of their actions, they acknowledge facts, and they don't whine. In "Death & Company" Moley does an aloof analysis of his capture, explaining that he dropped his gun when the Op shot him in the leg. And in the face of the Op's lecture about the futility of his actions and the specter of the gallows, Moley's only response is curiosity about Chappell's actions. Indeed, early on, when the cops discover Moley's connection with the crime, one of them, Callahan, observes that "he'll laugh while being tough" (124). So it is not the detective but the hard-boiled man who attracts more and more of Hammett's attention and admiration in stories beginning with "The Big Knock-Over."

If readers know the Op only from "Death & Company" and the other final stories, they have a far different conception of his character than that which Hammett crafted for his first run of Op stories in the early 1920s. For one thing, the Op's criminology became more sophisticated. Whereas in the early stories the Op's effectiveness depended upon his wits as well as his acquired skills as a detective and his knowledge of underworld characters, in the later stories Hammett adds to this expertise in historical crime. In "Fly Paper" there is the allusion to the historic arsenic-related Maybrick and Seddon cases and in "Death & Company" the Op rattles off the "history of kidnapping from the days of Charlie Ross" (119), alluding to the 1874 crime that was the earliest known case of kidnapping in the United States. Here, the influence of the golden age detective fiction makes itself felt: the new generation of detective writers that Hammett had been reviewing had made the citation of historic crimes like Crippen's a standard character feature. Hammett borrowed the device to supplement the authority he used to bring to his fiction from his years as a private detective. This minor addition goes along with Hammett's decreased attention to process — what the detective does — and increased use of the surprise ending.

A prominent sign of the subtle changes in Hammett's detective stories shows up in his new attitude toward the Op's height, weight, and age. Knowing only the late stories readers don't know anything about these things. As we have seen earlier, in the first stories Hammett made the Op regularly speak of himself as short, fat, and middle aged. Some of this was for marketing — to distinguish his hero from all of the young, tall, lean, muscular detective heroes that were the norm in the patently unrealistic detective stories of the early 1920s. More important, perhaps, is that Hammett used the short, fat, middle-aged references to both connect his hero with the average man and to develop the Op as not only a realistic but also as an ironically self-effacing hero. The Op may be smart and knowledgeable and willing to mix it up with the bad guys, but he is also an average person who has a realistic and ironic view of himself. In other words, when one has to wriggle and struggle to button one's trousers, the Op demonstrates the notion that it is best not to take oneself altogether seriously. All of this is an essential ingredient of the Op's character as Hammett developed him in the 1920s. But the short, fat business disappears in the last batch of Op stories. It's not that he didn't have ample opportunities to exploit this part of the Op's character. There exist in the later stories multiple occasions in which Hammett could have made the Op comment on being short and fat: the Op chases after bogeymen in the dark woods in "The Farewell Murder" he runs up the front steps of Chappell's house at the conclusion of "Death & Company." But there's no mention in these stories about height or girth. This corresponds with the Op's increased social sophistication — his knowledge of languages and how to behave in affluent surroundings— that seems to develop in the later stories. It also goes along with an increased aloofness on the Op's part toward truth and justice. The Op becomes more of a boss than a part of a team, and his friendship with fellow detectives O'Gar and Dick Foley has been lost. More important, perhaps, the late stories seem to manifest a different view of personal responsibility and justice. Thus, rather than feeling any personal or professional obligation to set things right, in "The Farewell Murder" the Op leaves Farewell without solving Kavalov's murder and does not return to unravel the plot until Mrs. Ringgo contracts with the agency to have him return to protect her husband. And in "Death & Company" the Op sits in a taxi waiting for Moley to arrive and execute Chappell rather than simply turning him over to the police.

5

Afterthoughts

In the eight years between the time that Hammett's first publication appeared in *The Smart Set* in 1922 and when "Death & Company" came out in *Black Mask* in 1930, he had written 63 magazine pieces (including two appearances in *Experience* that no one can locate and "A Man Named Thin," which remained unpublished until the 1960s), several poems, four novels, numerous pieces for literary periodicals, and a stack of book reviews. During that time Hammett struggled with poor health and near destitution as well as experiencing changing relationships with his wife, family, and assorted female companions. During that time he also tried to figure out what he wanted to be — a satirist, or a serious literary figure; an advertising executive or an expert on crime, criminals, and detectives; a popular mystery writer or just a man about town who didn't have to do anything. Throughout the twenties, much in the manner of the hero of his "Laughing Masks," Hammett took advantage of those things that circumstance put in his path: his Baltimore connections with H. L. Mencken led first to his lofty aspirations as a *Smart Set* writer as well as for a chance for quick cash writing for the Mencken-related pulps *Spicy Stories* and *The Black Mask*; his Pinkerton experience gave him something to write about; his job with Samuels Jewelry led him to write about advertising and to think more specifically about language; his association with Captain Shaw and then Blanche Knopf led him to write novels instead of novelettes; and the books he encountered in reviewing mysteries for *The Saturday Review of Literature* and *The New York Evening Post* changed the way he viewed his own role as a detective story writer. When

Hammett started to write he tried lots of things and he thought he could do anything.

The Persistence of Satire

Hammett broke into print as a satirist, as a wry observer of the follies of men, women, and society. Pretense, pomposity, arrogance, conceit, and vanity wrapped in naïveté form the subject matter for his first publications. In them he ridiculed those traits across the social board—from the grocer who believes he can buy immortality and the barber who believes manliness is the guide to behavior, to aristocrats reveling in their illusions about their own greatness, to petty criminals who have neither the brains nor the discipline nor the courage to do anything right. In terms of satire of social institutions, Hammett had a much narrower range. He started out with a caustic look at marriage, and "The Parthian Shot" and "The Barber and His Wife," published two months apart, skewer the ways that women and men undermine the institution. Relatively quickly he added to his satiric repertoire private detectives, the law, and criminals. "The Master Mind" ridicules the big-wig genius detective whether from fiction (a la Sherlock Holmes) or fact (Allan Pinkerton, William Burns, et al.). In "From the Memoirs of a Private Detective," just about everyone and everything connected with the detective business—crime prevention and apprehension, criminals, courts, detectives, and even public gullibility—gets the raspberry for simplemindedness. The pattern that Hammett followed in his first year as a writer was to take what amounted to satiric vignettes conceived for *The Smart Set* and expand them into short stories published wherever he could publish them. Thus, "From the Memoirs of a Private Detective" became "The Sardonic Star of Tom Doody," "The Vicious Cycle," and "The Green Elephant." And "The Parthian Shot" generated his run of sex stories. In a real sense, all of these played a role in the creation of Hammett's detective stories.

Indeed, after leaving *The Smart Set*, a good bit of Hammett's short fiction draws upon the satiric bent that he developed for his stories in Mencken's "magazine of cleverness." This is evident especially in his criminal stories. Thus, Hammett extends the comic ridicule of the bumbling, pathetic losers portrayed in "The Sardonic Star of Tom Doody" and "The Green Elephant" to "Itchy the Debonair" and "The New Racket." These pieces are both satiric in intent and comic in character, incident and dialogue, a combination that Hammett most happily executed in "The Second Story Angel," where criticism and irony combined with comic stereotypes, slapstick action, and appropriately amusing dialogue. Practiced first in his openly satiric stories, Hammett used some of these same techniques in his other kinds of fiction. They are all there, for instance, in "Ber-Bulu" with its stock characters and comic deflation of arrogance and bullying. And they are distributed in the detective stories, from the stereotype of the mincing detective Robin Thin, to the Keystone Kops opening of "Arson Plus" where all of the Irish deputies named Mac jam into Sheriff Jim Tarr's office door, to the bantering, mock Chinese hyperbole in "Dead Yellow Women." Most significantly, Hammett's practice and practices in satire extend to that part of the Continental Op's character that recognizes that he is an average man confronted with extraordinary events and demands. This comes up most clearly in passages about the Op's size and shape like the one in "The Girl with Silver Eyes" where he grouses about struggling out of his pajamas and then stuffing his bulk into his street clothes.

On top of this more or less lighthearted humor, Hammett often displays a more serious satiric bent. This appears most frequently in his sex stories where he intends to give everyone the business by revealing the shallowness and delusions of both partners. "Esther Entertains," for example, unfolds to show readers not only a woman who may or may not be vacuous and irritating, but also a man who is arrogant, self-deluded, and governed by his libido. More pointedly, "The Ruffian's Wife" shows a wife's loss of illusions about her husband and herself, coupled with the deflation of the husband from swashbuckling adventurer to repellent "sneak thief." Even though the early Op stories principally focus on process and not on satire, nonetheless Hammett often couples caricatures of semicomic bumbling criminal characters with characters with dangerous and repellent personalities. Thus, "Crooked Souls" brings together the hapless Penny Quale and the wild, spoiled, headstrong, perverse Audrey Gatewood; "The Zigzags of Treachery" couples the inept Estep with the sinister and murderous Ledwich; and "The Whosis Kid" contrasts Billie, the bone-headed bruiser, with the dangerous, hair-triggered, sociopathic Kid. The most significant impact of Hammett's *Smart Set* apprenticeship in satire and irony, however, resides in the larger ironies that emerged during the course of the Op stories. While early stories like "Arson Plus" and "Slippery Fingers" depended partly on the criminals' mistakes but mostly on the detective's skill, knowledge, and persistence, the later Op stories move, more and more, toward turning on circumstance, luck, and the inherent weakness of criminals. These things, rather than the detective's actions, bring about justice. In a number of stories after "The Whosis Kid," the Op is content to stir things up a bit, or, as in the case of "Death & Company," to simply watch while the bad guys slug it out among themselves. The ironic self-destructiveness of evil, then, becomes the central reality that affects the nature and actions of both the criminals and the detective in most of the later Op stories.

Criminals

Underneath the implicit and explicit irony that informs most of his detective fiction, Hammett devoted considerable attention to developing in the Op stories a variety of criminal character types who make the plots run. Taken as a whole, the Op stories alternate between three kinds of plots.

1. Standard detective story plots centering on domestic crimes based on passion or accident ("Crooked Souls," "It," "Nightshots," "Women, Politics and Murder," "Corkscrew," "The Creeping Siamese," "The Main Death," "The Farewell Murder," and "Death & Company")
2. Plots focused on what can be termed independent criminal contractors motivated only by greed ("Arson Plus," "Slippery Fingers," "The Tenth Clew," "The Zigzags of Treachery," "The House on Turk Street," and "The Golden Horseshoe")
3. Plots having to do with characters involved in organized crime ("The Bodies Piled Up," "The Girl with Silver Eyes," "The Whosis Kid," "One Hour," "The Scorched Face," "Dead Yellow Women," "The Big Knock-Over," and "$106,000 Blood Money")

While the domestic stories display little that is especially unique about Hammett's villains (in part because their motives necessarily remain hidden until the end of the narrative), in the organized crime and private contractor stories Hammett developed a cast of stock characters. There is, starting at the bottom, the violent, simian, knuckle dragger seen first with Hook in "The House of Turk Street" and then with Big Chin in "The Whosis Kid," Gooseneck Flinn in "The Golden Horseshoe," and, finally, in finished form, with Pogy in "The Big Knock-Over." The gigantic Billie in "The Whosis Kid" comes from the same mold, but instead of being solely motivated by crime and violence he is actuated, in beauty and the beast fashion, by love. With these characters Hammett clearly sides with the Lombroso camp and classifies them for his readers as "degenerates" by comparing them to apes and emphasizing their prominent jaws (one of Lombroso's characteristics for classifying devolved humans). At the other end of the pseudo-Darwinian criminal scale, Hammett flirted briefly with the character of the Napoleon of crime and the master criminal, but they appear mostly offstage. Thus, the motivation in "The Bodies Piled Up" depends on an unseen "mastermind of crime," and the organizer of the big knock-over in the story with that title is the inconspicuous and seldom seen criminal genius Papadopolos. A large group of characters who carry over Hammett's basic notion that criminals are stupid occupies the middle ground of criminal types. Most of them are inept confidence men, a character type that stretches from Clane in "Slippery Fingers" all the way through to Holy Joe Wales in "Fly Paper." In that middle ground between the brutal cretin and the mastermind, however, Hammett created a few competent criminal characters and, significantly, they tend to be foreigners—the Chinese Tai in "The House on Turk Street" and two Englishmen (the false Ashcraft in "The Golden Horseshoe" and Captain Sherry in "The Farewell Murder"). While the Op expresses some admiration for this last group, the half-smart characters in this criminal middle ground lay little claim to the Op's or the readers' sympathy, and that they are disposed of in the stories makes little difference. This is not the case with the last of Hammett's criminal types—the hard-boiled ones.

Hammett's first draft of this character type was in "The Bodies Piled Up." This early piece centers on two very, very dangerous men: "Guy Cudner, alias 'The Darkman,' was the most dangerous bird on the Coast, if not the country" (85), and Orrett who "dresses well and doesn't look like a rowdy—but harder than hell! A big game hunter!" (86). Indeed, when the Op looks into Orrett's eyes he sees in them the eyes of a "congenital killer." Both of these men are smart, efficient, single-minded, capable of immediate action and reaction, and immune to the views of others. When he meets them the Op simply gets out of the way. Unlike his later treatment of the sociopathic killer in the persons of the Whosis Kid and Wilmer in *The Maltese Falcon*, however, Hammett treats Cudner and Orrett with sympathy (as when the Op lies to the dying Cudner in an attempt to put his mind at ease) and awe (reflected in Orrett's final assurance that his revenge will be swift and complete). Significantly, perhaps, Hammett's description of Orrett's face as one composed of lines and angles looks forward to his description of Sam Spade's face in *The Maltese Falcon*. Nonetheless, as impressive as Cudner and Orrett are, readers see only glimpses of them in "The Bodies Piled Up." Hammett also shows brief glimpses of another pair of hard-boiled gangsters (Tin Star Joplin and Kilcourse) in "The Girl with Silver Eyes." But other than noting Kilcourse's "alertness hiding behind an amused half-smile on his handsome dark face" (174), Hammett did little to develop either of them as characters.

Such is not the case with Red O'Leary in "The Big Knock-Over."

O'Leary is the central character in the piece. He is a bad guy, of course, linked to Big Flora and Papadopolis. He is big, strong, courageous, confident, and self-possessed. Larger than life, almost a force of nature, he happily mixes it up with anyone and against any odds: in the fight at Larrouy's, for instance, he not only prevails against overwhelming odds but he also sweeps the Op, Jack Counihan, and Nancy Regan along with him. Perhaps just as important as his strength and confidence, Hammett includes as an essential part of Red's character an element of joy. When faced with the final battle in the story, Red laughs "a triumphant laugh that boasted of his toughness" (583). After "The Big Knock-Over," Hammett's next versions of the hard-boiled criminal were in the portraits of Whisper and Reno in *The Red Harvest*. They both of them possess the capacity for resolute, direct, and immediate action, act on principle, and, ultimately, are willing to accept the consequences of their actions without blinking or whining. As seen above, Hammett extended the hard-boiled criminal into his last stories with the characters of Babe McCloor in "Fly Paper" and Moley in "Death & Company."

Defining the Op

Throughout the Op stories, traditional or conventional attitudes toward crime do not have a lot to do with the way Hammett defines his hero. Indeed, with some exceptions— notably "Nightshots," "The Zigzags of Treachery," "Who Killed Bob Teal?" "The Golden Horseshoe," and "The Scorched Face"— the Op expresses little sympathy for the victims of crime. And in two of the stories in which he does do so ("The Zigzags of Treachery" and "The Golden Horseshoe"), Hammett deliberately contrasts the Op's modest concern for the victims with attorney Vance Richmond's overwrought reactions to his clients' predicaments. Likewise, the notions of upholding justice or avenging wrongs against society or humanity have little to do with why any of Hammett's detectives do what they do. At the beginning of the Op stories, the hero defines himself almost exclusively by his job, and, as often as not, he talks about his job as being a "manhunter." In these stories the Op explains for readers the finer points of how detectives track people down, and one of the reasons that Hammett adds the short, fat, middle-aged description to the Op's character is to focus on the detective's technique rather than the distracting attributes of the conventional, larger than life, romantic, neo-Sherlockian hero. Insofar as the Op demonstrates passion in the early stories, Hammett usually connects it with his job rather than with feelings for others or dedication to an abstract principle. Here lies the primary reason for the introduction of the chorus line of seductive women in the Op stories: from Evelyn Trowbridge in "Arson Plus" to the princess in "The Gutting of Couffignal," all of them exist to demonstrate the Op's choice of work versus sensuality. Insofar as he possesses other kinds of passions, they all relate to his job or his doing his job. Thus, the Op's stubbornness leads to the conclusion in "Slippery Fingers," revenge for the death of a coworker fuels "Who Killed Bob Teal?" and the Op punches Madden Dexter in "The Zigzags of Treachery" not because of his crime but because he has sapped him and tossed him in the bay. The whole issue of passion versus profession comes to a head in the Poisonville theme of *The Red Harvest* when the Op realizes that he has been poisoned by the infestation of violence in Personville. By the time of *The Red Harvest*, moreover, the Op has lost the most important thing that helped to sustain him in the early stories—his fraternal and paternal connection with the police (his intimacy with O'Gar and Pat Reedy disappears in *The Dain Curse*) and the fellowship of his colleagues at the agency: Bob Teal dies, Tommy Howd disappears, Jack Counihan betrays him, and Dick Foley becomes a foppish, prudish runt instead of the "shadow ace."

If Hammett characterizes the Op by his vocation in the early Op pieces, more and more, as the stories continue, he comes to define him by his attitudes toward the criminals in the stories. Originally, criminals existed to present problems for the detective to solve and to be put away at the end of the story. The bad guys may possess some degree of cunning, but they have little impact on the Op or on the reader. Then Hammett started to flesh out the hard-boiled criminal he introduced first in Orrett in "The Bodies Piled Up." Unlike his attitude toward earlier criminals, in the later stories the Op develops a degree of admiration for the essential and thorough toughness of Red O'Leary, Whisper, Reno, Babe McCloor, and Moley. Significantly, however, these late stories do not recount contests between bad tough and good tough men, between the criminals and the Op. Consistently, the violent, hard-boiled gangsters destroy themselves and the Op serves as an observer or, at best, a mopper-upper rather than a combatant. Just as the fat, laissez-faire minister of police prevails at the end of "This King Business," the Op wins in the late stories by doing little beyond seeing and knowing. It was not simply Hammett's using the new and popular surprise ending that made the Op start to withhold answers from his community and the readers, it was also a move on his part to make his hero separate and aloof from the world of criminals in which he worked. In some ways, in fact, the late incarnations of the Op look back to Hammett's beginnings as a writer and his initial definition of himself in print not as a detective story writer but as a satiric observer of folly and irony. Thus, in the late pieces the Op is no longer the short, fat, genial detective who wishes only to tell readers about his experiences and how real detectives do their jobs. Increasingly separate from civil and corporate law enforcement, in the later stories, the Op meets mostly stupid and venal people and tells stories heavy with irony about men possessed of great vitality and resolve, whose vitality and resolve contribute to their destruction of others and themselves.

Toward Hard-Boiled Style

When Raymond Chandler wrote that "I doubt that Hammett had any deliberate artistic aims whatever" in "The Simple Art of Murder" (16), he probably only had Hammett's detective stories to base his judgment on. Taking all of his early writings into account, it seems that rather than having no aims for his writing he initially had too many. His studies at Munson's business school aimed him at news reporting; his contributions to *The Smart Set* offered the prospect of a career as a clever and sophisticated observer of universal folly; his job at Samuels Jewelry convinced him as an advertising writer he could be what amounted to the unacknowledged legislator of his time; and his letters to highbrow journals showed an aspiration toward being a voice in the world of belle lettres. While during that time Hammett tested the marketplace for different kinds of fiction that would pay the landlord and the grocer, he also experimented with technique.

POINT OF VIEW

Most prominently, Hammett experimented with the way he told the stories and to that end he tested various kinds of third-person and first-person points of view. His success with point of view can be seen in stories such as "The New Racket" and "Esther Entertains" in which Hammett reveals the intent of the stories through the ways in which he narrates them. In a number of stories Hammett's interest in and manipulation of point of view connects with his *Smart Set* grounding in satire in that their narrators reveal aspects of character, unaware that they are doing so, thereby providing an additional, second perspective for readers beyond that which the narrators intend. The narrator of "Esther Entertains," for example, unintentionally reveals his superficiality and inconsistency as he describes his apparently trivial and dim-witted mistress. On the lighter side, in the Robin Thin stories, part of their point rests with the detective's abstracted obliviousness to the meaning of almost everything except his poetic endeavors and the summary solution of the crime puzzle that intrudes into his consciousness. It is point of view, in fact, that serves as one of the distinguishing features of the Op stories. As opposed to the aloof and cynical message about criminals and detectives expressed in the necessarily first-person "From the Memoirs of a Private Detective," for the early Op stories Hammett used a variety of first-person points of view that generate no second perspective: the entire intent of these stories is to portray an absolutely dependable, trustworthy narrator whose purpose is to objectively inform readers about what he sees, what he knows, and what he does. Unlike the Sherlock Holmes tradition, in the early stories the Op never springs whodunit surprises on his readers. This frankness of purpose also expands to include the short, fat, middle-aged characteristics of the hero as one of necessity, as someone who is what he is because of his honest appraisal of his own physical reality. And it also connects in its most austere form with the Op's rejection of the seductresses who doubt his purpose and self-definition as a detective. When Hammett shifted the Op stories from emphasizing process to stressing action and the self-destructive nature of evil, he also began to tinker with point of view. Along with the Op's increasing separation from the cops and the agency in the later stories, Hammett also adds an element of aloofness that distances the narrator from readers when he holds out on them, as he does in *The Red Harvest*. While part of this change was no doubt occasioned by Hammett's knowledge of the mechanics of the Van Dine, Queen, and Christie style of detective story, part of it came from Hammett's own exploration of point of view, its influence on character, and his changing attitude toward the kinds of attributes with which he wanted to invest his hero. Thus, near the end of the first run of Op stories, Hammett switched to third-person narration for "The Assistant Murderer," the story that was to be the practice run for the narrative technique of *The Maltese Falcon*. As he does with the Op, Hammett presented Alec Rush, the hero of "The Assistant Murderer," as someone grounded in physical reality (as the Op is short and fat, Rush is ugly), as someone technically proficient in detective tradecraft, and as someone who is ultimately kind and sympathetic. In spite of being burdened with a sensation novel conclusion, Hammett's narration in "The Assistant Murderer" coincides with the changes in the Op as narrator and in his relationship with readers. The narration of "The Assistant Murderer" raises unanswered questions about Alec Rush — such as why he was fired from the Baltimore police force — and suggests that he is a more complex and even more dangerous character than the third-person storyteller, obsessed by the man's ugliness, can convey.

HARD-BOILED SENTENCES

Another stylistic element with which Hammett experimented during the 1920s was sentence length. Short sentences made Hammett famous. It seems clear that terse style was something that Hammett worked out through experimentation, and that, in his early works at least, he made a distinction between literary style and what came to be known as hard-boiled style. Thus, in his nonfiction pieces (all of which were written for what Hammett considered middle- or highbrow magazines), from the *Smart Set* epigrams through "In Defence of the Sex Story," one finds moderately long sentences with piled-up clauses punctuated regularly with the same semicolons that he would condemn in 1926 as "a hangover from the days of lengthy sentences, as not suited to an age of telephones and airplanes" in "Advertisement Is Literature." By 1926, however, Hammett moved permanently away from the more complicated sentence structure of his "literary" style and provided both the theoretical justification for the short sentence school as well as a satire of prissy, convoluted prose in the narration of Robin Thin in "The Nails for Mr. Cayterer." Hammett's sentences have been dissected by a number of critics (see Walter Gibson's *Tough, Sweet & Stuffy* and William Marling's *Dashiell Hammett*) who present data and analysis of his short, active, monosyllabic, economical, speedy sentence structure. It wasn't long after the publication of *The Red Harvest* that reviewers began comparing Hammett to Hemingway as writers whose stripped-down prose radiated toughness (Layman 96).

While the short sentence along with its rhythm and timing became one of the essentials of what would come to be called hard-boiled prose, it is not the only feature of Hammett's syntax. Open any page of any Op story and one will most likely find it punctuated with dashes. Dashes appear in Hammett's prose all the way from "Arson Plus" to "The Big Knock-Over." Grammatically, they serve the same purpose as parentheses: dashes permit the writer to add material that is not (strictly speaking) essential to the sentence — digressions and afterthoughts. Then, too, dashes are speedier and are less formal than parentheses. That's part of their impact in the Op stories. But mostly dashes serve to encourage a certain relationship between the narrator and the reader. Almost the first thing that the Op says to readers in the first story, "Arson Plus," involves dashes:

> I had been doing business with this fat sheriff of Sacramento County for four or five years— ever since I came to the Continental Detective Agency's San Francisco office — and I had never known him to miss an opening for a sour crack; but that didn't mean anything [____].

Here, and throughout the Op stories, dashes signal the introduction of supplementary material and feature the narrator stepping out of the story to speak directly to the readers. In the earlier Op stories the material set off by dashes often tends to connect with Hammett's inserted descriptions of the way real detectives work. In the later pieces, dash-separated phrases and clauses become more familiar and descriptive as in the added phrase in the first paragraph of "The Big Knock-Over" that tells readers that Paddy the Mex was "an amiable con man who looked like the King of Spain." With the inserted comments, then, Hammett's prose does two things. The short, active, monosyllabic, economical, speedy sentences convey an objective, hard-boiled tone to the narration, and the inserted comments add a note of familiarity, even intimacy, to the prose. This combination of disparate elements presents the same paradox as that found in the Op as emotionless manhunter and paternal colleague, and in the Op as little middle-aged fat man and more than competent roughhouser. And from these paradoxes come some of the power of Hammett's prose.

HARD-BOILED DICTION

Much of the power of Hammett's prose rests on the language his characters speak. As Chandler would have it, "He put these people down on paper as they were, and he made them talk and think in the language they customarily used for these purposes" (16). But Hammett did not begin this way. In his earliest pieces the speech of the "common man" serves mainly as yet another object of ridicule. With the Op stories, however, Hammett consciously set out to objectively render the speech of characters who inhabit and make interesting the world in which the detective lives. By the time of "Advertisement Is Literature" moreover, he preaches that rendering common speech is art and one of the things that makes it art is that it's not as simple as it seems.

In the Op stories one finds three kinds of diction: that of the Op as narrator, that of the Op as character, and that of the cops and the underworld characters. Each differs. The Op as narrator tends to use standard diction; the Op as speaker occasionally uses slang, especially in the later stories; and the most memorable characters in the stories use both improper grammar and slang. A good bit about Hammett's use of slang has been said already. Part of the slang in his detective fiction simply follows a crime fiction tradition of defining criminal argot, a convention that goes back through Bulwer Lytton and eventually to Thomas Decker's 16th-century pamphlets. One can see this purpose in Hammett, for example, in "The Zigzags of Treachery," when the Op gives readers definitions of slang terms that they might not understand. Indeed, in "The New Racket," Hammett even takes an excursion into presenting and defining British thieves' cant. All of this, of course, probably reflects the way criminals spoke in the 1920s and possesses some etymological interest. But even though some of the flashiest and most original bits of 1920s gangster slang found in contemporary fiction become an integral part of the characterization of his hard-boiled tough guys, this use of slang in itself is not quite the element that makes Hammett's prose the springboard for the development of hard-boiled style in the 1930s. On top of his short, active, economical, speedy sentence structure, that element was Hammett's wordplay. Hammett's employment of slang can occasionally convey unique enthusiasm and power when the narrator plays with words—when he makes up what amounts to his own slang. Thus, Hammett's language is vital and arresting when he gives readers newly madeup words aptly suited to the speaker and the occasion. This is the kind of thing, for instance, that one finds when Hammett converts the noun "cigar" into "cigared" in "It" or when he makes a verb, "inch by inched," out of an adverb cluster at the close of *The Red Harvest*. The trouble is that this kind of language play only happens occasionally. The same holds true for the other elements of hard-boiled style — hyperboles, similes, and wisecracks. All of these occur in Hammett's style, but only occasionally. This is the kind of thing that probably gave rise to Chandler's notion that Hammett had no deliberate artistic aims—that he didn't take advantage of or work at the things that he did best. Thus, although Hammett may have had artistic aims when he started out, as a young, enthusiastic writer in the 1920s, he had neither the time nor the leisure nor the patience of Chandler who labored over each word he wrote.

And then when Hammett had the leisure to do this kind of thing, he wanted to move on to other kinds of writing. He left the world of the Op and O'Gar and Dick Foley and Red O'Leary—the world of cheap cigars, roadhouses, and tough talk—and ended in the world of penthouses and repartee with Nick and Nora Charles. He made himself into this country's first authentic detective story writer when he created the Continental Op. Then he tried to be a mystery writer. And then he wrote no more.

Works Cited

Hammett's Works (in Chronological Order)

"The Parthian Shot." *The Smart Set* 69.2, October 1922: 82.

"The Great Lovers." *The Smart Set* 69.3, November 1922: 4.

"Immortality." *10 Story Book*, November 1922. (Cited from www.miskatonic.org/rara-avis/biblio/lazy-gink.)

"The Barber and His Wife." *Brief Stories* 7.6, December 1922: 23–29. (Cited from *A Man Named Thin*. New York: Ferman, 1962, 54–63.)

"The Road Home." *The Black Mask*, December 1922. (Cited from Ruhm, Herbert, ed. *The Hard-Boiled Detective: Stories from Black Mask Magazine*. New York: Vintage, 1977, 31–34.)

"The Master Mind." *The Smart Set* 70.1, January 1923: 56.

"The Sardonic Star of Tom Doody." *Brief Stories* 8.2, February 1923: 103–6. (Cited from *A Man Named Thin*, 31–37.)

"From the Memoirs of a Private Detective." *The Smart Set* 70.3, March 1923: 87–90. (Cited from *Dashiell Hammett: Crime Stories and Other Writings*. New York: Library of America, 2001, 905–909.)

"The Vicious Circle." *The Black Mask* 6.6, June 1923: 106–11. (Cited from "The Man Who Stood in the Way" in *The Woman in the Dark*. New York: Spivak, 1951, 120–128.)

"The Man Who Stood in the Way." June 1923.

"The Joke on Eloise Morey." *Brief Stories* 8.4, June 1923: 295–98. (Cited from *The Creeping Siamese*. New York: Spivak, 1950, 71–78.)

"Holiday." *The New Pearsons* 49.7, July 1923: 30–32. (Cited from *Woman in the Dark*, 114–119.)

"The Crusader." *The Smart Set* 71.4, August 1923: 9–10.

"The Green Elephant." *The Smart Set* 71.–, October 1923: 103–8.

"Arson Plus." *The Black Mask* 6:13, October 1923: 25–36. (Cited from *Dashiell Hammett: Crime Stories and Other Writings*, 1–21.)

"Crooked Souls." *The Black Mask* 6.14, October 1923: 35–44. (Cited from *Dashiell Hammett: Crime Stories and Other Writings*, 35–51.)

"Slippery Fingers." *The Black Mask* 6.14, October 1923: 96–103. (Cited from *Dashiell Hammett: Crime Stories and Other Writings*, 22–34.)

"The Dimple." *Saucy Stories* 15.2, October 1923: 115–6. (Cited from "In the Morgue" in *A Man Named Thin*, 88–91.)

"The Green Elephant." *The Smart Set* 73.2, October 1923: 103–8. (Cited from *Dead Yellow Women*. New York: Dell, 1947, 163–175.)

"It." *The Black Mask* 6.15, November 1923: 110–18. (Cited from "The Black Hat That Wasn't There" in *Woman in the Dark*, 44–58.)

"The Second Story Angel." *The Black Mask* 6.16, November 1923:110–18. (Cited from *Dashiell Hammett Nightmare Town*. New York: Knopf, 1999, 214–226.)

"Laughing Masks." *Action Stories* 3.3, November 1923: 61–81. (Cited from "When Luck's Running Good" in *A Man Named Thin*, 91–127.)

"The Bodies Piled Up." *The Black Mask* 6.17, December 1923: 33–42. (Cited from "House Dick" in *Dashiell Hammett Nightmare Town*, 42–55.)

"Itchy the Debonair." *Brief Stories,* January 1924. (Cited from "Itchy the Debonair" in *A Man Named Thin*, 63–73.)

"The Tenth Clew." *The Black Mask* 6.19, January 1924: 3–23. (Cited from *Dashiell Hammett: Crime Stories and Other Writings*, 52–83.)

"The Man Who Killed Dan Odams." *The Black Mask* 6.20, January 1924: 35–41. (Cited from *Dashiell Hammett Nightmare Town*, 69–78.)

"Night Shots." *The Black Mask* 6.21, February 1924: 33–44. (Cited from *Dashiell Hammett Nightmare Town*, 79–84.)

"The New Racket." *The Black Mask* 6.21, February 1924: 34–37. (Cited from "The Judge Laughed Last" in *The Adventures of Sam Spade and Other Stories*. Cleveland: World, 1945, 160–168.)

"Esther Entertains." *Brief Stories* 9.6, February 1924: 524–26.

"Afraid of a Gun." *The Black Mask* 6.23, March 1924: 39–45. (Cited from *Dashiell Hammett Nightmare Town*, 227–235.)

"The Zigzags of Treachery." *The Black Mask* 6.23, March 1924: 80–102. (Cited from *Dashiell Hammett: Crime Stories and Other Writings*, 84–122.)

"One Hour." *The Black Mask* 7.1, April 1924: 44–52. (Cited from *Dashiell Hammett Nightmare Town*, 250–261.)

"The House on Turk Street." *The Black Mask* 7.1, April 1924: 9–22. (Cited from *Dashiell Hammett: Crime Stories and Other Writings*, 123–145.)

"The Girl with the Silver Eyes." *The Black Mask* 7.4, June 1924. (Cited from *Dashiell Hammett: Crime Stories and Other Writings*, 146–190.)

"In Defence [sic] of the Sex Story." *The Writer's Digest* 4.7, June 1924: 7–8.

"Women, Politics and Murder." *The Black Mask* 7.7, September 1924: 67–83. (Cited from "Death on Pine Street" in *Dashiell Hammett Nightmare Town*, 189–213.)

"Who Killed Bob Teal?" *True Detective* 2.2, November 1924: 60–64. (Cited from *Dashiell Hammett Nightmare Town*, 262–277.)

"The Golden Horseshoe." *The Black Mask* 7.9, November 1924: 37–62. (Cited from *Dashiell Hammett: Crime Stories and Other Writings*, 219–263.)

"Mr. Hergesheimer's Scenario." *The Forum,* November 1924: 720.

"Nightmare Town." *Argosy All-Story Weekly* 165.4, December 1924: 502–26. (Cited from *Dashiell Hammett Nightmare Town,* 3–41.)

"Mike, Alec or Rufus." *The Black Mask,* January 1925. (Cited from "Tom Dick or Harry" in *Dashiell Hammett Nightmare Town,* 236–249.)

"The Whosis Kid." *The Black Mask* 8.1, March 1925: 7–32. (Cited from *Dashiell Hammett: Crime Stories and Other Writings,* 310–355.)

"Ber-Bulu." *Sunset Magazine* 54, March 1925: 17–20.

"Vamping Samson." *The Editor* 69.6, May 1925: 41–43.

"The Scorched Face." *The Black Mask* 8.1, May 1925. (Cited from *Dashiell Hammett: Crime Stories and Other Writings,* 356–394.)

"Genius Made Easy." *The Forum* 74.2, July 1925: 316–17.

"Corkscrew." *The Black Mask,* September 1925. (Cited from *The Big Knockover: Selected Stories and Short Novels by Dashiell Hammett.* New York: Vintage, 1966, 250–304.)

"The Ruffian's Wife." *Sunset Magazine,* October 1925. (Cited from *Dashiell Hammett Nightmare Town,* 55–68.)

"Dead Yellow Women." *The Black Mask* 8.9, November 1925. (Cited from *Dashiell Hammett: Crime Stories and Other Writings,* 395–449.)

"The Gutting of Couffignal." *The Black Mask* 8.10, December 1925: 30–48. (Cited from *Dashiell Hammett: Crime Stories and Other Writings,* 450–482.)

"The Nails in Mr. Cayterer." *The Black Mask* 8.11, January 1926: 59–73. (Cited from *The Creeping Siamese,* 40–70.)

"The Assistant Murderer." *The Black Mask* 8.12, February 1926: 57–59. (Cited from *Dashiell Hammett: Crime Stories and Other Writings,* 383–521.)

"The Creeping Siamese" *Black Mask* 9.1, March 1926: 38–47. (Cited from *Dashiell Hammett: Crime Stories and Other Writings,* 522–537.)

"The Advertisement Is Literature." *Western Advertising,* October 1926: 35–36.

"The Big Knock-over." *Black Mask* 9.12, February 1927: 7–38. (Cited from *Dashiell Hammett: Crime Stories and Other Writings,* 538–592.)

"$106,000 Blood Money." *Black Mask* 10.3, May 1927. (Cited from *Dashiell Hammett: Crime Stories and Other Writings,* 593–635.)

"The Main Death." *Black Mask* 10.4, June 1927: 44–57. (Cited from *Dashiell Hammett: Crime Stories and Other Writings,* 636–658.)

"The Cleansing of Personville." *The Black Mask,* November 1927.

The Red Harvest. New York: Knopf, 1929. (*The Novels of Dashiell Hammett.* New York: Knopf, 1965.)

"This King Business." *Mystery Stories,* January 1928. (Cited from *Dashiell Hammett: Crime Stories and Other Writings,* 659–710.)

"Fly Paper." *Black Mask* 12.6, August 1929: 7–26. (Cited from *Dashiell Hammett: Crime Stories and Other Writings,* 711–744.)

The Dain Curse. New York: Knopf, 1929. (*The Novels of Dashiell Hammett.* New York: Knopf, 1965.)

"The Farewell Murder." *Black Mask* 12.12, February 1930:9–30. (Cited from *Dashiell Hammett: Crime Stories and Other Writings,* 745–782.)

The Maltese Falcon. New York: Knopf, 1930. (*The Novels of Dashiell Hammett.* New York: Knopf, 1965.)

"Death & Company." *Black Mask* 13.9, November 1930: 60–65. (Cited from *The Return of the Continental Op.* New York: Dell, 1945, 117–127.)

The Glass Key. New York: Knopf, 1931. (*The Novels of Dashiell Hammett.* New York: Knopf, 1965.)

"A Man Named Thin." n.d. (Cited from *Dashiell Hammett Nightmare Town*, 333–46.)

"Suggestions to Detective Story Writers." (*Dashiell Hammett: Crime Stories and Other Writings*, 910–12. Steven Marcus's assembly of Hammett's *New York Evening Post* "Crime Wave" column.)

Secondary Works

Chandler, Raymond. *The Simple Art of Murder.* New York: Ballantine, 1972.

Dooley, Dennis. *Dashiell Hammett.* New York: Ungar, 1984.

Gibson, Walker. *Tough, Sweet & Stuffy: An Essay on Modern American Prose Styles.* Bloomington, Indiana: Indiana University Press, 1975.

Gregory, Sinda. *Private Investigations: The Novels of Dashiell Hammett.* Carbondale, Illinois: Southern Illinois University Press, 1985.

Johnson, Diane. *Dashiell Hammett: A Life.* New York: Random House, 1983.

Layman, Richard. *Shadow Man: The Life of Dashiell Hammett.* New York: Harcourt Brace Jovanovich, 1981.

_____, ed. *Selected Letters of Dashiell Hammett: 1921–1960.* New York: Basic Books, 2001.

Marling, William. *Dashiell Hammett.* Boston: Twayne, 1983.

Mott, Frank Luther. *A History of American Magazines.* Cambridge, Massachusetts: Harvard University Press, 1938–68.

Nolan, William F. *The Black Mask Boys.* New York: Morrow, 1985.

_____. *Dashiell Hammett: A Casebook.* Santa Barbara, California: McNally & Loftin, 1969.

_____. *Hammett: A Life at the Edge.* New York: Congdon & Weed, 1983.

Wolfe, Peter. *Beams Falling: The Art of Dashiell Hammett.* Bowling Green, Ohio: The Popular Press, 1980.

Index

209